Education for the Professions

Quis custodiet . . . ?

Edited by
Sinclair Goodlad

Papers presented to the
20th annual conference of
the Society for Research
into Higher Education
1984

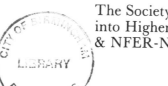

The Society for Research
into Higher Education
& NFER-NELSON

Published by SRHE & NFER-NELSON
At the University, Guildford, Surrey GU2 5XH

First published 1984
Reprinted 1985
© Society for Research into Higher Education

ISBN 1-85059-001-X
Code 8936 02 1

Typeset by FD Graphics, Fleet, Hampshire.

Printed in Great Britain by
Antony Rowe Ltd, Chippenham.

The Society for Research into Higher Education

The Society exists to encourage research and development in all aspects of higher education: highlighting both the importance of this and the needs of the research community. Its corporate members are universities, polytechnics, institutes of higher education, research institutions and professional and governmental bodies. Its individual members are teachers and researchers, administrators and students. Membership is worldwide, and the Society regards its international work as amongst its most important activities.

The Society discusses and comments on policy, organizes conferences and sponsors research. Under the imprint SRHE & NFER-NELSON it is a specialist publisher of research, with over thirty titles currently in print. It also publishes *Studies in Higher Education* (*SHE*) (twice a year), *Research into Higher Education Abstracts* (three times a year), *Evaluation Newsletter* (*EN*) (twice a year), *International Newsletter* (*IN*) (twice a year) and a *Bulletin* (six times a year).

The Society's committees, groups and local branches are run by members with limited help from a small secretariat and provide a forum for discussion and a platform for ideas. Some of the groups, at present the Teacher Education Study Group and the Staff Development Group, have their own subscriptions and organization, as do some local branches. The Governing Council, elected by members, comments on current issues and discusses policies with leading figures in politics and education. The Society organizes seminars on current research for officials of the DES and other ministries, and is in constant touch with officials of bodies such as the CNAA, NAB, CVCP, CDP, UGC and the British Council. The Society's annual conferences take up central themes, viz. Education for the Professions (1984, with the help and support of DTI, UNESCO and many professional bodies), Continuing Education (1985, organized in collaboration with Goldsmiths' College, the Open University and the University of Surrey, with advice from the

DES and the CBI) and Standards (1986). Special studies are being commissioned. Joint conferences are held, viz. Cognitive Processes (1985, with the Cognitive Psychology Section of the BPS). Members receive free of charge the Society's *Abstracts, SHE (corporate members only), annual conference proceedings, Bulletin* and *IN*, and may buy SRHE & NFER-NELSON books at discount. They may also obtain *EN* (published jointly with CRITE), *SHE* and certain other journals at discount.

Further information from the Society for Research into Higher Education, At the University, Guildford GU2 5XH, UK.

Contents

Preface and Acknowledgements

Education for the professions, because it involves both general education and job training, is subject to many significant pressures — from the state, from professional associations, from higher education institutions, from students, and (unlike non-vocational education) from the clients of professionals, the consumers of professional services. The interests of all of these groups are continually changing. For this reason, it is essential that the form and content of education for the professions be subjected to regular scrutiny and appropriate adjustments made to accommodate it both to underlying theoretical insights in academic disciplines and to the requirements of practice.

This book has been produced in preparation for the 1984 Annual Conference of the Society for Research into Higher Education, and perhaps raises more questions than it answers, its aim being to stimulate discussion — both among those attending the conference and among a wider readership.

Although the conference will deal with issues important to many occupations, three have been chosen for special treatment: one (medicine) which is often seen as an archetypal profession, another (management) which is not usually regarded as a profession at all, and a third (engineering) which has features shared by each of the other two. Papers were commissioned to (a) identify major developments in medicine, engineering, and management; (b) examine the implications of these developments for education; (c) review research on (a) and (b); (d) suggest possible research problems for the future; and (e) indicate how the research already done, and the likely outcome of research suggested, might influence policy and practice.

The first three chapters identify some broad issues relevant to the definition of professions and show what consequences they have for education. Chapters 4, 5 and 6 are overviews of issues in education for medicine, engineering, and management. Subsequent chapters examine specific topics in respect of the three occupations: access and recruitment; curricula and teaching methods; accreditation, validation, evaluation, and assessment; continuing education; and innovations. Chapter 26 discusses education for a nascent profession (biomedical engineering), an appropriately interesting combination of concerns forming legitimate parts of the three other occupations reviewed. The development of biomedical engineering also illustrates some of the problems which affect occupations which seek to become professions. Chapter 27, which examines how management techniques are involved in all professional practice, is seminal to the whole discussion.

Chapter 28 seeks to highlight issues relevant to *all* professions to which research and policy discussion need to be directed. This chapter is intended as a contribution to the agenda of discussion for the SRHE 1984 Conference (which will include an Inquiry by four wise persons before whom debate about issues relevant to education for the professions will take place); we hope it may also stimulate discussion elsewhere.

The Society is indebted to UNESCO and to the British Government's Department of Industry for generous grants towards the cost of commissioning and publishing these studies and holding the SRHE 1984 Conference for which they are preparation. The support and interest of a number of the professional bodies is also gratefully acknowledged.

My debts, as editor of this volume, are almost too numerous to mention. It is, however, my pleasure to acknowledge specific forms of help which were indispensable: The University of California, Berkeley, for appointing me a visiting associate in the Center for Studies in Higher Education during the summer of 1983 where I benefited from valuable discussions with Martin Trow (its director), Sheldon Rothblatt, Janet Ruyle, Barbara Shapiro and many others, from excellent research facilities including significant administrative help from Melissa Feldman, Wanda Mulcahy, Jonathan Bielak, Carolyn Duffey, and Marilyn Kinch, and help from Sonia Kaufman (Education and Psychology Library) with a literature search; the Trustees of the Higher Education Foundation, who contributed towards the costs of my visit to the USA; Burton Clark and Alexander Astin, at UCLA, with whom I enjoyed very valuable discussions; Ainslee Rutledge and Cynthia Collins who did a great deal of typing; and the authors of the chapters of this book who submitted to a somewhat 'dirigiste' regime from their editor and who cheerfully accepted modifications to their work so that all the pieces of the book fit together (I trust) reasonably coherently. In addition to the authors of chapters, several people made valuable suggestions concerning the list of questions in Chapter 28 − in particular, John Barcroft, Donald Bligh, Ernest Boyer, John Dancy, Roy Niblett, Desmond Ryan, Michael Shattock and Campbell Stewart. The Conference Organizing Committee

(Appendix B) made many valuable suggestions for contributors and offered comments on the content. In particular, David Jaques acting as agent of the SRHE Publications Committee (custodian of standards) offered many valuable suggestions about content, and also did a good deal of the house editing. Sally Kington, the SRHE Publications Officer, prepared the volume for publication with her renowned eye for detail.

January 1984

Sinclair Goodlad
Imperial College
London SW7 2BT

'Pone seram, prohibe.' Sed quis custodiet ipsos custodes? Cauta est et ab illis incipit uxor.

('Put on a lock! keep her in confinement!' But who is to guard the guards themselves? Your wife is as cunning as you, and begins with them.)

Juvenal, *Satires*, vi, 347.
(Translated by L. Evans)

Part 1

The Context

1 Introduction

Sinclair Goodlad

How may a greater flexibility of access to the professions be achieved compatible with efficiency and effectiveness of education to be given and the maintenance of public confidence in professional services?

How, through the design of curricula and the use of appropriate teaching methods, may intending professionals be encouraged to learn-how-to-learn and simultaneously to receive liberal education?

How may the mechanisms of accreditation and validation of education for the professions be based on appropriate evaluation of learning, and how may assessment measure legitimate professional competencies?

What are the most appropriate arrangements for continuing education for the professions, and how may these be suitably integrated with initial education?

Is there a case for the creation of a staff college for the professional educators for the professions, based, for example, on departments of higher education in universities?

These questions, like most issues in education for the professions, are ultimately reducible to questions about <u>control:</u> of definitions of legitimate knowledge; of licence to practise; of arrangements for providing service to the public; of entry to courses of education; of the form and content of curricula; of standards of achievement. Because all of these issues are systematically interrelated, it is neither possible nor appropriate to discuss one without reference to the others.

For example, when changes take place in what is defined as legitimate knowledge, professional practice must be adjusted; this must entail the continuing education of practising professionals. If it is assumed that the continuing education of practitioners can and must take place, there are obvious implications for the form and content of initial studies (it may be futile to try to 'cover the ground' in the sense of providing first-degree graduates with all the knowledge and skills they are ever going to need). A more relaxed attitude to the 'technical' content of initial studies may in turn permit and encourage systematic attention to the needs of students for general ('liberal') education in addition to purely vocational education. Similarly, if it is assumed that the primary function of initial education is to help students to learn how to learn (rather than to accumulate vast quantities of information in a fixed period of time), it becomes possible to contemplate less rigid entry requirements: this in turn may have beneficial effects on the pattern of recruitment to a profession, on the form and content of schooling, and so forth.

There are sufficient similarities between the ways in which different occupations confront these issues to merit discussion between practitioners, educationists, educational researchers, sociologists, and others about what control should be exercised by whom and in what areas. Compromises must inevitably be made between the legitimate interests, inter alia, of:

- The state for a guaranteed supply of professional/technical services at reasonable cost

- Practitioners for social identity/visibility and the security of employment/level of pay that this entails

- Higher education institutions for advancing the base of knowledge (in particular complex theoretical formulations) on which good professional practice is based and for constituting an independent source of reasonably disinterested criticism

- Students for education which is stimulating and fulfilling

- Consumers of professional services for reliable (and affordable) service

Medicine, engineering, and management are three occupations whose educational requirements highlight most of the crucial issues. Medicine, like law, is often regarded as an archetypal profession whose stigmata (high income, high social prestige, independence in professional judgement and practice), real or imagined, are sought by other (aspiring) professions. Management, although often involving complex technical knowledge with an elaborate theoretical base (eg operations research, organization theory), is not usually thought of as a profession, mainly because it lacks some of the institutionalized features of professions like medicine and law (such as a highly organized professional body or an association which guards standards of professional practice, controls entry, issues licences, etc.). Indeed, the more managers are seen to be 'owned' by organizations whose primary raison d'être is profit (rather than disinterested service to the public), the less 'professional' they are perceived to be.

Engineering is an illuminating intermediate case. It has well-organized and active professional bodies with routines, even rituals (cf Bledstein 1976, p.94), of entry, achievement, recognition, and so forth, abundant opportunities for updating of technical knowledge through meetings, journals, etc. However, most engineers are nowadays employed in organizations in which their conditions of work (choice of problems, even methods of practice) are constrained by the interests of people who are not engineers. This can be the case even when, as with biomedical engineers (see Chapter 26) they may, through their unique knowledge of the technicalities of life-support systems, have greater control over the lives of patients than the medical consultants who are nominally responsible.

Medicine, engineering, and management thus represent in various ways the complete spectrum from 'inner-directedness' to 'other-directedness' (to borrow Riesman's (1961) phrase). There are perhaps more occupations aspiring to professional status whose work approximates to the organizational complexities of management than whose work approximates to the individuality and independence sometimes believed (often incorrectly) to be the condition of medical or legal practice. Management techniques, as Charles Handy argues in a seminal chapter (27) of this volume, may be a crucial and indispensable part of all professional practice. Indeed, a possible title for this volume might have been 'The Management of Learning for the Learning of Management'.

What is a Profession?

Most occupations commonly recognized as professions control access to information valuable to the public. The key professional tasks may well be those of diagnosing and prescribing in matters technical (particularly where specialists draw on a comprehensive body of theory and information, and a repertoire of skills, which transcend those available to their colleagues or clients), followed by communicating to people less well-informed than the professionals the areas of their choice (cf Goodlad 1982b; Goodlad *et al.* 1983). The professional may then go on to execute the wishes of the client, or collaborate with other professionals in, for example, the design of physical systems or devices; but this should not disguise the fact that the effective communication to non-specialists of complex information (with a view to pointing up choices) is a fundamental part of most professional work. For example, a doctor describes a patient's physical condition as precisely as possible and explains forms of treatment available; the patient, however, must decide whether or not to follow the doctor's advice (possibly being required to sign a consent form). The control of knowledge (and, in consequence, education) is at the heart of the concept of a profession; because knowledge represents a form of power, professions are political phenomena. If knowledge is too vague to have ready application, it does not lead to power; if it is too precise, and therefore not difficult for lay people to acquire (eg building, car maintenance), it cannot form the basis of professional organization (cf Nilson 1979). This is not to say that, because of the specialization of the division of labour in society, the sudden withdrawal of non-complex labour cannot form a powerful bargaining tool!

From the difficulty of defining knowledge and the conditions through which specific social groups get control of its disposal stems the notorious difficulty in defining a profession. Is everyone becoming professionalized? (cf Wilensky 1964). Or are professionals becoming proletarianized? (cf Oppenheimer 1973). Do we know? Does it matter? What is, perhaps, more important is to ask (as Terry Johnson asks in Chapter 2 in this volume) why occupations should want to become professions in the first place. Likewise, in deciding what is appropriate education for the professions, it is extremely important to examine (as Michael Burrage does in Chapter 3) how varying social conditions determine what professionals do and what it is thereby appropriate that they learn.

What people perceive professionals to do may be as important as what they actually do − for example in ensuring a flow of recruits to the professions or in ensuring equitable treatment of professionals by those who pay for their services. The popular use of the word 'professional' may be some guide in this respect. Sometimes the word simply implies the world of work (rather than of leisure); the box of tissues on my desk is marked 'for professional use' − meaning (one gathers from the undecorated appearance of the box) for use in the office rather than at home. Or the sign on a shop 'Shoes professionally mended' may simply mean 'competently' mended. As so often, popular culture may contain hints of what people value. The TV series 'The Professionals' (concerning CI5, an agency for neutralizing terrorists and spies) depicts men (sic) of decisive action dedicated to public service regardless of personal risk (the credits show a car leaping through a plate-glass window), relentlessly pursuing the workers of iniquity. Backed by elaborate technical equipment (computers with files, it seems, on all of us), and with privileged links to the centres of power (Cowley, the chief, seems on first-name terms with ministers of state), 'The Professionals' show that work is their central life concern (personal pleasures are abandoned without hesitation when duty calls). Ruthless peer review ensures the right level of dedication to the cause (even Cowley is 'investigated' when it seems he may have been corrupted by the enemy). 'Continuing education' (karate lessons and whatnot) keep the agents ready to meet any demand upon their mental and physical fitness. 'The Professionals' do not act from naked self-interest or institutionalized self-interest (though the junior agents often ask for pay increases, and Cowley defends his jurisdictional 'patch' against the CID). Ruthless, tough, ambitious – but dedicated to the public good. This seems to be the popular expectation of professionals.

Hughes (1963, p.657) captures this ideal of professional practice by suggesting that the central feature of all professions is the motto (not, as far as he knows, used in this form): *credat emptor* (let the buyer trust). Thus, he suggests, is the professional relation distinguished from that of those markets in which the rule is *caveat emptor* (let the buyer beware). Although this ideal of disinterested service is in constant danger of being swamped or obliterated, it is perhaps the crucial component of professional work. For example, Millerson (1964) convincingly demonstrates that codes of 'professional conduct' are more concerned with defending the interests of the members of the profession than in advancing the interests of clients; nevertheless, the ideal is important.

An important part of the service which professionals offer (with whatever mixture of idealism or self-interest is brought to bear individually or corporately) is technical competence of high quality. In a useful definition of professionalization, Freidson (1973, p.22) uses these two notions of service and knowledge:

> Professionalization might be defined as a process by which an organized occupation, usually but not always by making a claim to special esoteric competence and to concern for the quality of its work and its benefits to society, obtains the exclusive right to perform a particular kind of work, control training for and access to it, and control the right of determining and evaluating the way the work is performed.

Some Issues in Education for the Professions

Special competence, implying complex formal education, is central to nearly all definitions of 'professional' and 'professionalization' (cf Moore 1970). Indeed, as the need for such education increases 'amateurs' may be edged out of occupations, such as geology, in which they once contributed significantly (cf O'Connor and Meadows 1976). However, the work of the professions is constantly changing and is the product of powerful competing interests which vary from country to country (as Michael Burrage demonstrates in Chapter 3). The innocent notion that professional groups are politically neutral, with decisions which are only 'technical', has long ago been abandoned (cf Gyarmati 1975). Professions are not static phenomena; as Bridgstock (1976), among others, comments it is no longer profitable to adopt an approach to the study of professions and education for the professions which consists of identifying assumed 'attributes'. We cannot plan professional education around an idealized (or 'ideal type') image of a profession. What we need to do is to study how professions emerge and how they have to co-operate with other professions (as Colin Roberts does in Chapter 26), ensure (by whatever 'political' action may be indicated) that their influence is beneficient, and devise whatever education seems most likely to benefit both students who wish to become professionals and the society they will eventually serve.

That education, as Schein urged twelve years ago, must now prepare professionals to work in organizations in collaboration with people from other professions (the 'management' model) and not just as isolated individuals (the traditional 'medical' model). Engel and Hall (1973, p.85) have provided a useful comparison of traditional and modified characteristics of the professional (see Table 1.1).

Table 1.1   Evolving professional characteristics

Traditional Characteristics*	Modified Characteristics
1 Isolated individual provides service	Team provides service
2 Knowledge from a single discipline typically utilized	Knowledge from diverse fields typically utilized
3 Remuneration predominantly fee-for-service	Remuneration predominantly by salary
4 Altruism: Selfless service limited by entrepreneurialism	Altruism: Increased opportunity for selfless service
5 Restricted colleague evaluation of product	Increased opportunity for colleague evaluation of product
6 Privacy in client-professional relationship	Decreased privacy in client-professional relationship.

* Engel and Hall note that each of the following authors has associated one or more of these characteristics with the professions: Carr-Saunders and Wilson (1933); Marshall (1939); Cogan (1953); Lewis and Maude (1953); Goode (1957); Hughes (1958); Bucher and Strauss (1961); Becker (in Henry 1962); Wilensky (1964); Sherlock and Morris (1967).

The suggestion by Engel and Hall that professionals may have greater opportunities to demonstrate altruism in complex organizations than by working as individual entrepreneurs is echoed by other writers. Equally, the independent judgement of professionals may, in some situations, be more difficult to sustain. Morrissey and Gillespie (1975), for example, having reviewed a multitude of studies dealing with the conflict between professional ideals and the requirements of employing organizations, suggest that the issue is not a simple one of the independent and informed judgement of professionals being subordinated. Sometimes, as Haug and Sussman have suggested (1973), the desire for individual mobility (which is involved in the professional mode of advancement) may be worse for clients than the effect of the 'all for one and one for all' of the collective action involved in unionization: professionals may be tempted to do what is good for their own careers (or for the collective interests of their occupational groups) rather than what is good for their clients.

One implication of this discussion seems self-evident: namely, that education for the professions must involve some conscious attention not only to the technical component of the professionals' service (physiology, circuit analysis, operational research, etc.) but also to the fundamentally moral issue of who is controlling what knowledge for whose benefit. As Jarvis (1983, p.127) aptly puts it:

> Professionalism is an ideal of commitment for the sake of service. It is, therefore, a moral issue which demands considerable study and discussion since there are no simple solutions. It does not involve indoctrination, rather it demands a considered examination of the values implicit in the concept and, as such, should form a major focus in the professional education curriculum.

How is this to be achieved? How can the curriculum of intending professionals be so arranged that questions of meaning, purpose, and social justice are considered alongside the acquisition of techniques with which professionals can take effective action? Among the many complex factors through which curricula are defined, two are crucial: the institutions through which political, social, intellectual, and other pressures defining legitimate knowledge are negotiated into a workable agenda; and the motivation of individuals which defines the de facto curriculum or, in Snyder's (1971) phrase, 'the hidden curriculum' (that which students discover that they have to learn rather than that which the prospectus suggests that they should learn).

A brief review of some of the major issues treated in the chapters of the present volume will indicate how these factors combine to establish the control of the learning of intending professionals. Chapter 28 offers some questions for debate which ask more precisely what action should be taken by whom. Access, curriculum and teaching methods, accreditation, validation, evaluation and assessment are areas where institutions at present dominate; in continuing education, by contrast, market forces dominate — individuals have to want to update their knowledge. (Re-licensing, as Innes-Williams argues in Chapter 19, is probably not at present politically viable, even in medicine where the knowledge-base doubles approximately every seven years.) The innovations described in Chapters 22, 23, 24 and 25 reflect attempts to accommodate and stimulate individual initiative in learning. Is it possible that professional education may be beginning a shift from <u>control</u> (through which institutions dominate individuals) to <u>facilitation</u> (in which individuals plan the form, pacing, and detail of their learning, aided rather than constrained by institutions)?

Access and Recruitment

Gatekeeping is one method by which professions define and defend their share of the job-market. An early stage of the 'professionalization' of an occupation has often been negotiation for a formal course of instruction at the highest possible level (cf Wilensky 1964, p.142). Access to higher education is often (as Oliver Fulton demonstrates in Chapter 7) in practice access to the professions. There is abundant evidence of patterns of recruitment to higher education which are unrepresentative of the population at large − in terms of sex, social class, ethnicity, etc. (cf Warren Piper (Ed.)1981). The phenomenon is not limited to the United Kingdom. Jones (1976), for example, offers evidence from Australia, Canada, and Sweden to show that there was substantial over-representation (compared with the social class distribution of the populations at large) of professional backgrounds among lawyers and physicians, compared with teachers and social workers, in all three countries.

It is of course possible that people with given social backgrounds are more interested in certain subjects than people with other backgrounds. Hardy (1974), for example, shows this with respect to scientists and scholars in America. His data (up to 1960) indicate that liberal Protestant sects, such as Unitarians and Quakers, and secularized Jewish groups are highly productive and that less liberal faiths are moderately productive. Again (as Sir John Ellis shows in Chapter 8), a disproportionate number of medical students come from medical families. Is this because of family tradition or because of bias in selection? We need to find out. <u>If</u> paper qualifications are becoming crucial in defining an individual's life chances (as Dore (1976) and Collins (1979) suggest), it must be a matter of some urgency to ensure equity of access and recruitment to the professions. Flexibility is crucial, as Carr-Saunders and Wilson urged over fifty years ago (Carr-Saunders and Wilson 1933, p.494):

> Certification may become a snare; the forcing of every one at an early age into watertight compartments may remove the sense of adventure

and impair the spirit of initiative. Hence the importance... of keeping doors open into every profession for those who do not enter by the usual gate, and decide, perhaps only relatively late in life, what vocation they wish to pursue.

Curriculum and Teaching Methods

Of the many pressures on professional curricula, three merit special mention: pacing, volume, and validity.

First, pacing. At present, most professional curricula are organized on the assumption that most students are of the same ability (and even age and family circumstances), and that all will learn at the same speed. However, even within individual departments there may be a very wide spread of ability, interest, background knowledge, and so forth. 'Convoying', which may be marginally convenient to the administration and teaching staff (who thereby have less course designing to do), is increasingly being perceived as unsatisfactory.

Second, volume. There seems to be an almost unlimited amount that students might be expected to know: Seager describes the problem vividly as it affects medical education (Chapter 11). In other professions, too, it is increasingly perceived to be impossible for students to learn everything they need to know through formal, initial education. Again, Jarvis (1983, p.43) aptly suggests:

> Competency to practise is not a legitimate aim in professional education. Rather, producing in the learner the ability to recognize good practice and the determination to ensure that his own future practice will not fall below this standard is a major aim.

The misguided attempt to 'cover the ground' can have damaging effects on the general education of students (for example, in crowding out of the studies of science and engineering students in many UK institutions any opportunity for personal enrichment through study of the arts or experience in organizing student activities), and by producing a cascade effect whereby schooling becomes over-specialized to accommodate the pressures of first-degree studies (cf Goodlad 1973).

Third, validity. How can all the contributory disciplines in professional education be welded into a credible and meaningful whole? Whole books (cf Gould 1968) and conferences (cf Indian Council on Social Science Research 1975) have been devoted to this problem, including the problem of offering reasonable career prospects to, for example, social scientists who teach in professional schools. In the United Kingdom, for example, successive high-level reports have urged the broader education of scientists and engineers (Robbins 1963; Dainton 1968; Swann 1968; Finniston 1980). Whole degree programmes have been designed with a view to achieving a greater inter-weaving of theory and practice (as Sir Monty Finniston explains in Chapter 5). Within degree courses, the General Education in Engineering (GEE) Project attempted to stimulate a merging of technical and policy interests through socio-technical projects (Goodlad 1977). Similarly, in the United States (as Lee Harrisberger reports in Chapter 12), there has been a strong movement towards competency-based learning in engineering, designed to teach what engineers really need to know. The Worcester Polytechnic Institute has been a pioneer in this type of work by arranging the integration of studies through project work.

Reforms aimed at achieving an integration of disciplines which is valid in terms of professional practice have, however, achieved only limited success. The dominant pedagogic mode is still parallel courses of lectures in basic disciplines. It is usually argued that students cannot be expected to tackle complex problems of professional practice until they have acquired considerable theoretical knowledge. The problem overlooked in this approach is that if students do not put their knowledge to use, they quickly forget it; by contrast, most of us can learn remarkably effectively if we have the incentive.

Some radical approaches to these three difficulties (pacing, volume, and validity) have involved giving more initiative to students themselves. The MacMaster medical scheme (described by Victor Neufeld and John P.Chong in Chapter 23) suggests that problem-based learning (where students have to get through their own devices what theoretical knowledge they need) is as effective as other pedagogic modes in preparing students for the examinations of the Canadian medical certification board. Similarly, the Undergraduate Research Opportunities Programme at the Massachusetts Institute of Technology (described by Margaret MacVicar and Norma McGavern in Chapter 24) has demonstrated that students are able to learn very quickly and become effective in advanced research if they are given motivation by being challenged.

The McMaster and MIT programmes have been running for only ten years — too short a time to convince sceptics that they are viable (though it is difficult to imagine by what process of longitudinal research they could be demonstrated to be better or worse than other modes of study). Suffice it to say that both programmes are highly attractive to students and act as powerful recruiting magnets for the two institutions.

It is possible that the interests of liberal education can also be well served by problem-based study of this sort. 'Authoritative uncertainty' could legitimately be regarded as the definitive quality of higher learning (cf Goodlad 1976); it has also been argued that coping with uncertainty is a fundamental task for most professionals (cf Nilson 1979). For this reason, education for the professions, if appropriately undertaken, can readily become one of the most searching, wide-ranging, and intellectually challenging forms of higher education. Projects or other types of study which constrain students to see 'technical' problems in their context can provoke thought about meaning, purpose, social justice, and so forth, and probably more effectively for many students than 'lateral enrichment' by the special, parallel courses in social sciences and humanities through which technical studies are sometimes given a veneer of liberality. More particularly, work which gives students a chance to combine academic reflection with work of direct practical utility to other people can be an excellent focus for essentially liberal education (cf Goodlad 1974, 1979, 1982a). It may, however, be desirable to clear space in professional studies (or in any studies in higher education for that matter) for a student's own project or other option (Goodlad and Pippard in Bligh 1982, p.94). Why should it be assumed that students who commit themselves to courses of ·professional education have ceased to desire intellectually-demanding study in fields outside their chosen vocation? Again, it is facilitation rather than control that is at issue.

Accreditation, Validation, Evaluation and Assessment

In Chapters 14,15,16, and 17, accreditation, validation, evaluation and assessment have been deliberately linked. The 'hidden curriculum' is dominated by what is assessed rather than by the broad goals, aims, and objectives listed in the prospectus. Evaluation, if effective, should demonstrate to both teacher and student (and to any interested third party) whether or not the real aims of a course are being achieved; evaluation should then influence how modes of assessment are used. Validation, in turn, is keyed into evaluation being the process by which the intellectual (academic) coherence of a course of study is ensured. Accreditation signals whether or not a given course is acceptable for specific purposes to a given constituency. In terms of the control of learning, these four processes are critical.

Chapter 16 of this volume (on how the Institute of Chemical Engineers goes about its work) raises very important questions about the autonomy of higher education institutions. Departments of chemical engineering which ignored the guidelines of the professional institution would very soon go out of business. A question central to this book is Who accredits the accreditors? Millerson (1964) shows how the 'qualifying associations' acquire their power (to issue, for example, licences to practise); but who can and should monitor the performance of the accrediting bodies? *Quis custodiet ipsos custodes?* The Monopolies Commission (1970) can, of course, swing into operation from time to time, or a Royal Commission may be appointed; but might there not be a case for some independent centres of criticism of the form and content of higher education, some of whose work could be dedicated to this purpose?

Continuing Education in the Professions

Perhaps, as Nancy Foy suggests (Chapter 25), the consumer-led styles of continuing education in management point the way to styles of education for the professions which more appropriately reflect the ethos of a society which may be moving (cf Turner 1960) from 'sponsored' to 'contest' forms of mobility. The highest rewards may, in future, go to those able and willing continuously and continually to refresh their knowledge by independent study, drawing on the services of institutions of higher education as facilitating agencies marketing their wares rather than as sorting houses controlling access to high status and income through selection.

Those responsible for programmes of continuing education have to undertake 'market research' and offer suitably attractive courses; if they do not, they will go out of business. Except in those professions which require their members to undertake a regular programme of professional updating, provision can be somewhat uneven, with opportunities for sustained study of complex issues difficult to finance. There is manifest need for some compromise between on the one hand the rigidities of education for the professions based on full-time study before professional practice and on the other the widespread chaos of much continuing education in the professions.

New Agencies to Manage Education for the Professions?

There is nothing radically new in most of the suggestions above. For example, in his study for the Carnegie Commission on Higher Education Schein (1972, p.70) noted four directions of change in professional education:

(1) more flexible professional schools that permit a variety of paths through the school leading to a variety of careers within the profession; (2) more flexible early career paths which stimulate role innovation and which enable and enhance the variety of career paths launched in professional schools; (3) more transdisciplinary curricula

that integrate several disciplines into new professions that will be more responsive to new social problems of today's and tomorrow's society; and (4) complete integration of the behavioural and social sciences into professional curricula at the basic science and applied skill level.

Schein's proposal (realized in some measure at the Open University, at the McMaster Medical School and elsewhere) was for new types of professional school with course design by faculty teams (Schein 1972, p.133). Interest, he urged, should focus on how students learn, not on how to teach something. This is also the burden of Warren Piper's chapter (Chapter 22). Such emphasis on design of professional courses may be achievable only if people are given the <u>incentive</u> to undertake the necessary hard work involved. At present, as Caplow and McGee (1958) observed a quarter of a century ago, and as is self-evident to even the most casual student of higher education, the rewards go to those who publish within mainstream disciplines. Can similar rewards be devised for educators?

Perhaps what is required is the creation of more chairs in professional education, possibly tenable (like deanships, to which they would be in many ways similar) on a short-contract basis. International visibility (and promotion at home) go at present to those who specialize in the academic disciplines (basic sciences) rather than in designing the interdisciplinary, synthesizing activities which nourish professional competence. What may be needed are not only chairs in medicine, but also chairs in medical education; not only chairs in engineering, but also chairs in engineering education; not only chairs in architecture, but also chairs in architectural education, and so forth.

The qualities of good teaching are different from those of good research (although the two are often successfully combined). The roles of professors of professional education would not be to advance knowledge in some small, specialized area (though they might still wish to do this); their task would be, rather, to keep up-to-date with developments in both theory and practice on a broad front and to <u>manage</u> the curriculum in the sense developed by Charles Handy (in Chapter 27). They would draw on the subject specialists to help to <u>execute</u> the curriculum — either by asking them to offer undergraduate research opportunities, or to act as subject-consultants in the design of problem-based learning materials or (if they were competent to do it) to give lectures or other direct modes of instruction.

Appointment of such professors of professional education might be undertaken by appointment committees including representatives of professional bodies, of the DES (or other relevant government agencies), of students and of the ultimate consumers of professional services (the lay public) as well as of the higher education institution in which the chair would be tenable. The skills sought would be those of effective course design, skills which (like the administrative skills of higher civil servants) are independent of the specific content of the professional education.

In the United States there are some eighty departments of higher education, whose graduates are primarily administrators of higher education institutions. This is not what is intended at all. What the professional schools may need are specialists in the <u>design of contexts for learning</u>. Special departments (or staff colleges) may be needed to train such people, who might come from the professions themselves (medicine, engineering, social work, etc.) or from academic specialisms which contribute to education for the professions. To a certain extent organizations already exist for the education of educators of professionals (the potential professors of professional education) — such as the Centre for Staff Development in the University of London, the Institute for Educational Development at the University of Surrey and the Teaching Services Unit at the University of Exeter. Perhaps what I am suggesting is the creation of another profession!

2 Professionalism: Occupation or Ideology?

Terry Johnson

It was more than fifty years ago now that Carr-Saunders and Wilson, in concluding their major study of the professions, suggested that an extension of these existing systems of colleagueship and training to more and more occupations offered the best defence against the 'crude forces which threaten steady and peaceful evolution' of society (Carr-Saunders and Wilson 1933, p.497). They identified these threats as arising both from the bureaucratic power of the expanding modern state and from the exploitability of public opinion by those whose 'ambitions know no bounds'.

> The family, the church, the universities, certain associations of intellectuals, and above all the great professions, stand like rocks against which the waves raised by these forces beat in vain. (p.497)

They had no doubt that professionalism in some form was bound to increase:

> In the long run technical advance implies an increase in the number of those doing more or less specialized intellectual work... (and) while the extension of professionalism upwards and outwards will be fairly rapid, its extension downwards, though gradual and almost imperceptible, will be continuous.
> (p.491)

Thus, while they saw professionalism rapidly pervading middle-class occupations, they saw the 'professionalization of everyone' taking a little longer. Associated with this view of a professionalized future was their belief that a massive expansion of education would be linked to such a trend:

> Opportunities for specialized training are being gradually extended to *all*, and we may therefore look forward to a system of careers open to trained and tested talents. (p.494)

While, fifty years on, we would wish to commend Carr-Saunders and Wilson for their informed foresight in predicting the massive expansion of claimants to professionalism and the associated increase in education and training, few would perhaps conclude that such developments had produced the utopia which those authors had in mind when extolling the virtues and potentialities of professionalism.

While in many respects the 'age of professionalism' is already with us, its benefits are not always clear. Far from accepting the defensive role of the professions, many now view any extension of professional power with alarm, as a threat to individual freedom. Perhaps the best known example of such a critique is the work of Ivan Illich (1976a, 1976b, 1977) who has suggested that professional dominance has progressively undermined the capacity of individuals and groups to assume responsibility and develop the means which would ensure their own welfare and well-being. A further example is the popular critique directed against social workers, who are seen as subverting the values and conditions of family life. Others consider that such 'trained and tested talents' exhibit not an ethic of service and social responsibility but a trained incapacity to understand a world beyond the demands of their narrow expertise and interest (cf Wilding 1982). Yet others would question the claim that professionalism rested securely on democratic foundations, as associations of occupational equals, arguing rather that such occupations are themselves bureaucratically organized; that they are hierarchies of professional command which mesh only too easily with the hierarchies of business and government (Mills 1956). In short, modern analysts and commentators have lost faith in professionalism as a necessarily beneficial social form.

It may, of course, be argued that the essence of what Carr-Saunders and Wilson found so attractive was not professionalism as such but its peculiar English form, that gentlemanly image and culture which so infected élite occupations in the course of their nineteenth-century formation and beyond (cf Reader 1966). There are certainly grounds for such a conclusion in the text, not least in their stress on the necessity of a liberal education as a foundation for a professional career.

What is of central importance in understanding the swing away from such faith in professionalism is the obvious diversity which characterizes those occupations which we today label professional. Carr-Saunders and Wilson merely assumed that some uniformity of organization, training and outlook not only characterized the occupations they surveyed but could and would characterize those which were to emerge.

The Heterogeneity of the Professions and the Role of Professionalism

Following the Second World War there grew up a literature on the sociology of the professions obsessed with asking What is a profession? (eg Greenwood 1957; Cogan 1953). With the benefit of hindsight it is possible securely to link this academic pursuit with the swelling chorus of those emergent and expanding occupations which shared in common the goal of professionalization. The effort to distil the essence of professionalism was of direct political relevance to social workers, librarians, teachers and the new technologically-based occupations who were engaged in a competitive struggle for recognition.

In more recent years sociologists have been forced by events – the patent failure of new claimants to professional status to establish themselves in the classical medical and legal moulds – to turn to the problem of why it is that many occupations, with the imprimatur of professionalism upon them at birth, have failed to attain the promised end-state (Etzioni 1967). A whole plethora of terms have been coined in the attempt to understand this phenomenon of stunted professionalization. The hybrids have been defined as quasi-professions, marginal professions, semi-professions, etc. In fact, we have long since reached the point at which those occupations requiring some such qualification far outnumber those enjoying full acceptance as professions. Both in academic and popular usage, then, the term profession has been extended to an increasingly large and diverse grouping of occupations, such that our identification of an occupation as professional has less to do with the reality of a division of labour in which an association of colleagues effectively controls its own work practices than with a recognition of the strategy of professionalism; a political strategy for occupational advancement (cf Johnson 1972; Larson 1977). What has become pervasive in our society is not, as Carr-Saunders and Wilson foresaw, professionalized work, but the occupational ideology of professionalism in the struggle for status.

Professionalism is an ideology and strategy for which the level and length of formal education undergone by practitioners is regarded as of crucial significance for professionalization, despite the fact that there is no clear historical example which would support such a belief. It is an ideology which stresses the primacy of the individual and personal relationship with a client, yet is espoused by occupations in which it is difficult to determine who the client is, and where the greater part of the work is of an impersonal nature (cf Halmos 1970). In short, professionalism has become an occupational ideal in a society in which its attainment becomes less and less likely as more and more work is routinized through technological advances and occupational practice increasingly finds its typical setting within bureaucratic organizations of various kinds.

To stress the social reality of professionalism as an occupational ideology rather than a form of the organization and control of work by a colleague network is not thereby to diminish its significance. That these otherwise heterogeneous occupations share a political strategy in common has the utmost significance for educational institutions in so far as they become subjected to consequential, competitive pressures. Nor should we suppose that, because the strategy of professionalism is often directed towards seemingly unattainable goals, it therefore has no real function or effects. For the contemporary salience of professionalism is that, more than anything else, it entails a sustained attempt to constitute a privileged relationship with the state, by way of official systems of recognition, licensing, regulated recruitment, and monopolistic practice. It is in this crucial respect that contemporary claimants to professional status are direct heirs to those occupations which underwent professionalization in the nineteenth century.

I have argued elsewhere (Johnson 1982) that professionalization and state formation have been intimately linked in the development of modern Britain, to the extent that what the state has become is in some measure dependent on its relationship with occupations whose practices generate those social definitions (of health and illness, deviancy and normality, educational success and failure, etc.) and categories which are relevant to state functions. At the same time the professions have been dependent on the state to secure various conditions of practice, including, paradoxically, the conditions of independent practice. While the state has been and is a common factor, it is also a source of the heterogeneity, in so far as different occupations have forged quite different relationships with the state. Barristers, for example, unlike solicitors, have both avoided legislative regulations of their professional organizations – the Inns of Court – while practising as officers of a state agency, the courts (cf Durnan 1983). The General Medical Council, the controlling body of medicine, is a state creation, yet has been a significant instrument of medical control over emergent occupations in the health field (cf Larkin 1983). Certain accountants have enjoyed state support through the licensing of their members as public auditors (Stacey 1954), while social work was effectively brought into being by the creation of state agencies such as the probation service. Thus, while the profession-state relationship is a constant factor, the forms it may take vary considerably, with important consequences for occupational organization and practice, as well as public image and prestige accorded.

In stressing the central significance of the relationship between state formation and professionalism in modern times, I wish to avoid the conventional view that such a relationship inevitably leads to the subordination of the professions to bureaucratic exigencies, for whatever autonomy these privileged occupations have enjoyed and continue to enjoy is in large part a product of the particular relationship with the state that exists. The institutionalized forms of recognition, licensing, granting of monopolistic advantages, etc. which have developed operate in many cases as institutional supports which constitute for the occupation independent arenas in which freedom of action is possible. The alternatives of state intervention versus professional autonomy do not, then, exist, because professionalization can only refer to a process toward partial autonomy, limited to specific areas of independent action which are defined by an occupation's relationship to the state. Areas of autonomy vary from profession to profession, and from time to time. Thus, despite the common factor of the state in the constitution of professionalism, there exists no common form of the relationship and, therefore, no common form of professionalism.

In stressing the interdependence of state and profession we should also avoid the conclusion that the relationship between the two is an easy or colluding one, amounting in George Bernard Shaw's words, to a 'conspiracy against the laity'. It is an interdependence which makes for an uneasy alliance in which professionals are constantly on the alert for signs of state encroachment upon what they regard as professional matters. Governments are not always clear about the degree to which the state depends upon the independence of professional services, in the sense that the legitimacy of the modern democratic state rests upon the independence of the courts as well as upon those 'experts' who effectively define crucial categories of social need in the field of health and welfare, or create the 'technically neutral' grounds for decision-making relating to policy formation and planning in numerous fields of government activity.

Such an argument leads us back to Carr-Saunders and Wilson's contention that the major defining function of professionalism is that it brings 'knowledge to the service of power'. In the discussion so far I have deliberately avoided confronting the assertion at the centre of much of the literature on the professions that the defining trait of the professions is their access to, control over, and transmission of an esoteric body of knowledge. This is because an explanation of the status of professional occupations in terms of their access to knowledge must at the same time involve an account of the context of power relations within which such access and control is achieved and of how it is maintained. In short, the role of the state has been crucial in determining the distribution, including the monopoly, of knowledge. Thus, while it is true that a patient entering a doctor's surgery is likely to defer to the medical man's superior knowledge, we still have to account for why a majority of patients are willing to take their professional guarantee of competence for granted; why is it that the established system of medicine is given greater official and public credence than alternative forms of treatment, such as osteopathy, or why are such alternatives excluded from the National Health Service? Nor does explanatory recourse to knowledge alone explain why the form of treatment of one health speciality, such as physiotherapy, should be institutionally subordinated to medical diagnosis and referral, while another, dentistry, should escape such medical control. These questions cannot be answered by reference to criteria such as relative complexity of knowledge or levels of technical skill, particularly as such variations are usually the historical product of occupational advantage and disadvantage rather than the reverse. The power context in which the various occupations we call professions have developed is, then, not reducible to the single criterion of knowledge and its effects. There is no doubt that the social distance between professional and client created by the knowledge-gap gives rise to a problem of control — a problem of control which agencies of the state have increasingly come to mediate (cf Johnson 1972, pp.41-52). However, the process of professionalization often proceeds in advance of substantial differentiation in this respect, with only a consequent formalization of the knowledge-base of an occupation and an inflation of its educational and training requirements (cf Larson 1977, pp.40-52). It is suggested, then, that the professions are a heterogeneous grouping of occupations in terms of status, forms of practice, complexity of knowledge base, etc., but sharing a common political strategy for advancement; a strategy which implies an intimate relationship with the state, which may itself be manifested in a variety of ways. Such a view of the professions has a number of important implications for any consideration of professional education and training.

Professionalism and Professional Education

When we compare the British professions with those in the United States or elsewhere in Europe we are very soon confronted with certain ways in which the British experience of professionalization has been peculiar. Characteristically, the British professional associations have enjoyed a much firmer control over the forms and content of training than has been the case elsewhere. Systems of apprenticeship or quasi-apprenticeship survived for a longer period (including the clinically-based medical training). and educational institutions have been relatively weak and less influential in establishing the forms of vocational training. Each of these 'peculiarities' has been associated with the historically specific relations between the professions and the British state. In particular, it was the relationship of the emergent professions with the imperial state which sustained the pre-eminence of the associations as examiners and qualifying bodies at the expense of educational institutions (Johnson 1982). For the British professions fulfilled an imperial role, either through the direct provision of examinations or as accrediting bodies for local courses and systems of training overseas. It was largely in the provision of such facilities that the British professions were forced to eliminate any nationalistic or particularistic criteria from their qualifying procedures. This was achieved by a variety of mechanisms: the creation of a 'colonial list' by the General Medical Council and the subsequent system of reciprocal recognition through which the Council accredited overseas medical schools; the extension of the RIBA accreditation system through a scheme which devolved its qualifying function to allied associations in the Empire and later the Commonwealth; and the direct provision and supervision of examination centres by accountancy bodies, which effectively opened up the field of professional education to private correspondence colleges. The associations became Empire-wide bodies by exporting their qualifications while maintaining a firm hold on examination standards and control over syllabuses. This system of qualification had the peculiar British consequence of subordinating academic professionals to the authority of practitioner associations and as a commentator on the architectural profession has pointed out '...the peculiar characteristics of architectural education in the UK are due to the fact that examinations preceded education instead of vice versa. ...Consequently architectural training has tended to be governed by the needs of the examination syllabus rather than the needs of architectural practice' (Barrington-Kaye 1960, p.159). The Empire role of the professions reinforced the balance of influence toward the associations and against the educational institutions. Also, in operating as effective gatekeepers to occupational practice throughout the Empire, the associations adopted a quasi-official role upon which British administration overseas was dependent.

This high level of control over the professional education achieved by the associations during the period of Empire is still with us today to the extent that many argue that the possibilities of innovation and rationalization in professional education are limited. In Britain, in particular, it is suggested that a narrow pragmatic view of education has been sustained despite mounting evidence that the consequences are undesirable in a number of respects. In medicine, for example, it has been understood for decades that training in the field of prevention is crucial for the improvement of modern systems of health provision, yet because of the low status of such a function in the practising profession, medical education has failed to respond to such needs.

We might even have the temerity to ask what the educational rationale is for the fact that doctors are trained for hospital practice when the working lives of a majority are spent in other locations, responding to a quite different set of demands and conditions. Also, at least since Snow's conception of the two cultures entered academic and political discourse, it has been clear that the engineering institutions and academics have only hesitantly and partially responded to the need significantly to extend the cultural horizons of future generations of engineers, and, in particular, to prepare them for the administrative, organizational and political contexts of their working lives.

There are undoubtedly many reasons, firmly embedded in British social structure, which help to account for such failures to respond to recognized problems. The burgeoning literature on the conditions of Britain's 'decline' is replete with alternative explanations for what is seen as a general social malaise. However, when we identify these specific problems associated with professional education, there can be little doubt that the balance of the relationships between practising professionals (through their associations) and academic professionals is a significant element, and that it is a balance of forces which is enshrined in state-mediated institutions of policy generation.

The dynamics affecting the reform of professional education today operate within a mould which was effectively cast by the successes of those occupational movements of doctors, lawyers, architects, etc. which emerged in the provincial towns of nineteenth-century England to overturn the metropolitan-based occupational élites whose influence had been dependent on patronage and social connection. This movement was an attack on the oligarchic structure of occupational practice, and stressed technical qualification and equal competence as central to professionalism. It was not until late in the century, for example, that the leadership of the architectural professional succumbed to the 'new' view that it was possible to train architects. Architects, they argued, were born with the requisite aesthetic sensibilities (cf Johnson and Caygill 1972). The success of the new men in radically shifting the criteria of occupational status set in motion a continuously shifting struggle for competitive advantage in a market whose potential volatility was from the beginning stabilized by government action and state mediation. The growing significance of this strategy of professionalism for the process of the division of labour has, in turn, ensured that these emergent status divisions and rivalries have been reproduced within the system of education. As a result, the direct relationship between educational provision and client-need has in many cases been displaced by the primacy of status demands, dressed up in the language of client-need. The root source of the problems faced by the educator in disentangling those training requirements which can be directly justified in terms of client-need and those which relate to occupational advantage and status was identified some years ago by T.H. Marshall (1963, p.156) in his attempt to define a profession as an occupation with the responsibility for giving clients what they need rather than what they want. Marshall's

definition represents a distilled expression of the strategy of professionalism, which in one stroke subordinates both client and educator to
occupational definitions of what client-needs are and how they should be
catered for in terms of both practice and training. Such views give
respectability to Illich's angry claim that:

> Need, used as a noun, became the fodder on which the professions
> were fattened into dominance.

The social services constitute an arena of professional practice where
definitions of need are particularly problematic, being subject to
constant review and revision as new social problems are identified and
the public gaze is diverted from one area of social concern to another
with great rapidity; a process which is reinforced and amplified by the
mass media. Nevertheless, the strategy of social workers has been to
adopt the medical model, stressing 'clinical freedom' and the therapeutic
basis of their relationship with the client, so focusing practice and
training on the individual expression of social problems – a symptomol-
ogy of the disease. A major organizational triumph in the progress of this
strategy was the creation in 1971 (following the publication of the
Seebohm Report (1968) and the passing of the Local Authority Social
Services Act of 1970) of a generic social work occupation with a unified
system of training resting on the primacy of the therapeutic principle.
Whether the 'best interests' and specific problems faced by the mentally
ill, the socially economically deprived, the old, the unemployed, the
socially incompetent, etc., are best served by the generic Jack-of-all-
social-services, trained in principles of individual and group counselling,
is a question which is foreclosed by the strategy adopted, and one which
remains contentious even as the educational foundations of such a
strategy are constructed.

Professional education, as it exists at a particular moment in time, is
then the sediment of the former struggles and strategies of occupations
for whom the images of success survive from an heroic past, and it is the
continuing contemporary vigour of professionalism as a strategy which
generates the heat fusing such sediment into the rocks on which
educational innovation and reform so often founders.

3 Practitioners, Professors and the State in France, the USA and England

Michael Burrage

Professions have been formed by the actions and interactions of three parties: the practitioners who invented and applied the techniques on which the profession was based and who established associations to represent and regulate the admission and conduct of those who wished to practise it; the professors who propagated, systematized and further developed the practitioners' knowledge; and the state, meaning the kings and councils, parliaments and legislatures, civil servants and courts which have either legitimized or limited the powers of professional associations and promoted or neglected the development of professional schools. The interrelationships of these three parties have been determined largely by political experiences, often in the distant past, and thus form a unique configuration in every country. Even though there are signs of convergence in the structure of professions in the contemporary world — principally because of the dependence of many professions on knowledge generated within universities — the roles of practitioners, professors and the state vary considerably from country to country, and in reflecting on the present condition and future prospects of the professions it is obviously essential to keep these variations in mind. Only then can we assess the incidence and severity of problems common to the professions in many western societies or decide whether reforms and innovations appropriate in one are practicable and relevant in another.

In this chapter I sketch the origins and development of the professional configuration of three societies: France, the United States, and England. These do not exhaust the possible permutations in the relationships between practitioners, professors and state but they illustrate some of their major variations. In each case I concentrate initially on the legal and medical professions since their history is better documented than that of other professions and, in any case, they established precedents which others sought to emulate. None of the others ever quite succeeded of course, but the ancient professions nevertheless provide a bench mark and one may then analyse the ways in which the later arrivals vary and deviate from them. There is however one extreme, deviant case, that of management, which is best discussed separately, and I therefore reserve my comments on it until the end.

In France, as one might expect, the Revolution constituted the critical period in the formation of the modern professions, and especially of law and medicine. Under the Ancien Régime both were governed by their own corporate bodies, the advocates by their *ordres* which controlled admission to the profession, upheld its rules of ethics and sought to protect both its jurisdiction and status against the claims and aspirations of the *procureurs* or attorneys. Though subject in the last resort to the authority of the king and of the *parlementaires* before whom they appeared, they seem in practice to have established complete autonomy in their professional affairs which they proudly asserted in the maxim *l'ordre est maître de son tableau* (Kehl 1956; Berlanstein 1975). Thus, whilst they were required, by a royal edict of 1653 to obtain a university law degree this appears to have been something of a formality. The advocates' own rules of admission, and in particular the need to obtain the sponsorship of a 'godfather' in the order and to complete a *stage* or apprenticeship seem in practice to have been the more significant requirements.

The three medical professions had similar corporate institutions, though only the physicians enjoyed the same degree of autonomy as the advocates. The other two, the surgeons and pharmacists, were subject in a number of ways to the supervision of the physicians, who claimed that medicine embraced both of these inferior crafts. In the decades before the Revolution, moreover, both Louis XV and Louis XVI had intervened in the affairs of the medical professions, the former to raise the surgeons from their craft status and to check the powers and prerogatives of the physicians. But despite these instances of state interference, the principle of practitioners' self-government appears nevertheless to have been the foundation of medical organization under the Ancien Régime (Léonard 1978; Gelfand 1974).

Between 1789 and 1793 the revolutionary assemblies challenged this principle and in the name of equality, of *carrières ouvertes aux talents*, and of the sovereignty of the people, destroyed the corporate institutions of all the professions and the crafts (Douarche 1905; Léonard 1978). In so doing they enlisted the support of large numbers of lawyers and physicians, since both professions were well represented in the revolutionary assemblies. The Revolution therefore did not merely destroy the professions' corporate bodies but simultaneously dissolved professional solidarity and professional loyalties, and introduced into the history of the professions that unusual phenomenon, the professional who in the service of higher ideals sets out to expose, humiliate and destroy his own profession.

In one respect the Convention quickly had second thoughts, for in 1794 it decided that the revolutionary armies needed trained medical and engineering personnel and it therefore established three *Ecoles de Santé* and the *Ecole Polytechnique*. It made no attempt however to review the civilian professional training or to reintroduce the regulation of legal and medical practice (Vess 1975). For more than a decade, therefore, both the legal and the medical practice were entirely unregulated and open to any citizen who had a mind to practise them. The reconstruction of the two professions only began under the Consulate. It continued under the Empire, but in a form that left no place for practitioner self-government. Both professions ceased to 'belong' to their members as they had done under the Ancien Régime. Instead the state determined their entry requirements, and in so doing emphatically reinforced, in both law and medicine, the importance of formal training, the duration and content of which were specified in detail by law. The state also rearranged the occupational jurisdictions of both professions, by refusing to grant the advocates any form of monopoly, by merging physicians and surgeons and by inventing a number of new medical occupations, most notably the *officier de santé* a sort of second-grade medical practitioner. Finally the state retained responsibility for supervising the conduct of practitioners. Advocates and others who represented clients in court were to be supervised by the local chief prosecutor, while medical practice was supervised by the Ministry of the Interior and the police, in accordance with the rules of medical practice promulgated in the Penal Code (Douarche 1905; Léonard 1978).

In 1810, some years after the new courts and law schools had been established and most of the new codes had been promulgated, Napoleon finally agreed to re-establish the orders of advocates, including their *bâtonniers* and disciplinary councils, their *tableaux* and *stage* or apprenticeship, but this was far from a restoration of the old régime, since the orders were to conduct all their business under strict state control, and could not in fact even call a meeting without the permission of the local *procureur-général* (Kehl 1956). Under successive régimes, the orders gradually managed to recover much of their old autonomy though they were never again *maîtres de ses tableaux*. The state intermittently used its authority first to restructure and formalize the *stage* and most emphatically in 1971-2 to merge the advocates and *avoués*, the successors of the Ancien Régime *procureurs*, and simultaneously create a new legal profession of *conseils juridiques* out of the large numbers of self-styled *conseils juridiques*, *agents d'affaires* and others who had practised since the late nineteenth century at least, though never subject to any form of state or practitioner control (Trouillat 1979).

By contrast with the lawyers, the doctors were unable or unwilling to mount a counter-attack against the revolutionary onslaught on their professional institutions. They did, of course, form societies after the Revolution and indeed began to do so in 1796, but these were voluntary societies whose main business was to arrange debates, lectures and demonstrations, to publish journals, to provide dissecting rooms and libraries, to honour distinguished contributions to medicine. None sought to organize the profession as a whole, or to exercise any representative or regulatory functions (Ackerknecht 1967). The profession therefore became internally divided, stratified and highly competitive. There were no professional bodies to restrain the competition between one doctor and another, while state officials were unable or unwilling to perform the regulatory functions they had been assigned by law or to supervise the other medical practitioners who had legal rights to practise, such as the *officiers de santé*, customary rights such as the nuns, *curés*, dentists and *bandagistes*, or the host of irregular practitioners without any rights at all (Léonard 1977; Zeldin 1973, pp.25-28).

The collapse of professional solidarity and the elimination of professional regulation may, as some doctors complained, have had an adverse effect on their incomes, but there is no reason to suppose it had an equally adverse effect on the advance of medical knowledge. On the contrary, it seems reasonable to suggest that the rearrangement of the division of medical labour contributed, along with the state funding and reorganization of hospitals and medical schools, to the dramatic advance of French medicine in the early decades of the nineteenth century and to the unquestioned leadership of Paris in the medical world until the rise of science and university-based medicine in the second half of the nineteenth century, to which the specialist French medical schools were slow to adapt.

In 1845 medical practitioners were permitted for the first time, along with pharmacists and veterinarians, to hold a congress which voiced the opinions of ordinary practitioners on professional matters, among which were proposals for re-establishing corporate bodies similar to those of the Ancien Régime. Their proposals were rejected, and it was not therefore until the last quarter of the nineteenth century, when they were allowed to form mutual benefit societies and trade unions, that medical practitioners were able to resume some responsibility for their professional activities. Like their manual counterparts, however, the medical trade unions often argued and competed with one another, and therefore never unified the profession, but they did at least prompt state officials to perform the regulatory functions which they had for long neglected (Léonard 1977). The medical profession and practice continued to be regulated by the *ministère public* and the police, who were urged on by the practitioners associations. In 1941, however, the Vichy régime, in deliberate opposition to the egalitarianism and individualism of the Revolution, sought to organize the entire labour force into self-governing professional families, and as part of this 'national revolution' created an *Ordre des Médecins*, which was authorized to control, subject to the law, the admission, training and conduct of French doctors (Chaigneau 1945). In this there was of course more than a little irony, for even the revival of practitioner self-government in French medicine required state action and a detailed statutory framework.

The Revolution had far less influence on the development of the engineering profession than on law and medicine, for while the engineers were a recognized *corps* before the revolution, they were a *corps* within the state with no tradition of self-government, trained mainly in royal schools, and employed entirely in civil or military branches of the state. The revolution therefore merely continued and reinforced state initiative in the formation of the engineering professions, by reviving the old training schools such as the *Ecole du Génie Militaire*, created in 1745, the *Ecole des Ponts et Chaussées*, created in 1747, and the *Ecole des Mines*, transformed in 1769 into specialized *écoles d'application* to follow the basic training provided by the *Ecole Polytechnique* (Ahlström 1982; Artz 1966). The French engineering profession therefore, to a greater extent than either the legal or the medical professions, is the result of state initiative, and it was the state, together with the professors of the leading schools, which determined the entry requirements of the profession, the level and content of their training and the scope and jurisdiction of engineering specialities.

A civilian engineering profession emerged only slowly in the nineteenth century from the trickle of the graduates *démissionaires* of the élite state schools into private industry, augmented after 1829 by the graduates of the *Ecole Centrale des Arts et Manufactures*. However this school was established by private initiative— an administrative official, an artillery officer and two professors – and it remained a private institution until 1857. About fifty more technical schools were established before 1850, many of them also by private initiative, but their distinctive feature was that they followed the precedents set by the state and sought to form a civil engineering profession by means of schools rather than by organizing practising engineers and establishing a system of professional representation and government. In 1848, the graduates of the *Ecole Centrale* formed the first association of practising engineers, the *Société des Ingénieurs Civils de France*, but this has played a minor role in the development of the profession, being a learned society rather than a professional association in the proper sense. It has never sought to control admission to the profession, to regulate members' behaviour or to make itself responsible for improving the status of French civil engineers in general. French engineers have never been in fact a corporate body, and their status has remained highly differentiated, according primarily to the kind of school they attended. This has, in turn, determined to a large extent their subsequent employment and career prospects (Ahlström 1982; Finniston 1980, pp.214-8).

Unlike the French, the American Revolution did not entail the violent, full-scale reconstruction of social institutions. Nevertheless it seems to have inspired aspirations for law without lawyers, comparable to those heard in revolutionary France, and subsequently to have provoked a wave of popular hostility towards the power, privileges and status of the legal profession. In the immediate post-revolutionary years nothing much came of these attacks, though many of the new state legislatures were unwilling to grant the bar the kind of autonomy it had enjoyed under colonial rule. The attacks, however, continued in many states through the early decades of the nineteenth century, and prompted many state legislatures to reduce or abolish the clerkship and educational requirements for admission to the bar. In 1835, Massachusetts, the heartland of bar organization both before and after the revolution, finally succumbed to these popular pressures, and as a result bar associations in the state collapsed and disappeared and the distinctions between attorney, counsellor, barrister and serjeant which it had adopted from England fell into disuse (Chroust 1965). Though a few states retained minimal entrance requirements for legal practice, there was, after this date, no organized legal profession in the United States.

The American medical profession had developed more slowly than the legal profession, no doubt because patients were rather more difficult to control than litigants, but in the eighteen twenties and thirties, the medical societies and medical licensing were subject to the same kind of popular attacks: the people and democracy against the 'favoured class', the 'privileged order' and the 'aristocracy' of licensed physicians. As a result, licensing legislation was diluted or repealed and by mid-century only New Jersey and the District of Columbia had any laws regulating the practice of medicine (Rothstein 1972). Unlike the bar associations many medical societies survived the repeal of licensing legislation, but they became, of necessity, voluntary and élitist associations, rather than the representative or governing bodies of the profession (McDaniel 1958). Inspired then by ideals similar to those of revolutionary France, the American state legislatures, over the first half of the nineteenh century, though never attacking bar or medical associations directly, also opened legal and medical practice to anyone who had a mind to practise. As in revolutionary France, some legal and medical practitioners had joined the popular critics of their own profession and helped to debunk the arguments commonly used to justify their prerogatives and pri-vileges and actively lobbied against them in state legislatures and conventions.

The long-term effects of these events were quite different from those of revolution in France, but no less decisive for the subsequent development of the professional configurations, for without strong practitioners associations to maintain fixed apprenticeship rules, the professors of law and medicine were free to develop their courses as they wished and to compete with one another in marketing their degrees and diplomas. They thereby gave their professions a distinctive character which they never quite lost, even after the revival of practitioner associations and practitioner power at the end of the nineteenth century. In the first place, law and medical school professors were not in the least interested in defining or protecting the occupational jurisdictions of practitioners, nor were they concerned or equipped to inculcate and uphold rules of etiquette or ethics, nor could they protect their collective honour and status. The professors' main concern was to enlarge the enrolments of their schools and to do this they competed aggressively with one another, by lowering admission requirements, by shortening courses and by offering advanced credit (Reed 1921; Norwood 1944).

The universities tended to win out in this competitive struggle, since they could offer the prestige of a university degree. But after the civil war the private commercial schools found themselves new markets in the immigrant communities of the Eastern cities. The total effect of this competition between the schools was to hasten the decline of apprenticeship, to boost the numbers entering the professions, and to open them to lower socio-economic groups. As a result, the two professions lost the social homogeneity of the early post-revolutionary decades and became highly differentiated, by their practitioners' own social and educational background as well as by the socio-economic background of their clientele.

When professional associations began to revive in the late nineteeenth century, they first sought to try and develop some sense of professional esprit after the interregnum decades, though many medical societies and bar associations believed that this could and should only include a minority of those actually practising medicine and law. They then sought to exercise some control over admission to their professions, that is, over the professors and the schools. In this respect, the medical profession was by far the more successful. With the support of the élite schools anxious to be rid of low-cost competitors, of the Carnegie Foundation, of state legislatures and licensing boards, and of public opinion the AMA succeeded by means of accreditation in controlling and upgrading the curricula of medical schools and therefore in drastically cutting their number (Stevens 1971). This alliance of professors, practitioners, legislatures, foundations and popular opinion could not, however, be mobilized in other areas of professional regulation and the AMA never became the legitimate representative or governing body of American medicine and could not therefore reinstate a system of practitioner self-government.

To begin with, having eventually decided to turn itself into a mass, representative association, it did not hold on for long to a substantial majority of American physicians, and currently represents certainly less than a half and probably little more than a third of American physicians (Schwartz 1981). For much of its history it seems to have had difficulties in enforcing its policies even on its own members, has often been obliged to apply politically counter-productive policies against them and as a result has provoked a good deal of opposition within the profession, especially from the schools of medicine and public health. Though it tried, it was never able to regulate the internal division of medical labour, to demarcate family practitioners and specialists, and this distinction has therefore remained largely unregulated, while the numerous specialty boards fought, often at cross purposes, with the AMA to establish their jurisdictional claims (Stevens 1971). Nor was the AMA particularly successful in preventing new medical occupations such as osteopaths, chiropractors and opticians establishing their rights to practice, for even though the need for medical licensing was accepted, state legislatures and the American public remained suspicious of the powers and pretensions of closed professional groups, and especially of the AMA, the most powerful of them all (Rayack 1967). The AMA has also contributed little to the maintenance of the ethical standards of the profession. During the interregnum decades, patients had begun to take action on these questions themselves via malpractice suits, and the courts, rather than any professional body, have remained the major disciplinary tribunal of the profession, though supplemented in recent times by government sponsored PSROs (Performance Standards Review Organizations) in federally-aided hospitals.

The AMA often serves as the archetypal illustration of entrenched and irresponsible professional power but, as these examples suggest, its power over medical practice is limited. The power of other American professional associations is even more limited. The bar associations which were created in the later nineteenth century, for instance, hoped that practitioner control of admission to the profession might be reimposed via compulsory clerkship, and the abolition of the 'diploma privilege' (Reed 1921; Stevens 1970). Their efforts were unsuccessful and they were therefore obliged to follow the 'accreditation' policy pioneered by the medical profession. State legislatures, however, despite the substantial number of lawyers in them, were reluctant to restrict severely entrance to the legal profession. They therefore gradually raised entrance requirements to high school, to a college degree and to years at an 'approved' or accredited law school only when it was clear that a substantial segment of school population could reasonably be expected to meet those requirements. Accreditation therefore never drastically reduced the number of law school places and admissions, though virtually all current entrants to the legal profession have attended an 'approved' school (Woodworth 1973). In engineering, accreditation has constituted even less of a barrier on admission to the profession, and though most schools, other than the élite institutions, currently seek accreditation of their courses, attendance at such courses does not constitute a requirement to practise as an engineer, except in certain special circumstances where a state license is required (Finniston 1980).

Moreover, both professions have suffered from the same kind of problems as the medical profession in trying to establish their authority: the indifference of many practitioners towards professional bodies, competition between rival associations, and in the case of the lawyers, outspoken opposition to the very idea of a bar association and even anti-bar associations (Melone 1977; Tierney 1979, pp.166-9; Black 1971). Like physicians the lawyers have also had to face a great deal of public criticism of bar association rules, criticism which has at times been supported by law school professors. In their efforts to regulate legal practice, the bar associations of many states therefore felt obliged to turn to the state to 'integrate' the bar, ie to make bar association compulsory, so that they might exercise some control over the practising lawyers in their jurisdictions (McKean 1963). Engineering associations have attracted little public antagonism, but then they appear merely to have voiced the grievances and aspirations of engineers and to have had very little impact on their admission, training, practice or status (Layton 1971).

In a manner of speaking the English revolution of 1642-49 was also a critical event in the history of the English legal profession for it prompted a considerable popular movement against the profession and the Inns of Court and demands for the deprofessionalization of the law, comparable to those heard later in Paris in 1791 and in the United States in the early nineteenth century (Veall 1970). Cromwell himself had great sympathy for these demands, but was forced to admit that the 'sons of Zeruiah' as he referred to the lawyers, 'are yet too strong for us' and the Inns of Court emerged therefore at the Restoration, intact. The principle of professional self-government again came under threat in the last years of the Stuarts when Charles II and then James II challenged and recalled the charters of most of the major city of London companies, as well as of the College of Physicians and the Society of Apothecaries, partly to raise money, but also to subject these chartered bodies to royal control (Wall 1963, pp.100-5). The Glorious Revolution of 1688-9 put an end to this policy however and, while the professional bodies have often been subect to criticism, the principle that practitioners had major responsibility for governing their professions seems rarely to have been seriously challenged in England, either by the state, by the universities, from within the professions themselves or by the public at large.

From this point on, one can trace the emergence of strong, autonomous institutions of practitioner self-government, and whilst none can rival the immunities and privileges of the Inns of Court, the associations of other professional practitioners which developed in subsequent generations, such as the Law Society, the Royal Colleges of Physicians and Surgeons, the Institution of Civil Engineers and the rest, have also been granted a high degree of autonomy by comparison with their counterparts, when they have any, in France or the United States. Charters and statutes seem very largely to have reinforced their authority over members of the profession, and to have helped them both to control admission and training, and to defend their occupational jurisdictions. The development of the English professions has depended primarily therefore on the practitioners themselves, with the state and the universities playing rather minor supportive roles.

These differences in the role of practitioners, professors and the state in the three countries prompt a number of hypotheses about the English professions in general, the present evidence for which is suggestive rather than conclusive, and to which there are no doubt a number of exceptions, but which may nevertheless serve as a useful baseline in attempting to identify 'the peculiarities of the English.'

— First, the English have preserved the apprenticeship method of professional training to a greater extent than either the French or the Americans, or indeed any other modern society, and have been reluctant to admit that universities might have something to contribute to the preliminary or professional training of their members, or even that university degrees had much to contribute to their status. Accordingly, a lower proportion of English professionals have received a university education.

— Second, as the English professions have come to admit that universities and polytechnics have a part to play in the education of their members, and that university degrees might indeed augment their status, they have sought to limit the universities to a preliminary or part-time role and have thereby created the distinctive English system of dual curricula and dual qualifications.

— Third, as a result perhaps of practitioner control of entry, the English professions have tended to be proportionately smaller than their counterparts elsewhere (Rueschemeyer 1978; Todd 1968, p.141; Ahlström 1982, pp.79-90).

— Fourth, as a result no doubt of apprenticeship training, they appear to have succeeded in recruiting a higher proportion of practitioners as members of professional associations, excluding from the comparison of course those cases where membership is compulsory, such as the Inns of Court or the American integrated bars. One may therefore reasonably suggest that the English have a higher sense of professional solidarity than their counterparts in France and the United States, and correspondingly also, though it would be extremely difficult to test, that they are more inclined to accept and conform to their profession's rules of etiquette and ethics (Johnstone and Hopson 1967, p.475). There is, at least, no English parallel to the French and American experience of large sectors of the professions developing for long periods without any form of professional regulation.

— Fifth, the English professions have demarcated and enforced an inter-professional division of labour far more effectively than either the French or the Americans, who have faint or no equivalents to the rules of etiquette which still govern relationships between the two branches of the English legal and medical professions.

— Sixth, and last, it would appear that English professions have always shown a greater concern for the corporate honour and prestige of their professions than their French and American counterparts. Their attempts to preserve an inter-professional division of labour are of course merely one indication of this concern. In France only the advocates constituted an analogous, distinct and cohesive status group. Other French professions, and even more so the American, seem to have remained less cohesive and homogeneous in status terms than their English counterparts.

All of these hypotheses require further investigation, but two related questions in particular require future comparative study: first, how far English professionals employed in industrial enterprises maintained a feeling of solidarity and corporate honour, a proprietary sense of their legitimate jurisdiction, and rules of etiquette in dealing with other professionals and outsiders similar to those which are so evident in the behaviour of English lawyers and doctors. There is some evidence to suggest that they have, most notably from Granick's investigation, which noted that the careers of British managers tended to be within a specific occupation or function, be it accounting, engineering, personnel or sales, in sharp contrast to the cross-occupational career patterns of American, and even of French and Soviet managers (Granick 1972). The second question is how far the occupational cohesiveness and solidarity implied by Granick's findings affect the innovativeness and efficiency of British industry. Since successful American and Japanese corporations seem to have made immense efforts to eliminate the occupational loyalties of both professional and manual workers in favour of loyalty to the enterprise as a whole it would appear to be wholly adverse, but this remains to be demonstrated.

Whether or not each and every one of the hypotheses proposed above is proven correct, it is nevertheles clear that the distribution of power and authority between practitioners, professors and the state is radically different in these three countries, and that some recognition and assessment of it is the first preliminary to any proposals for reform, since each configuration presents a distinct set of obstacles and opportunities. The French expect the initiative to rest with the state, the Americans can rely on their market-oriented universities, while the English seem to be obliged to work through practitioner associations, with long traditions of part-time education, and, with their ability to mobilize practitioners, a considerable power to veto unwelcome or threatening proposals.

The second preliminary to any discussion of reform is an explicit statement of value premises, since it is clear that professions may be judged by alternative and conflicting criteria. If, for instance, one believed that the best legal profession was one which minimized the resort to the courts and the best medical profession one which resisted the 'medicalization' of everyday life, then one would, in all probability, opt for the English model. If, however, one thinks that the business of the legal profession is to see that everyone is able to defend their legal rights and has access both to the courts and to adequate legal representation, and correspondingly that the business of the medical profession is to provide a universal, preventive care, then one might find the more entrepreneurial, American professions rather more promising, with their freedom to advertise and compete, and to develop new forms for the delivery of professional services, such as the new legal supermarkets and physician assistants (Gerson 1980; APAP 1980). The industry-based professions probably present rather fewer problems in this respect, since, in theory at least, there is one generally accepted criterion by which they all may be assessed, and that is their contribution to the economic performance of their industries.

Finally, there remains the deviant 'profession' of management. This does not fit the configuration outlined above very well, if at all. In the United States, it is true, the universities seem once again to have taken the lead, by the creation of business schools, but in France private initiative was crucial, at least in the development of management education, while in Britain the creation of the British Institute of Management (BIM) and of business schools depended on state initiatives wholly without precedent in the development of other established professions. From this one might conclude either that arguments based largely on the experience of medicine and law are inappropriate in analysing the development of newer professions or that management is not, in the same sense, a profession. For several reasons I am inclined to the latter alternative. In the first place, the members of this 'profession' cannot be readily defined, except in the rather special case of management consultants, and it is not surprising therefore that they do not appear to have developed much professional esprit; nor have management associations succeeded in recruiting substantial numbers of 'practitioners'. Furthermore, it is not clear how admission to this 'profession' could ever be controlled, or why it would ever be necessary or desirable to do so.

However, my main reason for doubting that management is properly considered among the professions is that it does not appear to have, or to have in prospect, an occupational jurisdiction comparable to that of any profession. The primary managerial task, I take it, is to organize, monitor and reorganize other people's work, which is to say that it is of necessity opposed to fixed occupational jurisdictions, to occupational solidarity and occupational status pretensions and is, or should be, forever seeking to re-arrange, re-deploy and re-structure work relationships as processes, products and markets change. Management's proper jurisdiction is, so to speak, everybody else's. For this reason it is entirely appropriate that many business degrees should have a kind of 'cuckoo' curriculum since managers require sufficient knowledge of law, accounting, personnel management, marketing and the like to be able to communicate and work with specialists in these areas. At the same time, however, they need to be permanently identified with none of them, since at times at least they have to question the assumptions and ideologies that professional specialists inevitably come to share, and to challenge the prerogatives they frequently contrive to establish. In the lay sense of 'expert', or 'trained' or 'efficient', managers may of course be professional; but if the term is used to describe or connote the kind of social institutions and attitudes that the English professions have developed, managers are not, or at least should not be, in the least professional. On the contrary, they should be profoundly anti-professional.

Part 2

Overview of Issues in Education
for the Professions

4 Overview of Themes in Medical Education

Henry Walton

This chapter presents key issues which the writer believes to be the most telling at present, although not all of them are widely acknowledged as crucial or generally accorded importance by medical teachers.

Later chapters will focus on particular aspects of medical education, and there recent research will be cited. The purpose here is to state some of the main contemporary themes in medical education, and to indicate crucial research contributions which should be taken further by new investigation.

Research in medical education, perhaps more extensive than in any other branch of higher education, is naturally of widely diverse sorts, ranging from comparisons between different teaching methods (Walton 1969; Stretton *et al* 1967) which may remind educational researchers of the classical design of drug trials, to painstaking longitudinal studies requiring the sociologist to enrol in the medical school and not only attend classes and clinics but to live in dormitories until the students in his cohort graduate (Fredericks and Mundy 1976). From these investigations a great deal of understanding has been obtained.

Conservatism about the Profession of Medicine

Radical criticisms are not given much attention by medical teachers, and hence have little impact. Only a minority of medical teachers are interested enough in teaching to read the medical education journals (*Medical Education* published in the UK and the *Journal of Medical Education* in the US) or to attend national or international conferences on education.

The global body formally representing medical education, recognized as such by the World Health Organization with which it is in non-governmental relationship, is the World Federation for Medical

Education: its Executive Council has representatives from the six sectors (Africa, the Americas, the Eastern Mediterranean area, Europe, South-East Asia and the Western Pacific). The aim of the Federation is to promote and maintain associations in each of these regions. That in Europe may be mentioned as an example.

The Association for Medical Education in Europe (AMEE), when founded at Copenhagen in 1972 contained two members, the UK association (ASME) and the Nordic Federation. At the 1983 Conference of AMEE in Prague − the Association meets each year in a different country − twenty-seven countries were represented in the meeting of its Advisory Board (there are thirty-two countries in the World Health Organization's regional European sector), most now with national associations. To involve the educational administrators, as well as medical teachers, AMEE helped set up an Association of Medical Deans in Europe, the two bodies meeting in sequence always in the same place. There are thus regional and global bodies concerned primarily with medical education. The innovations reported and the issues raised in their deliberations are not usually reflected in the practices or concerns of most teachers in medical schools; the mere mention of certain of the themes being reviewed will cause indignation to many medical teachers, who will not accord some of them 'any' importance and will dismiss others as immaterial, irrelevant and unsound.

Radical Criticisms

Trenchant criticisms of modern medicine have appeared recently in print (Illich 1975) and other media, such as a recent series of BBC Reith Lectures (Kennedy 1981). These polemical attacks have been the most obvious, but social scientists have also investigated the major shifts in attitude that have occurred in Western societies. For example Foucault, by 'archaeological' inquiry (1973) which cuts across boundaries applied by medical historians, claims that apparent clinical entities such as 'patients', 'medical history', 'lesions' and so on are not preformed entities in the real world but products of the professional discourse which embodies them. Until recently medicine was perceived as characterized by disinterested benevolence and scientific advance; now there is both public and professional questioning whether greater improvement in health might not more readily result from an approach other than that of the medical services as presently delivered.

Doctors themselves understandably subscribe to the public stereotypes, and would be enlightened were they to become aware of the sociologists' demonstration of the 'social construction' of medicine (Wright and Treacher 1982), which challenges traditional assumptions that the identification and definition of medicine and medical knowledge is self-evident, taken for granted, and consists of what doctors and their ancillary workers do, mediated by medical schools and teaching hospitals and disseminated through medical textbooks and journals. Another common assumption, that medical practice is built on the findings of modern science and is effective, has been challenged by a notable professor of social medicine (McKeown 1979); he demonstrated that the role of medicine in improving health has been less considerable than is generally believed, both by the public and doctors themselves. Much modern morbidity (such as heart disease, cancer, rheumatism and other chronic disorders) remains poorly treatable, although there have of course been notable advances in such fields as the infectious diseases. However, as Powles (1971) has argued, progress in this respect is also often exaggerated.

The Medical School as an Institution

There have been numerous classical studies of medical schools by social scientists, who have recognized, in Bloom's (1958) words:

> The institution which has evolved within the profession of medicine for the purpose of professionalizing its recruits is the medical school ... the medical school provides the social environment in which this process of maturation takes place.

Merton (1957) was a sociologist who also conducted pioneering investigations into the way in which the medical school mediates the emergence of the professional self, and the gradual identification of medical students, by themselves and by society, as doctors.

New studies are pressingly needed. The medical schools in Britain are weakened by university economic cuts, with deteriorating facilities, difficulty in recruitment (better salaries can be earned by doctors in the National Health Service), frozen posts and thus loss of teaching staff. Prestigious professorial chairs remain unfilled. Other important new chairs, with great implications for preventive medicine (such as genetics) on occasion as now at Edinburgh are discontinued. In the US as well, prediction for a 'no-growth' future for medical schools (Roger 1980) has proved over-optimistic: federal, state and philanthrophic support are all actually diminishing. At the same time, public demand is more insistent that medical schools must educate doctors better in clinical service, and become more responsive to community needs and available to social groups at present relatively neglected, such as the elderly, the disadvantaged and the chronically ill.

Clearly, if medical schools try to go on doing what they have always done the whole situation can only deteriorate. There is more need than ever to ensure that teaching and learning are effective. Short-sightedly, medical education provisions may be curtailed: medical teachers in administrative position have been heard to say, for example, that small group instruction must diminish and more lectures return. Such reasoning is dangerously fallacious, and reflects the scant understanding of educational issues, such as the need to devise a learning experience to be congruent with the new knowledge or skills to be acquired. Rather should the decision of the Karolinska Institute in Stockholm be followed, where all departments have now to assign a proportion of funding for central medical education developments.

If one attribute of established medical schools has to be singled out, the prominent feature is resistance to change. Sociologists, investigating medical schools as institutions, have a complex but rewarding task ahead. Medical schools, like all university faculties, will be seriously strained as institutions when priorities have to be revised, current commitments altered and traditions broken.

Science or Art

It is remarkable to observe that the practice of clinical medicine involves managerial decisions (about sick people, aiming to alter disease) which have as yet hardly been investigated at all (Feinstein 1970). Most erroneously, this sphere of medical practice, concerned with managerial decisions by the doctor about sick people, has glibly been explained away as 'the art of medicine'.

With the availability of X-rays, EMI scans, biopsies, histology reports, non-surgical exploration of body cavities, safer surgical investigation, etc. doctors can now more precisely diagnose many diseases. The challenge is not the intellectual act of explaining deductive decisions, but the managerial act of deciding which investigations to carry out. The same type of decision-making is involved in deciding which treatments to apply. The challenge in establishing clinical science is to create better, and recognizable, methods for observing, identifying and classifying patients. Improved medical education calls for clearer definition of the methods a doctor uses when providing therapeutic services.

It is remarkable that only meagre investigation has been made by direct observation of doctors at work (Peterson *et al* 1956): such work greatly needs to be extended.

Medicine is held to have become a science with the publication of the Flexner Report of 1910, when the teaching of medicine became integrated with the natural sciences (Flexner 1925). The disadvantages of this revolution have started to receive some research attention. Analysis of medical teaching rounds has shown that senior physicians at the bedside gave little emphasis to the approach to the patients, or to establishing a doctor-patient relationship (Payson and Barchas 1965). In arriving at clinical decisions and relating the case findings to medical theory, teachers at the bedside were found to pay very little attention to individual or personal aspects of the patients.

An undesired accompaniment of progress in science and its adoption in clinical medicine was diminished concern with patients as people.

Entering Medicine

Perhaps the most pressing concern in medical education, on a global level, is entry to medical school. Countries differ according to whether free entry is permitted to all qualified school-leavers seeking admission (open entry) or whether numbers of entrants are restricted.

Britain and the United States are examples of countries where the number of students allowed places in medical schools is fixed, and entry is by selection. In contrast, Spain and Italy are examples of countries where there is open access. A result is 'massification', the creation of vast classes. In Spain 8000 medical students graduated in 1979, vastly in excess of the doctors the country needs. The total number of medical students in the twenty-seven medical schools of Spain is 82,000, greatly exceeding the entire number of doctors in the country, 63,000.

When open entry is used, wastage inevitably becomes the means to bring about the necessary drop-out; the basis for eliminating a proportion of entrants is the examinations in the pre-clinical subjects.

Countries which are in serious difficulty from the impairment in medical education which results from vast entering classes are prevented from reform, by public objection to which politicians are responsive. In fact, the whole issue of entry demonstrates blatantly how political, cultural and national influences rather than educational considerations can affect medical training.

A most pressing area for intensive research is methods of selection. Usually educational attainment is the chief criterion (in countries with centralized, adequately monitored national examinations). The fallacy of this approach is that non-intellectual attributes, such as motivation, have now been shown to be too important to be ignored. There are medical schools which do not interview applicants, but make their selection decisions simply on the basis of application forms reporting school examination results and head teachers' appraisals. Interviewing, for long under a cloud, is beginning to receive more support (Rippey *et al* 1981), and that notably at innovative schools such as McMaster in Canada and Beersheva in Israel.

Sex

A considerable change in medical schools has been in the proportion of women entrants. The proportion of women applicants to US medical schools increased from 5.7 per cent in 1949-50 to 29.5 per cent in 1980-81; the proportion of women entrants increased from 5.5 per cent in 1949-50 to 28.9 per cent in 1980-81. In some UK schools women now form half the class. Investigations have found important differences between men and women medical students. Women have more concern than do men for the psychological aspects of illness in addition to the physical aspects; women do better in examinations; they are more anxious and less sociable (Walton 1968). Cartwright (1972) found that women students are more sensitive to relationships, values, feelings and ethical issues than are men students.

The hopeful view has been expressed that young women doctors will improve the medical profession and as longstanding prejudices are overcome will move into wider professional spheres, some previously closed to them. 'The special qualities and values that they bring into the profession will very likely influence the behaviour of all physicians' (Relman 1980). However, it seems that while much is expected of them as their numbers grow, their proportion among medical teachers is dropping in the US: from 12 per cent in 1975 to 11.5 per cent in 1978.

The Curriculum

How the very many different basic science and medical subjects should be selected, put together, taught, learned, evaluated, monitored, the students assessed, and necessary change instituted is at the very centre of what medical schools are about. (This assertion does not overlook the other responsibilities of medical schools, such as research and patient care.)

There is a vast literature dealing with the planning and implementation of medical curricula. Those of each of the thirty-eight British medical schools as taught in 1975-76 have been painstakingly surveyed by the General Medical Council (1977). The first volume contains a general section, dealing with size of intake and selection then with the curriculum, examination systems and new developments, and continuing with descriptive profiles of each of the medical schools. The second volume summarizes the teaching of each subject in the curriculum. The comprehensive information makes clear the similarities and − more interesting still − the differences among medical schools. Britain is a good example of a country in which wide variations are possible among schools, and uniformity is not sought: an advantage when the right and best way to educate doctors is unclear.

Objectives

During the decades 1960-80 very considerable attention was given by medical schools to specifying educational objectives, and many medical schools for the first time set down their goals. However, the evaluation system does not harmonize with the stated objectives, and medical students naturally give precedence to the demands of examinations.

Certain medical schools, such as the Abraham Lincoln School at Illinois, went to great lengths in meticulously deriving very detailed objectives for every subject (1973). One medical school in particular (Ohio State 1976) required 'clear and concise' objectives for every subect, complying with a standardized format, and developed an independent study programme (ISP) to replace the 'conventional lecture-discussion curriculum.'

In general, the trend now is to endorse the need for objectives, so that medical students are explicitly told what they must know and what they must be able to do and respond to in each of the subjects they study: but highly detailed specification is not generally favoured, an approach widely endorsed at an international conference in Edinburgh (Association for Medical Education in Europe 1974).

Integration

The affliction common in curricula is the claim staked by the different departments for teaching time, inevitable and sometimes almost immutable when the 'departmental' structure of the medical school is emphatic. The anatomy department, say, or the orthopaedic department and so on, consider their institutional standing ordained by the amount of teaching time each commands. In consequence, when professors have control of curriculum planning, great obstacles are offered. 'The administrative structure of the traditional medical school is, I suggest, designed to achieve maximum inflexibility and the greatest possible difficulty in adapting the school's policy and programmes to a rapidly changing world' (Maddison 1978).

Vertical integration is the catch-phrase for doing away with the out-moded belief that clinical studies must be preceded by basic science teaching. Horizontal integration, although very generally approved, is often surprisingly difficult to realize. A move to 'topic teaching' is the most usual remedy attempted, when physicians, surgeons, pathologists, histologists, etc. pool their resources to teach about a particular subject such as kidney disease. It is rare for the basic sciences, however, to feature in clinical topic teaching.

Chapter 7 on 'Interdisciplinary Teaching' in the General Medical Council (1977) survey reports on six schools where integration is a major goal, and more schools report planning such integration both vertically and among disciplines. However, the reverse trend also occurs: 'One school in which the majority of theoretical clinical teaching used to be interdisciplinary has reverted to single discipline teaching, and another one is likely to do so.'

Illnesses and their management increasingly transcend any disciplinary or departmental boundary. There is also much evidence that it is educationally wrong to confine a learner's attention artificially, by departmental fragmentation, to one sphere when comprehension requires multi-disciplinarity. At times it is hard, even when not the professors but a curriculum committee plans the teaching, for example, to have anatomy of the brain taught at the same time as the brain is being dealt with in the physiology department. Amelioration of this serious problem has been tried through adoption of a matrix system of medical school management at McMaster University in Canada. Departments there earn resources not in respect of disciplines represented, but by virtue of the actual contribution made by a department to the medical school as an institution, thus encouraging medical teachers to work for institutional rather than departmental goals (Mustard *et al* 1982).

Finding Time for New Subjects

A major problem in the curricula of medical schools is lack of capacity to incorporate new subjects, a crippling limitation when it is recognized that there is expansion in the knowledge that may be useful for medical care. Instead, established subjects maintain their hold on hallowed teaching time claimed as of right. Much is taught that all teachers except those in the subject concerned recognize as lacking in contemporary relevance in medical education, and in consequence the rapid changes in medical care and health services are not given proper attention or scope. Statistics, research design, science of science, ethics, and medical engineering (Areskog 1977) are only some subjects for which pressing claims have been made.

Training Settings

There is some awareness that to be 'relevant' (a favourite word, currently) teaching has to be provided and learning take place where the phenomena are actually present, that is to say, at the actual sites where the patients present their ailments and illnesses. The implication clearly is that the proper training setting is the community, with its homes, factories, schools etc.; health care clinics, of all types; primary medical care settings like general practices; and outpatient departments of quite unglamorous hospitals.

This recognition clearly calls on medical schools to bring into use for teaching purposes a range of health care facilities not customarily sanctioned as academically up to standard. The traditional status assignment in universities is upset when a range of health workers (not only doctors) in the institutions of the community have to become recognized teachers. McMaster University, for example, in order to take advantage of neighbourhood non-university health care facilities, had to insist: 'we could not be tied to narrow university requirements for promotion, tenure and salary increases based on research alone' (Mustard *et al* 1982, p.6). In the UK, the position fortunately is that all Health Service consultants by contract are required to teach; the same does not apply to general practitioners, which complicated the recent efforts to give primary medical care greater time in the undergraduate curriculum. Before practical teaching can be moved out into the community, potential teachers based there have to be prepared for their teaching role, and supported in providing an adequate learning environment.

That hospital medicine has been over-emphasized is now coming to be realized, although clear warnings were sounded long ago: 'All that can be obtained from the teaching centre is a restricted view of a limited class of patients ... an inadequate preparation for the realities of practice' (McKeown 1961).

Problem-based Learning

Because it will be dealt with in detail in Chapter 23, it need only be mentioned here that a problem-solving approach, rather than depart-mental teaching, has been proposed (Barrows and Tamblyn 1980). This is a rigorous, structured approach to learning, based on research and experience, and not simply on the presentation of problems to medical students. Harmen Tiddens, a founder of Maastricht Medical School in Holland, goes so far as to believe 'that evidence is accumulating that a curriculum based on the concept of "problem-based learning" offers the best solution' to the major obstacles medical education is facing (Mustard *et al* 1982, p.51). This is a large claim of such importance that it requires to be tested by evaluative research.

Motivation

This was the subject of the Annual Conference of the Association for

Medical Education in Europe in 1982. A matter for concern among investigators during previous decades was the evidence that medical students sometimes become demotivated by their studies. 'Growth of cynicism' was a phrase used to describe an aspect of the disillusionment sometimes detected; other investigators claimed the phenomenon was different, and represented the 'detached concern' appropriate for a future doctor.

As further investigation of non-cognitive attributes of students proceeds, the effect of the wrong sequencing of subjects will need to be studied further: in particular, the effect of basic science subjects, taught largely by non-doctors, during the first half of the curriculum, on entrants wanting to study medicine and make contact with patients. Another matter needing attention is the emphasis in medical schools on the extrinsic motivation proffered by a succession of examinations while intrinsic motivation, which could stem from the nature of the task itself, is neglected. There is great need for investigation of the attributes and activities of both students and teachers which impair or reduce motivation, and for identification of effective learning approaches and teaching (Miller 1980).

Medical Teachers as 'Role Models'

Sociological research has demonstrated the extent to which an important component of learning derives from the example given in their own person by teachers, who significantly influence medical students in many respects, such as in their choice of future career, their professional attitudes, and the importance they assign to different subjects.

The presentation by teachers of themselves is thus an important component of medical teaching. However, the influence now appears more subtle and pervasive than earlier research suggested; Funkenstein (1978) has shown that career choice is less influenced by medical teachers than they suppose, only a fifth of students surveyed at Harvard and in a national US sample considering that a particular medical teacher had influenced their choice of professional career.

A special problem is the dwindling number of teachers in the basic sciences who are medically qualified. The 'pre-clinical' student increasingly is taught by teachers who cannot fully sympathize with the need for a form of medical education closely integrating the basic sciences such as anatomy and physiology with the clinical disciplines. The basic scientists are often not perceived as acceptable teachers by medical students, because the role model they present is insufficiently related to the professional futures that medical students envisage for themselves.

Striking differences have been found between teachers in the basic sciences and in the clinical departments (Jason and Westberg 1982). Both groups of teachers derive much personal satisfaction from teaching – that is the one similarity. Otherwise, they differ in their backgrounds before becoming medical teachers, their orientations to teaching, their teaching styles, the settings in which they teach, their attitudes to students, their views about the goals of learning and their personal values. In particular, it has been found that teachers who are medically qualified do not identify with the academic profession to the extent that basic science (predominantly PhD) teachers do. Those medically qualified look to other physicians in the community as a preferred local reference group, not to other professors in the university (Blackburn and Fox 1976).

Only recently is the effect on students of these discrepancies in outlook among teaching staff being recognized as a matter for concern and investigation, particularly when reforms are proposed to reduce fragmentation of curricula.

Medical Teaching as a Distinct Ability

A main reason for setting up national and international associations of medical education is to promote the recognition of teaching as a profession. Medical teachers are largely amateurs, and need in the medical school an atmosphere encouraging interest in teaching and in the technical aspects of education. Usually, advancement in academic medicine is on the basis of research achievement or clinical competence. Interest in or ability for teaching rarely counts.

Efforts have been made to rectify this institutional disparagement of teaching, by individuals and at certain centres. 'If competence as an educator is to assume the importance it deserves in the repertoire of a medical school faculty member, then it must be honoured far more than it is now' (Miller 1980). The founders of McMaster University in Canada were emphatic from the start: 'We felt education was important and that it would have to be recognized. ... Thus a Faculty member can be rewarded because of his work in research, education or health services...' (Mustard *et al.* 1982, p.6).

'Traditional' Medical Schools

The vast majority of the world's medical schools fall into this category, and the bulk of the world's doctors emerge from them. To the extent that medical education is in need of change, development and reform, that must occur in these medical schools.

Famous medical teachers have so despaired of introducing reforms into the traditional medical schools in their charge that they have left them and established new schools instead: Prywes exchanged Jerusalem for Beersheva, and Maddison forsook Sydney to set up Newcastle in New South Wales. Their accomplishments in fresh pastures have been prodigious and enlightening; but it is in the traditional schools, such as those they deserted, that the changes have to be made to train the doctors to meet health needs brought about by the massive changes in contemporary society.

It is from studies of the means by which changes are accomplished in long-established medical schools that determinants of stasis on one hand or the possibility of development on the other can be identified (Walton 1980).

In point of fact, the most famous of innovations, integration of the curriculum, which occurred in Cleveland in 1952, advancing to its second stage in 1968, took place at an established school, Western Reserve. The celebrated 'uncontrolled experiment' was a change in an existing curriculum. It is true that the then dean, Joseph T. Wearn, had ten new departmental chairmen under the age of forty, and that without them the 'revolution' of a curriculum designed not by departments but by subject committees might not have occurred (Ham 1976; Williams 1980).

Unfortunately, educational research at Western Reserve was in some respects lacking, but how many current innovations are properly studied? Although the customary emphasis given to outcome criteria of medical education ('a good doctor') is irrelevant, because so many different types of doctor are needed, graduates from Western Reserve have in fact been followed up, a rare undertaking (Mawardi 1979).

New Medical Schools

The hope for the future of medical education is sometimes (erroneously) viewed as being located in new medical schools. Certainly, the innovations at Beersheva in Israel, McMaster in Canada, Maastricht in Holland, Tromsö in Norway, Tampere in Finland and Newcastle in New South Wales are now given the closest attention (Ström and Walton 1978). The Minutes of 2 March 1950 at Western Reserve recognized the '...challenge and opportunity to make a real contribution to medical education' which served as an example throughout the 1950s and 1960s.

At Kingston, Jamaica in June 1979 twenty medical schools were represented at a meeting where a *Network of Community-oriented Educational Institutions for the Health Sciences* was set up. The 'Network' has its cumbersome name in part because one of its major sponsoring bodies, the World Health Organization, opposes narrow emphasis on doctors (or 'physicians' in US influenced contexts) and advocates that wherever possible references should include other health professions also. The Network forms the part of the World Federation which may succeed in pioneering the necessary reforms. As its secretary, J. Greep, said at its meeting in Havana in 1983: 'The Network will sing in the church of the Federation'. The two criteria for participation of schools in the Network are community-oriented programmes and the use of a problem-solving educational process.

How Doctors Diagnose

Clinical interviewing in the different branches of medicine has been intensively investigated in recent years. The clinical reasoning process is largely unconscious: the empirical studies of the way a doctor approaches a patient have demonstrated that doctors are little aware of the technical approaches they use. It has become apparent that the clinician characteristically generates only a few hypotheses, usually between two and five, very soon after first encountering the patient. These ideas or hunches or guesses, based on first cues presented by the patient, then serve to focus the clinician's history-taking and examination. Investigation has shown that experienced doctors often err by failing to respond to cues given by patients about their chief concerns. Such research (Elstein *et al* 1978) has obvious relevance in the design of medical education. Medical students are trained to follow systematized history-taking, physical examination and ordering of special investigations in a standard sequence which experienced doctors themselves do not operate.

Other Major Issues

To be at all comprehensive, passing consideration should now be given to important matters many of which have been the subject of major international conferences. Each of the following areas is of the greatest importance, and the brevity with which they are mentioned should not be taken as under-estimation of their significance.

Primary Care

The relative neglect of primary medical care, as distinct from secondary and tertiary hospital-based curative medicine, is now being recognized more clearly, although pressingly needed reform is slow in materializing in many countries (Noack 1980). The situation in Britain has been surveyed recently (Walton 1983).

Evaluation and Assessment

How medical students and doctors in postgraduate training are assessed and how the quality of their teaching and learning is evaluated are of pressing concern, because of the extent to which examinations dominate curricula. Fortunately, intensive on-going research is being actively carried out in many aspects of education and training (Fabb and Marshall 1982; Fleming *et al* 1976; Hubbard 1978; Metz, Moll and Walton 1981; Rippey 1981).

Postgraduate Medical Education

This vast area, where perhaps the most decisive and influential recent developments in training doctors have occurred, has not been given place in this review. That is not because its profound importance is being overlooked. On the contrary, it must be emphasized that in some countries very elaborate postgraduate training programmes exist. In others, however, a free-for-all system operates: there are countries in Europe without organized postgraduate training and with insufficient training places, even though full recognition has now been accorded to the fact that graduates from medical school are not yet by any means doctors; they need further organized and formal postgraduate training.

Continuing Medical Education

Much promise attaches to the steps now being taken, as a result of both professional and public pressures, to ensure facilities for experienced doctors in practice to maintain and continually update their clinical competence. Among such developments is 'peer review', a method by which practising clinicians meet regularly as a group to evaluate the quality and efficiency of the services provided by themselves and their colleagues. Another method is 'audit', the sharing by a group of peers of information gained from personal experience and/or records in order to assess the care provided to their patients, to improve their own learning, and to contribute to medical knowledge. Distance learning is enabling new procedures to develop fostered by technology such as computers and videotape. The questions whether periodical 'recertification' of established doctors is also needed, by examination or required courses, and whether CME should be obligatory in the US or voluntary as elsewere, is keenly debated.

Divorce Between Education and Service

Disjunction between medical education and the Health Care Systems of different countries is one matter for most serious concern (Karatzas and Walton 1980), and attention to it is one of the prerequisites for improvement in medical education.

The Future

A great challenge which is now coming before the medical schools and the postgraduate training bodies derives from an international agreement reached in 1978 at Alma-Ata in the USSR. All countries adopted a resolution at the 34th World Health Assembly in 1979 proposing 'Health for All by the Year 2000'. The method proposed to promote this ambitious goal is a new concept of 'primary health care', which calls for developments now relatively lacking in most countries: education of the public about prevailing health problems; a major emphasis on promotion of health; a serious concern with prevention of illness; proper nutrition; provision of safe water and basic sanitation; attention to family health; and appropriate treatment of common illnesses.

If primary health care is to become a reality (it has been adopted as the official policy of the World Health Organization), a major change will be demanded of the medical schools, with vast organizational and educational implications; delivery of health care will also have to be modified extensively. Doctors will have to work much more closely with members of the other health professions, and training will have to be provided in common. As things stand, governments have so far failed adequately to convey to medical schools what their countries at the world health parliament have committed them to implement (Walton 1983). Medical education in every country unquestionably stands to gain greatly from the more effective contact and improved communication of medical schools with the country's health care system, and with the government's health department.

5 Overview of Issues in Engineering Education

Monty Finniston

In January 1980, after some two and a half years of research study and of wide consultation and deliberation, the Report of a government appointed Committee of Inquiry into the Engineering Profession entitled 'Engineering our Future' (Finniston 1980), an intentional double entendre, was issued. Its eighty or so recommendations covered the complex diverse problems related to the supply and employment of engineers, including the recruitment of women; the changes required in schools to give greater prominence to engineering in career terms; the requirements of engineers for formal education and training to the graduate level and continuing education beyond; the registration and licensing of engineers; the role of the professional engineering institutions; the relationship between professional engineers and trade unions; and the organization of engineers in a national context.

Each of these topics merited a chapter on its own, but if there was one common thread on which they could all be strung, it would be today's needs by a developed or developing society for professionalism: professionalism in the conduct of all activities whether in respect of social, domestic, industrial or commercial purposes, whether in primary concerns such as manufacture or in the supporting infra-structure disciplines of education, law, accountancy, medicine, etc. In an era of continuing change and of increasing complexity, the application of muscle and ignorance no longer serve the future. So what is professionalism?

Professionalism

Engineering professionalism has, according to an American source, six aspects.

Know-how: a set of skills for effecting certain procedures.
Know-what: practical understanding and direct immediate ac-
                 cess to facts, findings, methods.
Know-whom: knowing whom to turn to for referral, advice, help.
Know-how much: judgement about orders of magnitude in capaci-
                 ties, costs.
Know-why: justification for procedures.
Know-when: strategic timing, practical wisdom.

Professionals, by reason of their disciplinary knowledge, their traditions, their relationship to other professionals, and their recognition by
and status in society, are not all comparable, much less equal. Engineers
for example differ from other professional groups in three important
aspects. Firstly, the great majority of engineers are employees of
companies and other organizations; even consulting engineers rarely
work in isolation. Secondly, the nature of the engineer's work (compared
with that of the doctor or the lawyer) is not well understood by the lay
public, with whom engineers are seldom in direct professional contact.
Thirdly, the range of activities covered by engineers is greater than for
most other professions, as evidenced by such epithets prefixing the term
'engineer' as civil, mechanical, electrical, electronic, chemical, marine,
mining, naval, municipal, production, structural, etc.; and as the
professional interests of engineers become more diverse, such specialist
engineers as nuclear, public health, highway, agricultural, etc. give even
greater diversity in identification.

The development of professionalism requires the provision of facilities
for education, training and experience to standards set by those qualified
and respected as setting example and to the personal satisfaction of the
potential practitioner. The early seeds of professionalism are sown in
schools, but not with equal measure or success of planting.

Nobody would hesitate to tell you what a doctor, a lawyer or an
accountant would do. But in this country engineering falls into a
category of public ignorance. Sixty-eight per cent of the public at large,
when asked (NOP 1978) what kinds of things do you think an engineer
might actually do, considered engineering was a manual skill; only 13
per cent thought that engineering related to the professional level, to
design, planning or research; and 19 per cent just did not know. This
lack of understanding of the activities of professional engineers does not
obtain in other industrialized countries, or certainly not to the same
extent. France, Germany, Japan and the US all cater to the professional
engineer in recognition, status, etc. in a way which compares favourably
with other disciplinary professions.

Engineering is not a subordinate branch of science, although
engineering attempts to base itself on science where science is relevant

and applicable. Like technology, engineering certainly concerns itself with the application of science but engineering has its own modus operandi and character of knowledge, method, practice and objective. It is regrettable that the achievements of engineers, particularly when they succeed in high technology developments, are attributed by the media to scientists, but scientific projects if they fail are regarded as the fault of the engineer. The dependence of science on engineering for its fulfilment is to be seen in the physical realization of atom-smashers, satellites, instrumentation and controls, etc.

Engineering Dimension

There are various definitions of engineering and in a field as diverse as that which has been indicated earlier, it is perhaps difficult to find one which applies generally and without equivocation. Engineers are associated with the design, research, development, construction and production of artefacts or systems in an industrial environment and in the marketing of the product output from their factories; they are also concerned with the design, development and operation of processes relating to manufacture and service systems. Engineers and engineering, however, cannot remain in isolation from the world of other disciplines in which engineers operate; for example, in the field of manufacture account must be taken of a whole range of complex and interrelated factors, including the size, buoyancy and accessibility of world markets, the impact of policies and priorities determined in the political sphere, the availability of finance (in particular for innovation), the competence of company managements and the support and commitment of employees at all levels for the changes needed. The engineering performance of manufacturing enterprises and even service industries depends not only upon the numbers and qualities of engineers employed, but equally (if not more) on the effective priority accorded to engineering in that enterprise. To convey this interaction of engineering with the non-engineering factors mentioned above and the importance of considering the manufacturing system as a whole and not just aspects of it, the concept of the 'engineering dimension' was conceived by the Committee of Inquiry. This is defined as 'the capability of an organization as a system for translating engineering expertise into production and marketing of competitive products through efficient production processes'.

The engineering dimension involves all the factors and activities concerned in relating the technological capabilities in the expertise of an organization to its overall objectives; this includes governmental activities both national and local where the importance of engineering and engineers has hitherto not been sufficiently acknowledged. Engineers have to work in teams not only concerned with engineering but also with the other impacting disciplines in which the total expertise is co-ordinated to achieve maximum efficiency towards the stated objective. Engineering projects, to be realized and managed, involve planning — with all that that entails in co-ordinating efficiently a complex system of interrelated disciplines in a given time frame.

Preparing Schoolchildren for the Professions

There is much talk of core curriculum subjects for schoolchildren. In the preparation of every professional for any career, there are some essential disciplines to be taught and learned. Firstly, communication in the form of language either verbal or written has to be mastered. Although language as generally defined means both words and grammar, in the context of professionalism it means more; it means the rational use of language, that is language expressed in logical terms. Yet surprisingly, logic is not taught in its own right in school education. It is true that mathematics and in particular geometry classify as symbolic logic but that does not translate easily if at all into everyday language. Logic in the conduct of one's professionalism, whether in debate, planning or decision-making, is learned subconsciously rather than by conscious preparation.

The second skill required by all scientific, technological and engineering practitioners is a grasp of mathematics; the level to which this is possible or needed in school may be debatable but the capabilities of many to assimilate understanding and use should not be underrated or underestimated.

The third element is an understanding of at least one if not more of the science divisions — physics, chemistry, biology — and of engineering, which itself can be sub-divided into mechanics, electronics and other sub-disciplines. This appreciation is essential for two reasons: to show how scientific research and development extends the boundaries of new knowledge and hence capability; and because it has an impact upon the development of engineering principles and purposes.

As a further input, since most careers are concerned with solving problems in real life, there would seem to be a case for relating subjects taken as part of the school curriculum to the solving of such problems rather than just to abstract academic exercises. Furthermore, since the British economy depends upon the economic success of its industries whether these be in manufacture or in services and since these industries relate in some way or other to professional use of machines whether as single units or when grouped in some system, it would seem appropriate that schoolchildren should be given some understanding of machines and their capabilities, and this more particularly because the further development of new products and systems is likely to be part of the future of these same children in their careers. To this extent, for example, knowledge of the internal combustion engine, the electric motor, the telephone, television, the computer, processes of manufacture of basic materials, is all relevant to education generally – and to engineering in particular. These subjects and many more not only provide understanding of the world in which the individuals will live, but properly taught also afford possible areas of interest from which potential careers might derive. This is not to argue against education in the classics or in such matters as history, geography, languages, etc., or in adult life against philosophy, politics, or economics or whatever. What is being argued is that the real world, in which children will be contributing to their own future and that of a dependent society, will demand some participation by them in the process of wealth creation. Their minds should be exposed to these possibilities (some might even say future responsibilities) directly; they should not be left with the infrastructure of their education made up of purely cultural aims unrelated to future vocation.

Academic Ability is not All

The exercise of professionalism does not depend wholly upon academic ability, essential and important though this latter is. To imagine that the standard of entry is set only by the 'O' and 'A' level, with its academic bias as the measure of ability predicting future career success, does not accord with fact. There is no high degree of correlation in predicting from entry qualifications an individual's degree performance in engineering or, from later academic qualifications, performance in later life as a practising professional. (Of course by definition high fliers will justify themselves in all ways.) Employers on the whole have given the view that their best engineers have sometimes had poor academic qualifications and that they prefer to recruit well-rounded individuals with perhaps a 2:1 or 2:2 degree than academically bright but personally less capable PhDs or first class Honours students. In fact, as in all professions, what count just as much as academic qualifications are personal characteristics which are not necessarily capable of being judged at an early age or of being tested by examination or of being learned: courage, resilience, judgement and energy, for example, are all characteristics which play their part in life and which are not necessarily brought out or determined by 'A' levels or even by academic degree performance. In continental Europe, in Japan and to an extent in the

USA, the demand to become an engineer is such that only able and determined candidates, ie individuals of character, can gain entry to courses, and employers are able to recruit from a large pool of high-calibre graduates and can offer the incentive of good career prospects and rewards.

There have been attempts in the UK to try and match demand for engineers with their supply. This, as in other professions, has been shown not to be capable of very accurate determination, because of the time gap and potential mismatch between recruitment to a discipline and the finished output. This may be anything up to seven years, during which time significant economic and technical changes nationally and internationally may occur. On the whole, however, professional engineers are more likely even in excess supply to find alternative employment to which they can turn their minds as well as hands if necessary, since the engineering degree of today is more generalist than the qualifications set for other professions and likely to be even more so in the future. Most engineers can turn from one particular specialist aspect to another if not with ease at least with less difficulty than it would be to turn, say, from law or accountancy to some other activity.

The Curriculum for Engineering Education

A professional qualification requires the acquisition of a knowledge and understanding of the discipline, eg engineering, which one intends to pursue as a career. The first stage in this process, generally after school (but there may be preparatory introduction to the subject at school), is at university or polytechnic. This stage covers three or four years of study of various relevant branches of learning leading to a degree. The Committee of Inquiry tended to favour the four-year course, recognizing the increasing complexity of engineering and the need to acquire knowledge of supporting disciplines particularly in industry (see p.58). Degree-level courses in engineering are offered at forty-eight universities and university colleges, twenty-eight polytechnics and twelve other institutions, although the size of establishment varies considerably among these. Some have small intakes of fifty students each year (or even less) while the largest ex-CATs take over 600. The eighteen biggest schools (those graduating over 200 students a year) provide some 70 per cent of the total output. Over 16,300 students embarked on engineering-related degree courses in these institutions in 1978 — about 11,200 in universities and another 5,100 on CNAA courses in polytechnics, etc. On past indications, around 80 per cent of this number will graduate in engineering.

Much argument goes on over the nature of the curriculum for degree standards of achievement, and opinions as to content differ in detail between universities and polytechnics. Attempts to define a core curriculum for engineers as a whole, much less a preferred total curriculum, have not crystallized, notwithstanding a review of course structures in foreign countries. Some general pointers to what might obtain in a core curriculum can however be given.

   i One cannot just add on new knowledge to a course ad infinitum when there is a finite time in which to qualify. Continuing development during the later career of engineers can look after gaps.

   ii The computer and recorded teaching have extended the tools of learning for many aspects and branches of engineering, eg design, manufacture, inspection, etc.

   iii Training and academic study should be distinct but closely related. Many of the conditions in which industry is practised cannot be produced in the academic world; for example the urgency of a time-scale for maintaining a factory operation in progress or improving the performance of a product against competition. To gain a feel for this environment requires the experience of industry itself and in the very broadest of senses through involvement and association with other functions and disciplines in industry. To gain this skill efficiently requires guidance by managers or senior personnel who structure and plan training in as much detail and instructive purpose as the academic arranges lectures or his laboratory work.

   iv Employers should take a more direct interest in the courses of study set by universities. The accreditation system of the Engineering Council for Professional Development (ECPD) in the US, and similar intervention by outside authorities elsewhere in the world, can be cited as beneficial.

The Committee of Inquiry attempted to apportion part of this training to the academic institutions, eg in the BEng course an *introduction to the fabrication and use of materials* (EA1) and the *application of engineering principles to the solution of practical problems* based on engineering systems and processes (EA2) were recommended. To industry was left a programme in two phases of planned accredited training after graduation. EA3 was a structured introduction to industry under supervision and involved a range of practical assignments: EA4 was specific preparation for a first responsible post under decreasingly close supervision.

The Entrance Course

Engineering education must give engineers some knowledge and understanding of those other disciplines with which they will come into contact and interrelate, including relevant institutional constraints: eg the law (on industrial relations and public company obligations), accountancy, economics and management (including appreciation of human as distinct from industrial relations), the infra-structure of local and national government, etc. This proper need of the modern engineer was the motivating influence in the concept of the enhanced course supported by the University Grants Committee in a number of universities and polytechnics. 'Enhanced' in this context means the inclusion of a substantial component of business topics and engineering management plus some required experience in industry. Since this is a novel concept which has only just been introduced in the UK educational system, the Committee of Inquiry sought a critical review of its usefulness after graduation from the first three generations of students. This review is due in 1985. The enhanced degree course in engineering could well replace the present generalist degree in politics, philosophy, economics (PPE) for undergraduates who cannot make up their minds what to do with their lives.

Teaching Design

Engineering has as the first stage of its practice a concept, followed by a design based on that concept, to achieve the performance and objectives specified by engineer, client or employer. When one speaks about a good design, however, one is speaking with several voices. Design for the lay person may just involve an appreciation of aesthetic appearance; for the manufacturer it may determine the ease with which a particular product can be made and assembled at the highest level of economy; for the engineer it may be the technical capability or performance of artefact or system that determines the preferred option; and for the client it may be safety, reliability in service, ease of maintenance, etc.

There are educationists in art and engineering who consider that design should be taught in the sense that product detail or assembly should be recorded or registered before an article or system is produced. Yet what one cannot inculcate is the imagination or creativity of design − the lateral thinking on existing artefacts or the radical innovation, which are certainly specific to an individual; and for many problems, imaginative creativity may be at high levels of understanding but may still require conventional logical thought based on analytical assessment, the normal features of engineering practice.

The process of imaginative creation has been extended by the tool of the computer. At present it is possible by appropriate soft programming to draw in various perspectives a design which will meet a given specification, to modify weaknesses which are shown up in a particular design; and to detail modifications in appropriate places where desired without having to build a prototype and without having to test out actual machines by trial and error. What the computer has in fact released is the controlled (and uncontrolled) imaginative energies for people to work out on a VDU various options and to choose the one which optimizes the characterstics called for in the specification for engineering courses. Knowledge updated by research and development supplemented by individual imaginative thought (which is unteachable) all come together in design; to that extent, design-orientated courses require a shift in educational emphasis including the use of the computer rather than the introduction of radically different engineering/scientific courses.

Structured Training

The essential element in achieving professional status in engineering is not just the academic education which one achieves in universities, polytechnics or other institutions; nor does it derive from assiduous study of the journals or publications of the professional institutes or scientific societies. Engineers (and this applies to other professions as well) do require some structured experience (which includes planning) in the wealth creating world in which they will participate in due course. Nowhere is this better expressed than by the Committee of Engineering Professors' Conference:

> The three-year degree is mainly devoted to engineering science, though in some courses, especially in sandwich courses having integrated practical experience, a somewhat greater emphasis is given to design. Generally however the time available in the academic part of all courses is insufficient for professional topics and for the study of engineering practice, although most courses allow some exposure to the elements of management studies, including economics. ... Students thus typically reach the graduation stage with a knowledge of engineering science and of analytical tools but they usually have little experience and skill in their application to engineering tasks as they occur in practice; they are also often without an understanding of the constraints under which engineering work is conducted in practice. Under the present arrangements the development of this experience and these skills in professional practice must be developed after graduation in industry. (See comment on EA3 and EA4 above)

This experience can, of course, be gained through sandwich courses while at university or polytechnic.

Sandwich Courses

The sandwich course is one in which academic study and employer-based professional training can be more closely related. To be effective, there has to be co-operation between university staff and the training organized by the personnel departments of the companies involved at the least. Employers however (as compared with the personnel function) must also involve themselves directly.

The thin sandwich course is one in which periods of employment in industry alternate with periods at college. Their common pattern is the alternating period of six months to be spent in each situation for a total of four years. Payment is made during the work period in each year with a normal grant paid for the two terms of academic study.

The thick sandwich course is of two generic types. The technological universities seek two years of study followed by one year in a job with a final year's study. Other institutions tend to go for a year in a job followed by a normal three years in degree study followed by a further one year in employment. These divisions of time and training are determined more for administrative convenience than for an optimum education and training schedule. The sandwich course seems to create the benefits of preparation for a career more directly and at an earlier stage when the energy, initiative, inquisitiveness and acquisitiveness of youth is more acute and absorptive.

Engineers, like other professionals, are problem-solvers. Students at the undergraduate level are given guidance in many ways of going about achieving solutions, eg by case studies, by project involvement at university, by vacation experience, etc. These are not of themselves sufficient to measure the capability of individuals to meet their own real life problems in engineering. This is best done by guidance from people who have experience of problem-solving either at the academic phase of education or in training.

Immediately after graduation the student should receive a structured introduction to industry under supervision. This would involve a range of practical assignments (EA3) and the final specific preparation for the first post under close supervision (EA4). The objectives of the penulti-mate training phase EA3 are to achieve the following:

a An understanding of the operation of an industrial organization and the nature and importance of the engineering dimension within it.

b An understanding of systems of communications and control within organizations.

c Personal skills of working with other people at all levels in an organization.

d An understanding of the organizational and administrative principles of running a business, particularly the roles of financial control, costing and marketing.

e An appreciation for the kinds of work in which they can best contribute to the business and most effectively develop their own potential.

f Experience in carrying out engineering tasks to build confidence in the application of knowledge to the solution of real problems.

The final phase of instruction (EA4) provides the bridge between formal training and the first commission of a responsible post. Decisions regarding the post to be filled depend upon not just the academic standing of the individual; personal qualities have to be considered and judged by the industrial employer. One cannot underestimate the responsibility of employers to engage their assets (graduates) to the greatest advantage, a compromise decision based on the observed needs of graduate, company and the future. It was the view of the Committee that wherever possible the decision over each individual's first substantive post is better left towards the end of the phase of postgraduate training and should be taken in consultation with the graduate.

It is particularly important that employers accept responsibility for developing the abilities of newly recruited engineers in completing their professional formation. The best and most successful companies do, but too often this does not happen. Because each industry, and in fact all companies, differ in their requirements and internal procedure, it is difficult to determine the balance between academic education and industrial training but some balance approaching 60:40 education to training is about right at the start of a career.

Continuing Development

The combination of education and training is described under the single term 'formation' borrowed from the French. The practice of formation is common in West Germany, Scandinavia, Holland, Switzerland, France, Japan and the United States. In these countries, too, the concept of continuing formation is expected to persist throughout the working life of the individual. The assumption that one's knowledge at graduation is sufficient to see one through one's further career of some forty years is absurd in the light of technological and other changes during that period. At present only about ten to fifteen per cent of the membership of most professions is involved in continuing professional development. In a period when the pace of technological and social change is accelerating at rates barely dreamed of by most professional people who qualified 15-20 years ago, this reluctance to update is deeply disturbing. Much of Britain's industrial and social progress, even its survival, depends upon the rapidity with which professional men and women seek new solutions to develop new skills and prepare the ground for others. It is in this area of continuing education and training that the professional institutions can, through their organization and membership (who are practising practitioners), make their greatest contribution to engineering and engineers (members or not), and not just through the exercise of existing facilities but their extension through the newer communication devices: eg cassette, Open University, or Open Tech (in due course). Only three professions in the UK — accountants, surveyors and very recently planners — have committed the members of their professional institutions to any kind of formal requirement for updating themselves and developing new expertise. The medical profession had a scheme for general practitioners based on giving seniority allowances to those who attended but when this carrot was dropped, attendance at continuation courses also dropped.

Continuing education of engineers must pre-suppose that the teachers of engineering are not to be considered immune from this process of training as well. Many industrial concerns, particularly in the electronics field but also in materials generally where individuals have established their reputation, could well benefit from short periods of instruction in industrial centres of excellence or in advanced technological companies specializing in these fields. In some cases this is done with an added element of contribution through the concept of the teaching company or through development contracts which bring universities and companies into direct exchange. Exchanges of this kind could be enhanced if certain aspects of curricula were so arranged that they could be taught within an industrial company which has a structured plan as well as a commitment to training. It is of interest that the training scheme of the Manpower Services Commission is intended as a temporary instruction employment to provide people leaving school with some skills which they would not otherwise have the opportunity to acquire. This scheme is one end of the concept of structured employment. What is required is something at the professional level which has the same objective in mind.

Institutional Organization of Engineers

One of the major considerations for any profession is that it should look after the disciplinary interests of its members, interests which are continually changing in the face of new technology and its practise. There are as well responsibilities for setting the moral and ethical standards of conduct of those who practise their particular profession, to this end the legal profession has its Law Society, the accountants have their Chartered Institute, the medical profession has its General Medical Council. Engineering professions have their institutions, which have a long tradition of overseeing their particular and specialist activities. There are over eighty national engineering institutes besides other numerous ad hoc and local associations of engineers. In 1962, thirteen of the largest institutions established the Engineering Institutions Joint Council to provide a single forum and representative voice for all professional engineers. This body changed its name to the Council of Engineering Institutions on securing its own Royal Charter in 1965.

The Institutions started off mainly as learned societies for the exchange of views and the dissemination of information among people with a shared interest in a particular branch of engineering. With the passage of time and as a result of trying to raise the quality of its membership in terms of educational attainment, practical training and public status required, the Institutions took on a qualifying function for professional engineers establishing membership criteria which specified minimum requirements for education training and responsible experience and which also imposed a code of professional conduct upon those wishing to join the institution.

Institutions have as a most important role in the world of changing technology the communication of new knowledge and best practice as quickly and as informatively as possible. Institutions already have close association with the academic world but it is even more important that the various techniques for communicating and transferring technology from and to industry be strengthened.

Following the formation of the Engineering Council, the CEI has passed over its responsibilities for setting qualification standards and titles to that Council. This latter body (granted a Charter in 1981) was set up by Privy Council and was the alternative to the Engineering Authority recommended by the Committee of Inquiry Report. That Engineering Authority would have had a statutory responsibility which the Engineering Council does not have. It would have kept the world of engineering and its practitioners in the influential oversight of Parliament and Government — the only continuing forum in which the problems, contribution, supply and status of engineers in the body politic might seek beneficial improvement to their profession. It would have undertaken a wide range of functions within a general remit to further the engineering dimension in Britain. Among these functions would have been the responsibility of maintaining the sole statutory register of engineers qualified to standards and criteria laid down in conjunction with employers, engineers and others with a direct interest in engineering formation and practice.

Registration would demonstrate an individual's fitness to begin practice as a qualified engineer, having satisfactorily completed an accredited formation package. It would also entail a commitment from registered engineers to develop and maintain that 'fitness-to-practise' throughout their careers.

Statutory registration on these lines must not be seen as an end in itself. What it provides is an ordered, structured and authoritative means towards implementing some of the changes required in the formation of professional engineers. In particular it provides machinery for employers, engineers (through their institutions), and engineering teachers to work together in establishing and maintaining new models of engineering formation, more acceptable to industry than the current system has been, and for engineers to obtain an integrated formation, and a consequent qualification, recognized and valued by employers and (by reason of its statutory basis) by society at large.

Trade Union Membership

The growing tendency for white collar workers to associate themselves in trade unions, has been a significant element in trade unionism for the past two decades. The basic concern of all trade unions is that they act in the interests of their members. If these interests happen to conflict with other concerns of the professional, it would be expected by the union that the professional would put his trade union rules before his other concerns; the professional code would expect otherwise. Although many professionals will join trade unions, they can thus create dilemmas for themselves in certain situations. Strikes by professionals are infrequent even rare; although there are other methods of influencing the resolution of trade unions disputes which are equally unacceptable professionally, eg by work-to-rule, embargoes, etc. Professionals who are important and even essential to the existence, viability and future of companies should be able to resolve with management (of which they are a part) the problems peculiar to themselves without resort to the trade union practices of the blue-coated worker. Some engineers (particularly affected by the moral dilemmas of war, pollution, use of scarce resources as these might handicap future generations) have argued for the equivalent of a Hippocratic Oath – but we are a long way from this. In general, since unemployment among professional engineers is small compared to general unemployment even in recession, and while there is a continuing considerable demand for their services, perhaps unacceptable conditions of service are better resolved by the professional changing employment than by discussion and persuasion.

Women – not a Very Special Case

The qualities of engineering professionals are as good and evident in women as in men, and women constitute the major pool of quality recruitment for the future. There is no intrinsic reason why women should not become engineers, as many have proved. Few engineers' jobs entail heavy or dirty work; indeed, one of the reasons that some people are keen to attract women into engineering is that they might help demolish the myth of the 'boiler-suits and spanners' image which engineers have long been trying, with limited success, to shake off. Reasons why more women have not entered engineering include:

- Sex differentiation in the curriculum: conventional school programmes for girls, reinforced by attitudes of parents and teachers, tend to steer them away from educational choices which might lead to engineering careers.

- The lack of precedents: girls may know women who are doctors or solicitors and will certainly know women teachers, but they are less likely to know, or even to know of, women engineers.

- Working patterns: the need to keep abreast of continually developing technologies is sometimes a deterrent to women who envisage breaking their careers to raise a family – and employers may be reluctant to provide expensive training for women who might leave work soon after they have qualified. Women engineers share with other working women with dependent children the problem and expense of employing childminders if they wish to return to work, a problem exacerbated by the lack of any tax relief upon such expenses.

Among the recommendations suggested in evidence to the Committee of Inquiry (notably evidence from the Women's Engineering Society (WES), the Equal Opportunities Commission (EOC) and the Engineering Industry Training Board (EITB)) which were endorsed wholeheartedly were:

a The many schools/industry liaison schemes should make special efforts to ensure that teachers and careers advisers are properly informed about the many opportunities open to girls from an engineering formation.

b Schemes such as the IMechE/ICI/IEE's 'Opening Windows on Engineering' which enable enthusiastic young engineers to talk about their work in schools, should be expanded, placing special emphasis on involving young women engineers.

c Engineering departments in universities and polytechnics should enable and encourage women (as well as men) who have developed an interest in engineering after they have embarked upon maths or science courses to transfer to engineering after their first year, providing such bridging programmes as may be necessary.

d Women wishing to maintain their expertise and confidence in a technical field during a break from full-time practice should be provided with opportunities to work on a part-time basis, employers would thereby be increasing their prospects of longer-term returns on their initial training investment.

e The MSC, through the Industry Training Boards, should initiate a scheme whereby women re-entering engineering practice after a break could be attached to a company for a practical on-the-job retraining course of, say, six months with a nominated tutor.

Finally, education and training for special categories of people who can advance the interests of an industrially-based society should be catered for. These include:

a Engineers re-entering the engineering dimension after a period of absence, including women engineers returning to work after raising a family.

b Scientists and others employed in engineering jobs who may need training in engineering practice.

c Those engineers whose formation has been predominantly engineering-science based.

d Engineers changing disciplines.

e Those upgrading their qualifications, eg promoted technicians.

f People managing or needing a working knowledge of technical operations whose initial formation was inadequate to equip them in this respect: eg 'technological literacy' for non-engineers.

Technician Support

One of the difficulties facing the professional engineer is in obtaining sufficient support skills from the technician. The weakening of the complement of technicians and technician engineers resulting from changes in opportunities in tertiary education has had the effect of graduates being employed to do their own support work at a relatively low-level routine of employ.

The main recommendation of the Committee of Inquiry was that urgent action be initiated to review and where necessary increase the supply of engineering technicians and to review their formation in relation to the professional engineers whom they support. If this were to be implemented, then the further education and training of technicians to professional levels would be facilitated. In present schemes the educational gap between technicians and professional engineers is too wide to allow an easy transition. It may well be that technicians of the future will find greater opportunity for employment and the use of their skills, to the advantage of industry and society, in the service-based industries, since these generally involve the operation, maintenance and even improvements in performance of physical systems which require engineering knowledge at a lesser level than is required of the professional engineer.

Conclusion

There is growing recognition of the importance of engineering and hence of engineers to the competitive world of the national economy, and the formation of The Engineering Council could do much to build upon this through organization of the education and training of professional engineers and technicians.

Such education and training should adopt an integrated approach to theoretical and practical teaching related to the needs of industry. Since these latter are subject to change, education and training need constant updating and accreditation (by the Council through nominated bodies, eg the Institutions). Because of the broad spectrum of specialist disciplines covered by the umbrella of engineering and its interdependence on other disciplines in academic and industrial environments, education and training can take many forms in its curricular organization. This lends itself to experiment, and benefit will derive from inter-comparisons between universities and polytechnics (at home and abroad) and the training experience of companies.

Essential to this whole process is the support of employers (particularly at the highest level of authority in companies or public organizations) in on-the-job training and in influencing though not determining the academic curriculum. Education and training should be a continuous process, postgraduate and post-experience.

In the final analysis, however, employers must use their professional asset of engineering staff to the full in advancing the engineering dimension, giving engineers the influence, authority and status to generate the products and systems on which the economy depends for the nation's standard of living in the complex world of international trading.

6 Overview of Issues in Management Education

Peter Moore

Management is not a recognized profession in the sense that medicine is, or accounting or the law. These professions are controlled by governing bodies which themselves have defined legal status, and the title of, for example, solicitor has a recognized definition in official parlance, whilst a doctor to practise must be on the official register of the General Medical Council. Engineers have been for some time in the same position as managers, with the title being widely used for a wide variety of activities, although strenuous attempts are now being made through the Engineering Council to turn the more advanced practitioners into a recognized profession with the Chartered Engineer status being the recognized status that is controlled from a central body. The lack of professional status (as opposed to professionalism) has very significant implications in the case of management education. Anybody can call himself or herself a manager, so that the term manager can just as easily denote somebody in charge of a small sweet shop as the boss of a multi-national company with a turnover of billions and with thousands of employees.

The Labour Force Survey (1981) gives a breakdown of educational attainments amongst those holding managerial positions. Some 15 per cent (or 390,000) of the 2.6 million described as managers had a degree or professional qualification. Moreover men who achieve this status tended to be slightly better qualified than women.

These numbers have to be compared with 1.75 million aged between 16 and 59 in active employment who have degrees or professional qualifications. A recent study made by the Institute of Employment Research at Warwick University (1983) suggested that the management group might rise by some 5 per cent by 1990, against a general decline of 5 per cent in employment overall.

Table 6.1 indicates not only the very wide definition clearly accorded to the title of manager, but also the large numbers of managers (about 27 per cent or 700,000) who have no formal education requirements at all.

This shows that complex management education does not face a single homogeneous task but a complex pyramidal one where a very wide range of educational and training needs have to be met.

Table 6.1

Higher qualification		Men (%)	Women (%)
University degree		9.5	6.3
Professional institution		7.8	1.5
HND/HNC		4.1	1.2
Nursing/Teaching qualification		1.4	10.4
Apprenticeship		19.8	5.2
ONC/OND 'A' level		11.7	12.0
'O' level		12.8	16.2
CSE		1.8	2.1
Other		3.8	6.2
None		24.6	36.4
Not known		2.7	2.5
	Number	2.04m	0.56m

The implications are that, whilst it is true that many successful managers have had little or no formal training or education as such, many less successful managers are also in that position. What cannot be denied is that it is the professions which in general tend to cream off the top graduates to the detriment of the management cadre. Admittedly some of the former subsequently enter management (the transfer of accountants into management is a good example of this); but in general the status and reward system operates negatively. It is interesting in recent years to note how the Civil Service is now trying to incorporate managerial skills amongst its requirements for top mandarins whose primary role up to now has been seen to be one of analysis of policy options, oblivious to the need to manage the actual spending of some £120 billion of public money – an enormous administrative task that can easily become wasteful if not handled with extremely high competence.

Educational Strata

The pressure to make management more accountable has in turn pointed up the need for more structured and qualification-based forms of management education. Four formal levels of work can be discerned: the BEC (Business Education Council) awards, the Diploma in Management Studies, first degrees in business and management studies, and, finally, awards of the Master in Business Administration format. There are further courses of varying lengths and level for practising managers, but these are commonly aimed at specific issues rather than being of a general educative format. All the four levels listed above have systems for their award but, it is important to note, there is no common agreement as to curricula and the contents can differ widely from one educational institution to another although some common features are discernible and some, eg the Diploma in Management Studies, are validated centrally. The task of curricula co-ordination has been seen most clearly as a means of enforcing some minimum common core without giving particular weight to the application areas in which the manager may be given to practise later. The tug-of-war between academic (qua intellectual) considerations in formulating curricula and the need for direct practical relevance in everything that is done is strong. A delicate balance must perforce be maintained.

In general the definition of manager in the Labour Force Survey is too wide for educational consideration in higher education terms. Probably the group that could be considered legitimately to warrant the title manager is no larger than 200,000. If we assume that each of these persons spends on average twenty years as such a manager, then we need an annual intake of 10,000 (quite apart from any catching up there may be that remains to be done to ensure that the current stock is reasonably well educated). First degree or BEC diplomates do not enter management in this sense directly as their qualifications are geared more to entering business or commerce in a functional capacity; a better comparator is the prevalence of MBAs and some fraction of the DMSs. This would be well short of 10,000 per annum and would thus make no advance on the backlog. The conclusion must be that educationally we are walking up the down escalator and only going upwards very slowly.

Education and experience are not by any means alternatives or opposites. It is undoubtedly true that intelligent people can learn a great deal about management through experience. They may make some expensive mistakes en route but, provided the tasks that face them have parallels with tasks facing them or their colleagues in the past, they should be able to cope. Where they commonly fall down is in facing a task that has no parallel with their previous experience, when they have neither precedent nor educational background on which to draw. It is indeed the problem of change that creates the most powerful incentive for managers to have a deep understanding of the system for which they are responsible.

Education can indeed provide two things: first, it can be an experience accelerator. No longer is it so essential to accumulate a full quiver of experience, possibly at random over a long period of time. Peak performance can be achieved earlier and thus the period of such performance extended. Secondly, education can provide managers with a background of information and modes of diagnosis and analysis that will enable them to examine problems that are new to their (or their colleagues') experience. Confidence in this aspect of management is essential in a fast moving and fast evolving world economy of the kind that we are dealing with today.

Some Comparisons

A useful analogy with commercial management is that of the officer cadre in the military. Whilst it is possible to enter the officer cadre from within, this is relatively uncommon and direct entry is the norm. For this group a basic grounding is given whatever the background of the recruit. For the Army, this is the Sandhurst experience lasting a year or so. About ten years later a selected group of officers (perhaps a fifth or less of the original group) attend Staff College for a year. The aim now is not only to fit officers for staff appointments with the requisite knowledge and skills, but also to impart the breadth of background desirable for a man to command a specialist unit and co-operate effectively with other specialist units. About ten or twelve years further on, those who are to be selected for the very senior positions, about a fifth again, attend the Royal College of Defence Studies (again for a year). The important thing to notice in this process is that those who are going to reach the top are given the most education and training. This approach ironically is rather different in many commercial organizations where it is often asserted that those who are going to undertake senior tasks are unable to spare the time, nor have the need for further education. Consequently management education is commonly seen as a way of motivating and improving the ongoing performance of those who will not reach the top, rather than the converse.

Comparisons with management education in other countries show a number of fundamental differences. Looking at our principal economic competitors such as Western Germany and Japan, we see an enormous educational effort made in preparing people for entry into business. The effort is made essentially at the first degree level, where degrees in subjects such as engineering are considerably longer than in the UK and contain a great deal concerning administration and managerial skills. In both North America and the United Kingdom, first degree studies commonly bear much less relation to the ultimate possibility of successful employment in business and commerce. This is then reflected in the subsequent felt need for graduate education in both countries in preparing young people for an industrial or commercial career.

It has been a British tradition to be somewhat suspicious of management studies at the undergraduate level and postgraduate training is relatively sparse. Indeed it is still true that industry generally expects and demands more experienced, rather than less experienced, graduates to enter areas involving managerial skills. One cannot have it both ways. One must either support management education at one level or the other, or deny that, in any specific sense, a university education is relevant to management performance other than as an exercise in intellectual gymnastics (see Bull 1983). In the United States there are some 50,000 MBA graduates a year and the medium has been developed as the primary vehicle for initial entry into areas of business and commerce leading to management. In the UK, whilst schools and university undergraduate degrees have prepared young people to follow many specialized professional occupations in society, they have done precious little to prepare those young people to win the economic war facing the country. Moreover, the number of MBA graduates is about 1200 per annum (of whom one quarter or so are from overseas). The disparity with the United States, even allowing for population differences, is very marked indeed. It is perhaps noteworthy that the USA turns out about four times as many doctors a year as the UK (which accurately reflects the population size differential), but forty times as many MBAs.

Because management education is not controlled by any central validating body, it is exposed to the winds of competitive forces. Students will, hopefully, select for themselves the course of programme that they feel most appropriate for their needs. Thus courses, and possibly institutions, will rise and fall according to student choice, or company choice in the case of post-experience programmes. This is healthy for institutions in a direct sense, but may not be quite so healthy for the economy in the long run as the short-term maximization principle (so beloved of politicians) can be incompatible with long-term optimization. Not only is this true of the type of programme offered, but it may also be true of the subject content. For example, even in institutions with high quality teaching and with many students with a technical background, few will opt for production management specialisms and subsequently enter operational management. This is commonly held to be a fault of the management schools and an indication of their bias against manufacturing (or operations). Yet many of these graduates do enter manufacturing industry, in jobs relating to marketing, or finance, or corporate planning, at significantly higher salaries than those offered were they to enter operations management. If this is felt to be non-optimal nationally, where does the blame lie? It can hardly be with the students, who are responding to market demand as indicated by salaries. The companies themselves tend to argue that production is only 'worth' the lower salary. Hence the implication is that the marginal gain by having a better than less well-educated manager in these areas is negative. If this is so, why all the fuss about the loss of competitiveness in manufacturing industry, low productivity, etc? Perhaps we are dealing here with a more deep-seated problem relating to societal preferences and attitudes.

There have commonly been two main routes to senior management positions in the UK. The first is to enter as a management trainee, either in fact or in name, and to work through from junior supervisory roles to more senior roles, with or without the aid of external (or internal) training and development. The success rate with this form of entry has generally not been very high. The second route is for those who have some area of specialization (engineer, lawyer, chemist, patent agent, etc), which they have acquired and are practising, to undertake formal studies that fit them to move into positions either of contolling experts (eg director of engineering) or of managing more general units of people and equipment. The danger with this route is that the switch is made with little or no formal preparation and the individual is left to sink or swim. The USA (and some other countries) have a third route via the MBA whereby such graduates at the age of 28 to 32 enter junior management roles directly and develop a career in management per se. It is open to debate as to whether this should best happen immediately after a first degree or after a few years' experience, the balance of opinion in the UK, but not in the USA, favouring the later entry.

A number of important issues for debate arise from the foregoing discussion.

First, when talking of management education, it seems most appropriate to talk about the process that leads to the formation of the core of 200,000 top managers in the UK, as these are the lay positions that control the economy. This is not to belittle the other 90 per cent of managers that are so rated in official statistics, but to emphasize the distinction between management, supervisor and general training for functional activities in business and commerce.

Secondly, should management seek to move towards formal professional status or not? If the former route is to be followed then the form of such status needs consideration, and whether there are to be various levels of recognition. Who is to provide recognition, and how, needs consideration, as would the role of the various educational institutions. Would other existing professional qualifications provide part of the whole of the requirements for recognition? Would formal status recognition of an individual be a legal requirement for holding a directorship of a publicly quoted company?

Thirdly, should we in the UK encourage greater pre-entry training in management-related subjects, or should we use training programmes at later stages? Is there any mileage in such ideas as a pre-entry course followed by a later full-time course lasting to an MBA, or a training contract for young entrants leading to a part-time MBA, as accountants and lawyers effectively have? How can the partnership between the management education institution and the practitioners be made most fruitful?

Fourthly, and finally, management is an evolving activity. Research is needed to ensure that management constantly looks forward and not backward, and that experience does not imply carrying forward outworn procedures from one generation to the next. How can this research best be carried out and the results disseminated to the management cadre?

Part 3

Access and Recruitment

7 Overview of Access and Recruitment to the Professions

Oliver Fulton

There are two ways of looking at the professions. One, the viewpoint of many ('professional') social scientists, is to see them as guild monopolies. In this interpretation, professionals earn their rewards and privileges (class, status and power) through their monopoly ownership of scarce knowledge and skills. If they are to keep or improve their economic, social and political position, these skills and knowledge have to remain scarce, and must certainly be inaccessible to lay people. Moreover, as a guild, professionals are likely not only to restrict the total number of entrants but also to select these entrants on the basis of compatibility with themselves.

The other viewpoint, commoner among the professions themselves, emphasizes not restriction but ease of access. To survive and prosper, professions must be open to talent. Self-regulation (which is in any case not an unconditional privilege of most modern professions) is only granted by society in exchange for ethical, and specifically disinterested, behaviour, including access on merit. In any case, modern society is notable for a huge expansion both in the size and in the number of the professions: the 'professionalization of everyone' is scarcely compatible with monopoly behaviour. And finally, even if some older professions still keep certification and regulation in their own hands, selection has nearly always been handed over to the disinterested institutions of higher education − the academic profession. This may be called the functionalist perspective.

Both views can obviously be criticized. It is not my purpose to choose between them − indeed it is possible that both can be 'true', since both represent useful ways of posing questions about higher education. For in either case it is clear that higher education is central to the modern problem of access. As more professions are invented and more become 'all-graduate', higher education increasingly becomes the primary gatekeeper, the provider of training, the conveyer of prestige, and the certifier of eligibility for professional membership. These vicarious functions, especially those of selection and certification, are the main topic in this chapter, but since we are concerned with access to the professions themselves, I shall also discuss what we know of the fate of graduates once they have been trained or at least certified in institutions of higher education.

Control of Numbers

Clearly we must begin with student numbers. The monopoly perspective suggests that there will be pressure, at least from the established professions, to keep numbers down. If so, it is presumably to the advantage of a profession to delegate to higher education any desired restriction of numbers, since it is then apparently out of its own hands and so more legitimate. Restrictions will also have the advantage, other things being equal, of increasing entry 'standards' to pre-professional courses, and so enhancing the profession's prestige. Upward pressure on numbers will mainly be exerted by those who want to improve the availability of professional services, or perhaps to reduce their costs. In the case of emergent professions, the pressures will be different: increasing the proportion of graduates in a profession should improve its prestige and enable it to charge higher fees. Again, how far outsiders will co-operate may depend on other circumstances: but clearly there will be considerable pressure from those young people who see in expansion an opportunity to achieve professional status and rewards.

What has happened in practice in recent years? If we interpret the concept of a profession sufficiently generously, almost all higher education graduates are potential professionals; and if so, it is clear that it is the upward pressures that have been highly successful in all the advanced economies, while control has been relatively weak. In Britain, the 'Robbins principle' of matching the supply of full-time student places to the demand from young people endorsed and encouraged a huge surge in the production of professional fodder between the late 1950s and the early 1970s (and did so, incidentally, against the wishes of at least one professional group, the university staff who would have to teach them (Halsey and Trow 1970)). But although most existing professions grew larger, it was other occupations which were mainly affected. They took the opportunity to claim professional status for themselves by recruiting large numbers of 'new' graduates, especially in public sector jobs – teaching, social work, local government administration and many of the smaller quasi-professions (planning, public health, etc.) – but also in business. And it is clear that the rising participation rate owes much to the attraction of young people to these essentially new or much expanded professions. Since then, and at least partly because of deteriorating employment prospects, the participation rate has ceased to rise, even though higher education's capacity has continued to grow to accommodate the birthrate bulge which has now just passed its peak among 18-year-olds. With the possible exception of teachers concerned for their pupils, however, it is hard to think of any professional group who campaigned during the 1970s for measures to encourage greater participation – not even university teachers, who might have found new clients but in fact were mainly concerned to preserve their status and style of life; and only developed a half-hearted interest when the declining birthrate threatened to cost some of them their jobs. The Conservative government's much-publicized 'abandonment' of the Robbins principle (still in late 1983 not quite abandoned in practice) was objected to only by parents and by school teachers. Professionals – and their employers – were notably silent, or even approving.

But although the Robbins principle required a place to be provided for every qualified applicant somewhere in higher education, it never stipulated that the applicant's choice of subject should be satisfied. Places in medicine and teacher training have long been planned – by government but with the advice of members of those professions – on the basis of forecasts of manpower needs. In other subjects governments have consistently tried to 'steer' the system towards science and technology and away from arts and social science, on the basis of assumptions about 'real' manpower needs but without the use of serious forecasting methods. The effects have been quite striking (see Farrant 1981). In medicine, restrictions on numbers have led to steadily fiercer competition for places, making the profession look still more attractive. In teacher training, however, violent oscillations (to adapt at inescapably short notice to changing school populations and teacher career patterns) have led at times to excessively low demand. Elsewhere, the 'steer' of higher education places towards science has combined with the 'swing' from science in schools (more accurately a failure of newer sixth-formers to specialize in science in the same proportions as their predecessors) to make arts and social science places for some years considerably harder to get than places in science and especially in technology. (This in turn encourages employers in uncharitable remarks about the quality of science and technology graduates.)

The difficulty in interpreting these trends is that even if graduates are for the most part fodder for the professions, most courses in arts and social science, and many in natural science, cannot be described as vocational training for a single identifiable profession. In engineering, where this is the case, the profession and its supporters in higher education have wavered revealingly between expansiveness and restrictiveness, insisting on a 'real' need in the economy for more engineers despite the evident failure of the labour market to demonstrate any shortage by offering high salaries, while devising schemes for training 'better' — ie more highly selected and so scarcer — graduates in special programmes. But in general the professions have not been inclined to form any strong views on student numbers in different subjects.

As for other pressures on numbers, potential students have found it hard to respond to this kind of 'steer', partly because of inflexibility in the secondary school system and in entry requirements for higher education: but they have also been encouraged by the continuing (until very recently) high employability of most arts and social science graduates. This has contributed to the disparity in admission rates and 'standards' through most of the 1970s. As far as government influence is concerned, the pressures of rising unemployment and rising expenditure are serious everywhere. But where, as in Britain, much of higher education is only loosely connected to jobs, manpower-based planning or steering of higher education, however technically difficult, is likely to prove politically easier than in Germany, for example, where courses have a much clearer professional focus, and all attempts at diverting access meet fierce resistance from would-be students and their families.

Recruitment and Selection for Higher Education

Whatever the causes of subject biases and restrictions, their consequences are fairly straightforward. Courses with a clear vocational focus, especially those with high competition for entry (often but not always the same thing, as we have seen) make the achievement of equity in recruitment and selection both especially desirable and especially difficult. The desirability is obvious enough: if access to an attractive career is channelled through access to specific courses, with few or no alternative routes, it is at this first point that justice should be seen to be done. It may be convenient for the professions to turn over the responsibility to higher education, but it does not make the responsibility any less. And if governments are creating these conditions through manpower planning, they too share the responsibility, but are likely to put pressure on higher education to discharge it. The difficulty arises in several different ways.

Most seriously, there is the problem of selection among applicants. There has certainly been, in the past, the temptation to discriminate in favour of certain categories of applicant. Some medical schools operated declared or undeclared quotas for female applicants until the Sex Discrimination Act. Many practised — and may still legally do so — discrimination in favour of candidates from medical families. Both kinds of discrimination were justified on pseudo-functional grounds: women, on average, were likely to work fewer person-years than men, so reducing the return to the state on its investment in medical education; those with experience of medical life would adapt more easily to its heavy emotional and life-style demands. Neither would now generally be regarded as legitimate, and both would be seen to be designed more to ensure a comfortably homogeneous profession than to serve any truly functional purpose.

There is little prima facie evidence to suggest that any such discrimination now occurs on a wide scale. Taking applicants to university as a whole, UCCA figures for 1981 show that 49.86 per cent of male 'home' candidates were successful and 49.96 per cent of females. In earlier years (but using a different residence classification) the difference was further to women's advantage. Similarly, an apparent slight bias in favour of 'middle class' applicants can be accounted for by their slightly higher 'A' level scores on average. Grade for grade, there is no difference.

This is too good to be true, and ought even to make us suspicious − not of wrong-doing but of coincidence. If we concentrate on gender differences, where far more published data are available, it is immediately clear (see Table 7.1) that women and men apply in very different proportions for subjects where admission rates are also very different.

Table 7.1   University home candidates 1981 (by domicile)

	Women as % of men applicants	Admissions as % of applications		Women as % of men admitted
		Men	Women	
Languages	233.9	52.8	49.5	219.2
Education	171.5	24.6	37.9	264.3
Humanities other than languages	119.8	63.5	62.9	118.6
Health other than medicine	104.6	33.3	37.4	117.2
Social science other than business etc. and law	99.1	47.3	47.0	98.6
Veterinary medicine	92.1	26.3	24.3	85.2
Law	78.6	45.2	44.0	76.4
Medicine	72.5	40.7	42.5	75.7
Architecture etc.	61.2	35.2	38.6	67.0
Science	47.0	66.3	67.4	47.7
Agriculture etc.	46.7	50.8	55.7	51.2
Business, economics, accountancy	40.1	39.3	38.2	39.0
Engineering	7.6	53.8	65.6	9.2

Source: UCCA Statistical Supplement, 1980-81

To take three examples, in languages in 1981 there were twenty-four women applicants for every ten men, and roughly half of all applicants were successful; in other humanities subjects there were twelve women to ten men and nearly two-thirds were successful; in business there were four women to ten men, and fewer than two-fifths were successful. If all this adds up to exact parity across the board this year, it only tells us that an invisible hand is skilfully at work. We need to look at the fate of applications within subjects.

In fact there are few substantial differences between men and women's success within groups of subjects. Women were far more successful than men in education (38 per cent to 25 per cent) – but education is both a choice of last resort for more men than women and a subject to which many applicants are diverted from other preferences. In medicine, architecture, science, agriculture and engineering women were slightly more successful (in engineering 66 per cent of women and 54 per cent of men – otherwise the difference is less than 5 per cent); in languages, arts, social science, veterinary medicine, law and business, men were more successful – never by more than 3 per cent. However, none of these differences takes account of qualifications, and it is clear from other figures that at least the large discrepancy in engineering, and possibly some of the others in women's favour, are justified by women applicants' higher qualifications. Women do not apply to engineering unless they have an exceptionally strong academic backing. Discrimination, then, is not an issue (negative or positive): universities at least seem to respond neutrally to applications before them. But this raises two questions.

First, does not this neutrality in fact discriminate against some applicants? Is there not a case for ensuring that grade for grade, more applicants from working-class backgrounds are admitted; or if not on a direct class basis, for discriminating in favour of candidates who did not attend experienced schools with a tradition of selection – a policy which would undoubtedly show up in the 'class' distribution to the same effect? Do those with 'mixed' 'A' levels (ie science and non-science), who more often come from comprehensive schools with a smaller curricular choice, deserve special treatment? How valid, or fair, is the use of 'A' levels at all, and could we not encourage a wider choice of entry criteria (Fulton 1981)?

But none of this answers the problem of differential application rates. We have just seen that women applicants to engineering have higher grades than men. Why do not women with lower grades apply? The proportion of women students in higher education has of course been growing for many years, apart from the period when places on teacher training courses were sharply cut back and the minimum qualification raised; but it has still not reached parity, and is very far from it in subjects like engineering. And the proportion of working-class children has not risen and seems now to be falling. Of course, many of these differences have little or nothing to do with higher education: both opportunities and aspirations for higher education depend in large part on powerful influences and opportunities far earlier in young people's lives than when the prospect of higher education first arises. Nevertheless, differential application rates within higher education are suggestive. Why should nine women apply to veterinary medicine for every ten men, compared with seven to medicine, five to science and less than one to engineering? Or twenty-three to languages, twelve to humanities, eight to law and four to business? Is it not likely that many women with 'A' levels identical to those of men are applying to different courses, and in doing so are performing the professions' work of selection for them? As we shall see, this process occurs even among graduates with identical qualifications.

If we use the individualist language of 'vocational choice', there may seem to be no problem, for society or for the occupations and professions affected. But even if pupils and students can be said to be 'choosing' at various decision or selection points, these choices are in fact limited by differential opportunities to pursue them, by differential access to information on which to base them, by differential recruitment strategies and, possibly most important and least regarded, by stereotyped images of higher education and of occupations which, being based on existing disparities, tend to reinforce existing patterns of aspiration. Bill Williamson (1981) has summarized much of the literature on this last point, and I have argued elsewhere (Fulton 1981) that the only hope of changing these patterns in a progressive direction, short of massive social change (of which the women's movement of the last fifteen years is the nearest we have to an example) is to attempt major changes not just in entry criteria but also in the structure of higher education (for which the only irresistible lever available to governments may be finance). But even if we can change overall participation rates, changing subject or occupational choice within them will probably be much harder. (And the evidence with which to work is much thinner.) Probably the best general recipe is simply to delay choice by delaying specialization. This will not prevent the most resourceful students making the most profitable choices – indeed by reducing the time-lag between labour market demand and graduate supply it may even benefit those with the sharpest eye to the main chance; but it will at least reduce the effects of stereotyping and misinformation.

Certification in Higher Education

Possibly the most important point to make about certification by higher education is that it is not very important. We know, admittedly, that the mere possession of a degree is still important: despite declining differentials, lifetime earnings of graduates are still healthily higher than those of non-graduates. We know very little about the fate of drop-outs from higher education, except for a suspicion that more than might be guessed do subsequently acquire a degree. But among the mass of successful graduates, most evidence suggests that it is the simple degree itself that counts for most. It used to be said that a person's degree classification dogged them for life: in British academic life, at least, it was more important than any subsequent achievements. Certainly the first employment statistics still show differences, in the expected direction, in unemployment rates by degree class. And the UMS survey of 1970 graduates (Williamson, P. 1981) shows that degree class continued to affect employment rates and earnings over a seven-year period. But these differences were much smaller than those between graduates in different subjects – and between men and women. It seems from the recent Brunel study (Roizen and Jepson 1983) that not only the subject, but the name of the institution conferring the degree is often of much more importance to employers than any statements the institution can make about the quality of a candidate for employment. In other words, whether or not employers value whatever higher education may have added to its graduates, they make their selection on the basis of characteristics which are determined on entry. Selection by university, polytechnic or college, and by departments within them, is of far more consequence than certification.

Recruitment to the Professions

If the evidence on access to higher education and its predisposing causes is so plentiful as to confuse, we know much less about the recruitment of graduates on exit from higher education. The 'first employment' statistics, although regularly collected for polytechnics as well as universities, are surprisingly uninformative, mostly because fewer than half of all graduates from either sector had taken up a 'permanent' job by the time of the latest surveys available, which were for 1982. And although it is possible to compare men and women, there is no evidence on social class or other possible biases. But allowing for these limitations, the evidence of the first employment figures on sex differences is clear. We find, on the one hand, that in each major subject group (arts, social science, science, applied science and medicine), except for applied science, women university graduates were slightly less likely than men to be unemployed six months after graduating in 1982; and the same is broadly true for polytechnic graduates. But women were also considerably less likely to have found permanent employment. The only university subjects where this was not the case were science and medicine. This is because, in every subject, men were considerably more likely to have gone into research training (which is most common for science and medicine graduates); while women, failing (or instead of) permanent employment, were more likely to have gone into other forms of training (for example teaching, law or 'other' careers – probably largely clerical). In other words, access to the professions direct on graduation is generally less common for women than for men. For those professions requiring further training, access to that training is more common for men in academic research and for women in teaching and law. (But this tells us nothing about eventual access to these professions themselves.)

A closer look at the data reveals something more disturbing: the diversion of women from permanent employment to further training is part of a wider phenomenon. Even in subjects like engineering, women are less likely to be employed in what might be called the core profession or occupation. Not only do more men get immediate jobs as language or social science graduates, while women train as teachers, but men get jobs as engineers while women take support jobs in engineering firms. It is perhaps little wonder that women's salaries are lower (holding constant degree subjects, employment sectors, marital status, hours of work, etc. (Williamson, p. 1981)).

Although it antedates most of the postwar expansion of higher education, the survey of 1960 graduates by Kelsall *et al* (1972) is still the best evidence we have on unequal access of graduates to the professions – and it still fits what we know of more recent trends. While the 'dominant ideology' of women's ambivalence about careers may have changed enough to propel far more women into higher education, and opportunities for teaching careers (which fit that ideology) are much reduced, we still find women graduates in subordinate or lower-status professions and jobs. However, deserving particular attention in the Kelsall study are their findings about social class. Although class backgrounds undoubtedly affected aspirations and so, presumably, job applications even among graduates, there was a substantial further difference, net of aspirations, in the jobs which graduates from different social classes actually entered, with some of the older professions, especially the civil service, law and management, as the most socially exclusive. There is in fact little reason to suppose that this has changed radically. The civil service still recruits its graduate intake largely from a few universities; and the UMS survey found in 1977 that social class still had a major effect on graduates' salaries, both overall and especially within management occupations (but not within the (traditional) professions). It is certainly possible that women too face barriers, net of any differences in aspiration which persist throughout higher education.

Conclusion

What all this implies is that access to the professions is a lengthy process of gradual selection and restriction. Whatever the formalities, the professions are not in fact equally open to all talents. In the first place, their numbers are generally restricted, whereas presumably the most effectively meritocratic method of selection would be to admit probationers and choose among them on the basis of their talents in the profession itself. And selection, beginning with subject choice and levels of aspiration at school, moving through access to higher education to access to the professions themselves, gradually constrains the 'choices' of certain social groups more than others. The three professions discussed in the following chapters differ from each other in important ways: medicine has tightly-controlled student numbers, high admissions requirements, and a finely-honed prestige which, as Liam Hudson has shown, even creates a status hierarchy among its specialists which is reflected in their gender and class origin, despite the fact that entry to higher education virtually guarantees entry to the profession. Engineering's student numbers are more responsive to market forces, but it too is heavily socially biased, with clear gender differences at entry to and exit from higher education. Management, an emergent profession recruiting from a wide range of specialist graduates, despite the growth of specifically vocational courses, seems to become differentiated mostly on exit from higher education, and indeed later in professional careers, although business and management courses also have their biases. Possibly the moral is that higher education can at best help to postpone the point at which ascription takes over from achievement, and that to some degree it does so already. But to some extent, evidently, it does not; it is co-opted into the ascriptive process. To reflect on and even to resist that would be no bad start.

8 Access and Recruitment to the Medical Profession

John Ellis

There are some 75,000 doctors working in Britain, half of them in hospitals, a third in general practice and the rest in a wide variety of posts in community health services, the universities, the armed forces, industry and research. Less than a third of those in hospital are consultants, and these are divided into some thirty-six specialties.

Recruitment is partly from among home-based students selected by the medical schools in Britain each year to fill around 3,800 places (1500 in 1960), and partly from among doctors selected and trained in other countries, particularly in Ireland, India, Pakistan, Australia, New Zealand and the younger Commonwealth states. Those recruited from overseas have had a different secondary education from those recruited from within Britain, have been selected by different methods, have received a different basic medical education, and may well be differently motivated.

Home-based Applicants for Medicine

Medicine has long been the most popular of the subjects offered by universities. The total number of applicants has been as high as 13,000 and is now around 10,000. It seems to have been little affected by reports of doctors being dissatisfied with their conditions of service, the changing nature of medical practice, or insufficient funding of the Health Service. Rumours of future medical unemployment seem to have had little impact. Recent reductions in the total number of applicants have been largely due to a decrease in those from overseas since the recent increase in fees.

Most applicants seek admission at eighteen and have made their career choice at or before sixteen years of age, in time to choose 'A' level subjects. At that age one of the attractions of medicine may be that within it is a wide range of different jobs. To choose it is, to some extent, to put off a final career choice until later. Older applicants have, however, increased in recent years, including many with first degrees in other subjects. Women applicants have increased steadily since the sixties.

Few universities now offer a pre-medical year to students gaining entrance through non-scientific subjects. Most applicants seek admission to the medical course on the basis of a range of subjects passed at 'O' level in the GCE and of passes at 'A' level in chemistry, physics and mathematics or biology, taken from secondary school, sixth form, technical or tutorial college. For the past ten years some medical schools have been willing to accept candidates with 'A' levels in chemistry, one other scientific subject and one non-scientific subject — but relatively few offer such a permutation.

This may be because of difficulties in combining scientific and non-scientific subjects in 'A' level courses, or because a majority of sixteen-year-olds contemplating medicine prefer scientific subjects. It could be because candidates, knowing that some medical schools demand, and that all will accept, three scientific subjects, feel that they offer the best chance of entry. Applicants and their advisers see admission to medical school not only as highly competitive but as extremely complicated. Each school begins its selection by considering those who put it as their first choice on the UCCA application form, but applicants often have little information about the schools, whose admission policies are the subject of much mythology. Relatively small differences in requirements, which could encourage diversity of educational background, probably lead to greater uniformity in it.

The number of applicants likely to gain higher than grade C in three subjects at 'A' level annually exceeds the number of places available.

The Selection Process

Beyond the requirement of three 'A' level passes (of which one must be in chemistry or physical science and at least one other in a scientific subject) national policy in regard to admission to medicine is the summation of the policies of upwards of thirty separate schools, as interpreted by admission officers or teams. The latter are composed wholly or mainly of medical school staff, including practising clinicians, except at Oxford and Cambridge where College selectors include few practising doctors. There is no national aptitude test, as in the United States, and GCE examinations may differ from board to board. Individual medical schools have, from time to time, applied some form of intelligence or aptitude testing but none has persisted. Experience has shown that students capable of grade C at Advanced level in three subjects are not intellectually extended by the medical course.

Ten schools offer places without interview to candidates who name them as first preference and who have a good 'O' level record, high 'A' level predictions and a satisfactory teachers' report. Their offers are conditional on gaining grade B or higher in the three subjects preferred by the school.

At other schools the UCCA form is used to select applicants for interview, after which offers are made on conditions tailored to take account of factors such as age, educational opportunity, personal circumstances and impressions gained at interview. Interviewing panels usually report to a dean or admissions officer who may attempt to put together a 'balanced' entry, appropriate to the school, from among those recommended for admission.

The factor which across the country plays the greatest part in deciding whether or not an applicant is offered a place is the 'O' level record. The factor which plays the greatest part in deciding which of those offered places are actually admitted is the 'A' level record.

The Entry

The UCCA Statistical Supplement provides a profile of the entry except in regard to religious affiliations, political interests and motivation. The profile gives the following information.

Age

Two-thirds of home-based medical students begin their medical studies between eighteen and nineteen. Most of the remainder are nineteen. Some are accepted at every age up to thirty, but few older. As many as 200 are under eighteen at entry. Most overseas students admitted to British medical schools are nineteen or older. Elsewhere in the world students begin the study of medicine at an older age than here. In the USA students enter medical school at about twenty-two, after four years at college. In the USSR, high school and medical school are separated by at least two years in some other occupation. Recent attempts to broaden the entry to medicine in Sweden, by taking account in the selection process of time spent in other fields, have resulted in an average age on entry of twenty-five.

Sex

Over the past decade the proportion of female applicants gaining admission has been higher than the proportion of male applicants who suceed. Between one-third and a half of the entry are women.

Social Class

There has been little change over the past two decades in the social classes from which British medical students are drawn. Most are the children of parents in Classes I and II (professional and intermediate occupations). Few come from Classes IV and V (partly skilled and unskilled). The pattern reflects that of all university entrants, sharpened by the fact that entry to medicine requires three 'A' level passes. Usually a slightly higher proportion of candidates from Classes IV and V than from Classes I and II are successful in gaining places.

The proportion of total entry who have a medical parent is not recorded in the UCCA document. Studies made by the Association for the Study of Medical Education in 1961 and 1966 showed that the proportion rose from 17.1 per cent to 21.2 per cent over those years. It is unlikely to be less today, and is certainly higher in some schools.

Religion

The intake includes active members of all religions practised in this country, along with inactive members, atheists and agnostics. The impression is that each year sees much the same mix, and always a large entry of committed Christians, many of whom express interest in serving in the Third World. The relationship of religion to final career choice has not been studied, but there is no evidence of any religion being an impassable barrier to entering any specialty.

Politics

Few medical students seem to have strong political affiliations or aspirations. Few medical schools belong to the National Union of Students. Pressure of examinations from the age of fifteen to twenty provides one, but probably not the only, reason. There are many signs that most medical students today have a more alert social conscience than their predecessors, contrasting sharply with the image of British medical students up to the 1950s. During the 1960s British medicals differed from their contemporaries in many countries by their lack of participation in student unrest. This may have been due to their not being confronted with the factors which roused medical students elsewhere. They were not confronted with the massive poverty and underprivilege which activated South American students, or the failure to provide medical care for large sections of the population which angered medical students in the United States, or (in the context of a Royal Commission on Medical Education) the resistance to reform of medical schools which roused students in much of Western Europe and Japan. British students have shown no great or widespread interest in sharing in the governance of medical schools or universities, or even in the management, as opposed to participation in the activities of student unions, clubs and societies.

Domicile

In 1966 the entry was drawn from across the country but with a disproportionately high number from Scotland and the 'South East and London' and a disproportionately low input from East Anglia. There is no record of the present situation which includes students whose home-based status depends on three years' secondary schooling in Britain. The ethnic mix of the entry has also been broadened in recent years by the inclusion of the children of immigrants, among whom medicine is popular as a career and who apply themselves with great determination to achieving high grades in GCE examinations.

Schooling

In 1966, 43-4 per cent of students entering English and Welsh medical schools had previously attended state schools, 22.1 per cent grant-aided schools, 31.2 per cent independent schools, and 3.3 per cent had had private education. More Scottish students had been to state and fewer to independent schools. No information is available on the present situation, but undoubtedly more medical students now take 'A' levels from technical and tutorial colleges than in the past.

Education
The academic attainments of entering medical students, as measured by GCE results, are high; higher than those of students entering other faculties and considerably higher than those of students entering medicine twenty years ago. The majority have achieved grades higher

than C at 'A' level in three subjects, most commonly chemistry, physics and mathematics (or biology) and an increasing number have passed a fourth subject at 'A' level, sometimes in a non-scientific subject.

Motivation

There is little hard data regarding the motivation of present medical students. A personal view, based on thirty-five years of interviewing candidates for admission and individual students after entry, is that the great majority are genuinely attracted by the concept of a 'satisfying' occupation, and although recently some see the satisfaction as intellectual, that which most hope for is the satisfaction of helping others.

Few sixteen-year-olds in Britain choose medicine with a view to raising their social status or achieving a high income — though these reasons may be important in some countries. The idea that doctors will always be wanted, whether correct or not, may motivate some. Parental pressure undoubtedly plays a part sometimes, exerted mainly by non-medical parents seeking the vicarious fulfilment of their own ambitions. Not infrequently death or serious illness in the family appears at least to have triggered off the decision to choose medicine. A strong desire to take it up is usually found in the children of doctors who died at an early age. Doctors' children seldom, however, have that clear vision of 'what medicine is all about' to which teachers so often refer in UCCA reports. They rarely have an opportunity to observe a medical parent at work.

For many, the career choice is made in childhood, reinforced over the years by the family ('Willie is going to be a doctor'), and questioned only when choosing 'A' level subjects. Early deciders include a few who choose a specific branch from which they never veer. The Association for the Study of Medical Education (ASME) studies of 1961 and 1966 identified profiles of would-be surgeons and, less precisely, of would-be psychiatrists. Others make their broad career choice at about sixteen, sometimes prompted by an interest in the 'A' level subjects thought to lead to medicine and often confident, despite a very hazy concept of the profession's current and possible future functions, that they will later find one of its many different branches very much to their liking.

The desire to be involved in making sick individuals better is the dominant feature of the motivation of British medical students, irrespective of when they made their career choice. It distinguishes them from those who choose medicine in many other countries and it is a feature which does not seem to have changed appreciably in the past thirty-five years, though the ways in which they would like to help the sick have altered. Thirty years ago the great majority wished to do so by the use of their own hands, counteracting physical disease by physical means such as surgery. Gradually the majority have come to favour what, though often described as 'applying science to human problems', is no more than a medical rather than a surgical approach. More recently the idea of psychological means of restoring health has become more attractive, but commonly more as an adjunct to other therapeutic measures than alone. More recently still a small stream of students has become discernible whose concern seems to be for society as a whole and who see in medicine a chance to change it by the psycho-social care of individuals.

Social service in secondary schools has brought many medical students into contact with some aspects of medical care, especially that of the old and the handicapped. Both appear to be considered important, but are unattractive to most by virtue of offering doctors too little scope for 'making people better'. Likewise the importance of preventive medicine is universally recognized but, as applied to the masses as opposed to individuals, is seldom seen as an attractive or even proper activity for doctors. Much the same applies to administration and management in medicine. The need for research is accepted but very few express any burning desire to become research workers. Few show any interest in a career in scientific medicine or in basic medical sciences. Most of those with first degrees in a basic science appear anxious to become clinicians, frequently in general practice.

These impressions of the interests of current recruits are in accord with the findings of the studies made of first and final-year medical students across the country by ASME in 1961 and 1966, and by Donnan in 1975.

The Rejects

Many try again the next year, retaking 'A' levels in the same subjects in the hope of better grades. Some medical schools have no interest in second-time takers: others are prepared to consider them, and at times offer places to applicants with low but adequate grades on condition that the year is spent in ways which complement their life experience to date.

Johnson compared a sample of 453 applicants who between 1961 and 1965 were unsuccessful in gaining admission (despite having at least minimum requirements) with students admitted and studied by ASME. He found the difference to lie almost entirely in the superior academic achievements of those selected. Analysis of five non-academic factors believed to affect selection indicated that none had a substantial and independent effect on it. Many applicants with at least minimum entrance requirements continue to be rejected each year in favour of others with higher qualifications. Some, who have been interviewed and offered places, fail to achieve even minimum requirements and cannot enter. They presumably include those with greatest difficulty in the basic sciences, a difficulty which possibly accompanies those personality traits which lead to interest in the psycho-social aspects of medicine.

Finance, or lack of it, is a barrier to admission only in the case of graduate applicants and those applying from overseas.

Results

The wastage rate in medical schools was running at 10 per cent for many years but may be falling. Whether withdrawal is voluntary or enforced for examination failure, the major cause is loss of motivation.

The relationship of academic achievement at entry to later success is difficult to establish. Medical examinations are conducted on a pass/fail basis and there are no qualifying Honours degrees. Recent studies in London have shown that schools taking entrants with the lowest 'A' level scores can achieve the highest pass rate for first-time takers in the final MB. There is as yet no way of objectively testing and comparing the performance of established doctors and no agreed criteria as to what constitutes a good one in most branches of medicine.

Final Distribution of the Medical School Entry

The final distribution of the students entering British medical schools in any one year is not completed until at least fifteen years later. The majority will have made a final career choice by that time, ten years after graduation, but many will still be completing the relevant postgraduate training. The time taken to achieve a career post (not necessarily carrying permanent tenure) varies: general practitioners usually taking less than six years from registration, non-hospital specialists the same, and hospital specialists taking some eleven years. British hospital specialists have longer training than anywhere else, and it is still possible to become an independent general practitioner at an earlier age in Britain than anywhere else.

Three years' vocational training is now mandatory for principals in general practice — those taking independent clinical responsibility. The minimum duration of training for all other specialties is much longer but varies considerably. Minimal requirements are laid down for each, specifying the time to be spent in approved training posts in various related subjects at increasing levels of responsibility under supervision. In all specialties, except general practice, one or more postgraduate examinations must be passed at some stage, more often early than late.

The duration of individual training posts ranges from six months to four years. Each must be obtained in open competition. Appointment committees are concerned not only with training but also with choosing young doctors capable of fulfilling the service commitments of the post. Recently, national policy has aimed at reducing the number of the most junior posts and increasing the number of consultants.

An early career choice allows an early start to training, quickly builds experience in it and shows commitment to it. The early deciders, pursuing a choice made even before medical school, lose no time in appointments outside the minimum requirements of their chosen specialty, provided they can obtain prescribed posts without delay. Early deciders, however, are a minority. Last and Stanley (1968) found almost no relationship between students' career preferences and the work they were doing five years later. Since then studies made between 1976 and 1979 by the Institute of Manpower Studies for the Department of Health indicated an increase in the number of young doctors making a career choice within five years of qualifying, without of course any evidence as to what proportion may later change direction, as a result of examination difficulties, failure to obtain posts, or the development of new interests.

The combination of a long undergraduate course with long post-graduate training requirements, is tending to curtail the currently undefined period of 'general professional training' which is intended to provide that exposure to a wide range of illness which is essential if career choice is to be based on experience.

The determinants of doctors' final career decisions are complex and interactive. The IMS enquiry identified the following factors and rated them in order of the proportion of doctors claiming to have been influenced by them: a positive interest in the work (99%), likelihood of obtaining posts (81%), fitting in with family circumstances (76%), good equipment (71%), geographical location (70%), good buildings (66%), and a previous experience in the specialty (55%).

The importance of the likelihood of obtaining posts is a reminder that at this stage there is not equal access to all branches of medicine. At any particular time graduates may find one specialty expanding and another virtually closed. Chance openings at junior level may, and frequently must, decide in which direction an individual moves. The further progress is made in one direction the less opportunity remains for change to another.

The Outcome

Probably more than one-third of British graduates end up in a specialty other than their first choice, some reluctantly. More women than men fail to achieve their first preference. They have particular difficulties in completing postgraduate training and in selecting a specialty. A much wider range of female graduates is faced with a range of specialties in some of which few if any women have ever practised.

Many of those who change direction, for whatever reason, acquire a broader-based training thereby. In contrast the experience of early deciders who achieve their first choice in minimum time is limited to a narrow range of illness related only to that specialty; and is likely to result in a blinkered approach to medicine as a whole and diminished potential as teachers.

There is little objective evidence as to the quality of the final product in any branch. Individual observers periodically assert that many people find doctors in Britain too concerned with the scientific and technological aspects of medicine, too little interested in its psychological and social aspects, and insufficiently 'caring'. Within the profession, however, there is anxiety that British medical education too often fails to confer the faculty of independent critical thinking, the ability to reason and apply scientific method to unfamiliar situations or to complex clinical problems involving psychological and social as well as physical and chemical variables.

For over forty years, efforts have been continuing to adapt British medical education to contemporary medicine by replacing the old medical school course of vocational training with a university education in medicine, following it with a period of wide clinical experience, and concluding with a postgraduate training tailored to provide the knowledge and skills relevant to the current practice of a given branch. The adaptation is not yet complete. The medical school course is not yet the university education on broad and liberal lines recommended forty years ago. The period of general experience is frequently lacking. If and when these long awaited reforms have been achieved, however, British doctors will have an educational foundation and a basis of experience which should help them more easily to find the right niche, and enable them to move more freely from one branch to another if necessary, while providing them with a more holistic view of medicine and a broader insight into the problems of sick people.

Educational reform by itself, however, is unlikely to alter the fact that there is insufficient recruitment to certain specialties, exacerbated at times by an increasing demand for them. They include the basic medical sciences, some sections of pathology and some areas of technical expertise such as radiology and anaesthetics; all of which are scientific in nature and exclude, or limit, patient contact. 'Shortage' specialties also include psychiatry and geriatrics (clinical specialties in which it is difficult to achieve rapid improvement in response to therapy), and community medicine which offers little opportunity to deal with individual patients and brings increasing administrative duties.

Finding that 'positive interest in the work' was the factor most often influencing career choice, the Institute of Manpower Studies attempted to analyse those aspects of work which appealed most. Over three-quarters of doctors liked treating and diagnosing illness, close patient contact, treating acute cases and affecting complete cures. Less than a third liked long diagnostic investigations, dealing with social problems or basically healthy people, and only 3 per cent liked treating old people only. Over 80 per cent liked personal independence, variety and using the skills of a physician. Less than a quarter liked working with complex machinery and apparatus or laboratory work. Few liked research work or administration.

These findings tally precisely with the impressions described earlier of the medical school entry and of the majority of the pool of applicants from which it is drawn. Present medical education does not appear to alter this motivation, but if the undergraduate course becomes more of a preparation for a changing future (and less concerned with vocationally orientated knowledge) it may do so.

There seems to have been little change in the interests of those admitted to medicine in Britain over the past few decades, in contrast to at least some other countries where the proportion interested in scientific aspects has long been higher, but has increased, as has the proportion interested in psychological and, more recently, social aspects. This may reflect other differences between medicine in Britain and elsewhere. Long ago British medicine developed particular characteristics: a conviction that the care of the individual patient is more important than anything else, and that observation rather than experiment is the method by which medicine should be advanced. These attitudes led to, and have since been fostered by, a unique pattern of hospital organization and a strict system of referral between hospital and outside practitioner, which are only now beginning to change. The British people as a whole, though not noticeably scientifically-minded, have been slower than many others to recognize mental disorder and welcome psychiatric care. The existence of a national health service in the context of a welfare state may have prevented that concern by doctors for the social aspects of medicine which has recently been more noticeable in the United States. Moreover, in few other countries does the decision to take up medicine have to be made commonly at sixteen.

These differences are likely to lessen, and any effect they may have had on recruitment to medicine could decline. It is reasonable to expect that medicine in Britain will attract a broader range of recruits in the future than in the recent past. This will almost certainly mean that more British doctors than now will be primarily interested in the scientific aspects of medicine, even if others are mainly concerned with the psychological or social. It will then be all the more important to ensure that round pegs are fitted into round holes. It will also be increasingly necessary to realize that doctors in every branch and specialty are engaged in the process of caring, and that the extent to which they are also engaged in giving comfort will depend, as it does now to a large extent, less on the selection and preparation (here and elsewhere) of the doctors, and more on the priorities established for the NHS.

9 Access and Recruitment to Engineering

Robert Smith

Access and recruitment to engineering is both open and flexible, principally because there are several levels at which engineers may practice. In this respect, engineering may be a better model for other (perhaps nascent) professions than, say, medicine or law.

History

Prior to the 1960s, the main route into the engineering profession, to full chartered engineer status, was by part-time study for the Higher National Certificate (HNC), followed by an examination set by one of the professional engineering institutions. Engineers at that time combined an educational programme with relevant practical experience at work. With the expansion of the universities and polytechnics in the 1960s came a growth in engineering degree courses; as a result, the profession decided to restrict entry from 1971 onwards only to people with degrees. Only a fraction of one per cent of engineers now achieve chartered status without a degree. Thus from 1971, the engineering profession became effectively an all-graduate one: a similar movement to that in many other professions.

One consequence of these developments is that engineers in senior and middle management positions most probably came up the HNC route. There is some tension between them and the new entrants who started with degrees, whom they see as 'callow'. The sandwich course was developed as partial compensation for the loss of practical experience commensurate with the HNC. Sandwich courses are identified only with the technological universities (Salford, Loughborough, Bradford, etc.) and with the polytechnics. Thus although perhaps 40 per cent of engineering students may be following sandwich courses, they are in institutions associated with lower entry standards than the top band of universities.

Very recently, from the late 1970s, there has been a growth of extended 4-year degree courses directed at engineering 'high-fliers'. All of these courses have some industrial experience built into them, thereby providing for a proportion of the most able students something of the experience a sandwich course student gets. There is a good example of a 4-year degree at Brunel University, where the 'Special Engineering Programme' normally requires three grade As at GCE 'A' level for entry. About 5 per cent of university engineering entrants are now entering 4-year degree courses. Such courses attract the top ability students both academically and in personal qualities.

The HNC still exists, but has been effectively supplanted by degree courses for those aspiring to chartered status.

Definitions

There are four levels of engineering preparation now recognized for different occupational levels within engineering:

a *Craftsman engineers* who would typically have a City and Guilds Certificate.
b *Engineering technicians* who will have taken the old Ordinary National Certificate (ONC) or its Technician Education Council (TEC) equivalent, normally starting at age 16.
c *Technician engineers* who will have taken the HNC (or HND, see below); entry to these courses being either by the ONC or by one GCE 'A' level (ie two streams entering, one straight from school with GCE 'A' levels, the other from technical college with ONC). Graduates with Ordinary degrees (or in certain disciplines even those with third-class Honours degrees) cannot proceed beyond the technician engineer level.
d *Professional engineers* who will have taken an engineering degree accredited by an engineering institution under the general overview of the Engineering Council.

There is a significant input to degree courses, particularly in the polytechnics, of those with technician engineer qualifications. About 50 per cent of students on polytechnic engineering degree courses have technician engineer qualifications. In some polytechnics it is possible for students to start by doing one year of an HND course and then switch to the second year of the degree course.

The ONC and HNC are qualifications taken by part-time study interleaved with periods of industrial experience; full-time equivalents of them are known as Ordinary National Diploma (OND) and Higher

National Diploma (HND) respectively. These Diplomas may be taken by two years of full-time study each; by contrast, the Certificate courses (ONC and HNC) usually take three years of combined part-time study and work experience. Someone leaving school at 16 could qualify as a technician engineer through the part-time route by age 22.

Entry to Engineering Degrees

Modes of Entry

About 18,000 students entered degree courses in 1983, about 40 per cent of them being in polytechnics. Three-quarters of the entry came direct from sixth forms with GCE 'A' levels; the other 25 per cent came from technical colleges with OND or HND qualifications.

The minimum requirement for those entering with GCE 'A' levels is two subjects, usually maths and physics, although chemistry is demanded for those who wish to become chemical engineers. There has been some limited experiment with a maths-only entry following publication of a British Association report in 1977 (British Association 1977), which suggested that many more students would be eligible to study engineering if higher education institutions dropped the requirement for physics. The number entering with just maths is, however, very small and tends to be restricted to courses related to computer engineering.

Two GCE 'A' levels will obtain entry to a polytechnic course, and, in 1983, two D grades would have been adequate, although the better polytechnics would have been demanding two Cs. For a university course, three GCE 'A' levels are normally required; in 1983, the requirement was for three grade Cs. The university entrant will offer maths and physics, with a good deal of flexibility now being permitted or even encouraged for the third 'A' level. In the past, applicants came forward with chemistry or further mathematics as the third GCE 'A' level, but there has been pressure for a broader sixth-form programme as it has become appreciated that engineers need a wider range of skills than just the scientific ones. A number of course selectors now welcome economics or a language as the third 'A' level, while there is also a strong movement afoot to include design and technology as an acceptable third 'A' level.

Competition with Science

The students entering universities or polytechnics with GCE 'A' level qualifications will have come from the science sixth form; engineering degree courses are, therefore, in competition with those in the physical sciences. In the past, the sciences had a greater status in Britain than engineering, and until the late 1970s the entry standard into science courses was higher than that into engineering courses. There has been a change in the last two to three years, with entry standards to engineering courses now being higher than those to science courses. This phenomenon reflects not only the publicity following the publication of the Finniston Report, but also the recession, in which young people are seeking out degree courses which they believe will give them the best chance of finding jobs at the end of their studies.

The problem of 'empty places' in science and engineering courses which existed in the 1970s has now disappeared. At that time there had been a move away from science subjects in the sixth form which resulted in lower application rates to both science and engineering. In engineering departments, the empty places were filled by overseas students — with, in the mid-1970s, something over 25 per cent of students coming from overseas. The overseas proportion has, however, fallen dramatically, following the increase in overseas students' fees, the swing back to science in the schools, and the movement towards engineering courses. The problem now is to find places for all the young people who want to study engineering. Students who a few years ago might have entered a polytechnic engineering degree course may now be having to undertake an HND (at least for the first year — see below).

Women in Engineering

Two factors militate against girls entering engineering degree courses. First is the public perception of engineering not being a female activity, with pressure being put on girls by their parents, their teachers, and (above all) by their peer group to conform to the female model and not to apply for engineering. Secondly, the problem is exacerbated by the normal requirement for entry being maths and physics at GCE 'A' level, and the fact that at mixed schools, and even in girls' schools, girls tend not to choose maths and physics at 'A' level.

In 1983, around 5 per cent of the entry nationally to engineering degree courses was girls. The percentage has been increasing slowly through the years; the 1971 Census recorded 182,000 practising engineers, of whom 700 were women; a proportion of only 0.4 per cent. If the percentage is to rise further, both the image of engineering and the maths plus physics entry question will have to be tackled.

Girls do, however, enter computer science in large numbers: the subject is one part of computer engineering. At Kingston Polytechnic, for example, the computer science course has 35 per cent women, but the electronic engineering course, with much the same subject-matter, has only 5 per cent of women. The computer science course does not require physics at GCE 'A' level: the electronics course does.

A major initiative in 1984, the Women into Science and Engineering (WISE) programme, will try to encourage more women to take science and engineering courses. It is being promoted jointly by the Engineering Council and the Equal Opportunities Commission.

Working-Class and Ethnic Minority Students

As indicated, there is a significant entry to engineering degree courses mainly in the polytechnics, by the technician engineer route: about 25 per cent of the entry across the system as a whole. This provides an entry for working class and/or ethnic minority students where sixth-form 'A' level study may not have been possible or attractive. (The sixth-form 'A' level entry is likely to be mainly middle class; the technician entry route is likely to be mainly working class.)

The British Association Report (1977) showed that engineering degree courses had the largest proportion of working-class students of any degree subject in universities. In part this is because of the technician entry route; in part it is because engineering is seen as an acceptable subject for working-class young people to study. Similarly, because there were many overseas students on engineering degree courses in the 1970s, ethnic minority students saw engineering as an acceptable occupation. The engineering profession does not have the middle-class stamp of many others.

The Degree Course

The Branches of Engineering

The majority of degree courses specialize in one of the main branches of engineering − electrical and electronic, mechanical and production, civil, and chemical engineering. Within these, electronics is a growth area, overlapping with computer engineering and information technology. Mechanical engineering is comparatively stable. Civil and chemical engineering are, at present, over-supplied: this is reflected in reduced numbers of applicants for courses in these areas.

There are some broad-based general engineering courses where the students take the whole range (electrical, mechanical, civil, etc.) or at where there is a common first year or two before students specialize in one or other of the main branches.

The Format

There are two standard formats: first, the 3-year straight-through degree, with a mixture of lectures, laboratories, etc. in the first two years and a project included in the third year; second, the 4-year sandwich course which combines about the same amount of academic study as the 3-year course but with industrial experience, which ideally is integrated with the academic work. About 40 per cent of students are on sandwich courses. Graduates emerge with Honours degrees, which is the normal entry requirement for professional status, or with an Ordinary degree which constrains them to becoming technician engineers.

Since 1978 certain new types of degree have been developed, particularly following the publication of the Finniston Report (1980). These new courses include, in addition to the technical material covered in the 3-year straight-through or the sandwich course, material on engineering applications and give an appreciation of the business environment in which engineering is practised. Engineering applications concerns design and production.

There are two types of new degree. The 'extended' 4-year degrees (the first one started in 1978 and there are now 40-50 such courses being offered) are directed at the most able entrants, with constraints of about 20 per cent maximum of engineering entry to universities and 10 per cent to polytechnics. Following pronouncements by the Engineering Council in the summer of 1983, there has been a move to include a number of the so-called enhancing elements of the 4-year course in the 3-year degree: engineering applications and business and management studies. The first steps towards a 3-year 'enhanced' degree are taking place in the polytechnic sector, with the new degrees being validated by the Council for National Academic Awards (CNAA). It is proposed that the 3-year 'enhanced' course should lead to BEng and the 4-year 'extended' course to MEng. The intention of the Engineering Council is that accreditation will be given only to these two kinds of courses in the future. Students who follow the older type of BSc course (with technical material, but no study of its applications, etc.) will have to take a longer time after their degree to log up relevant experience to achieve full professional status. The fast route to becoming a chartered engineer will therefore demand a place on an accredited degree course.

After the Degree

The engineering profession is now controlled nationally by the Engineering Council, working through some fifty or so specialist engineering Institutions. Professional status (giving the title of chartered engineer) requires study on an accredited degree course; then postgraduate training in a relevant company; and finally a period of practice as an engineer. Each of these stages is accredited by one of the specialist engineering Institutions working on behalf of the Engineering Council. With three or four years spent on a degree course followed by two to four years in subsequent training and relevant experience, it is not until their mid-twenties that young engineers can achieve full professional status: the majority do not achieve it until their late twenties.

It is estimated that 15,000 engineering graduates emerged from universities and polytechnics in 1983, of which at least 10,000 graduated with Honours degrees at the level appropriate to chartered engineer status. Engineering graduates tend to enter employment closely matching their first degree. A 'feed' of 10,000 new engineers into the profession is more than adequate to maintain the stock of just over 200,000 professional engineers now in employment. It can be argued that there should be some production of engineering graduates beyond the numbers required immediately to match the needs of the profession, in that there are benefits to be had from having people with engineering degrees entering other spheres of industrial and commercial life.

Typical Career of an Engineer

Engineers in manufacturing industry have a fairly common career pattern: entry into industry after a first degree; if lucky, a year or more of post-graduation training (increasingly a luxury); certainly work fairly soon as specialist engineers in design, development, or some similar technical area. Engineers will typically stay in one of the specialist areas until achieving chartered engineer status. In their late twenties or early thirties, engineers are likely to acquire some management responsibilities, probably as project managers or section leaders. The management element will grow through their thirties so that, by mid-career, their job will be more managerial than technical. Only a limited number of engineers in their late forties to early fifties are left in specialized engineering areas. It is for this reason particularly important that some appreciation of management matters is included in engineering degrees; management skills will be vital to most engineers from their early thirties.

As engineers move through their careers, the nature of their tasks changes substantially – starting from technical skills and moving to management skills – perhaps more markedly so than in other professions. It may only be a measure of the low status which has been accorded to engineers, but one of the standard tests is how people answer the question on the Census form of what is their main professional activity: engineers in manufacturing industry who have some management responsibilities insert 'Manager' rather than 'Engineer', in complete contrast to engineers in civil or chemical engineering who are proud to be recognized as 'Engineer'. It is unusual to come across civil engineers who hold senior management positions in civil engineering companies calling themselves anything other than 'Civil Engineer'; they tend to play down their managerial responsibilities and to play up their engineering ones.

A Closed Profession?

The engineering profession is not a closed one. For the majority of employers, the knowledge and experience of an engineer are much more important than the chartered engineer qualification. There are exceptions, notably in chemical, civil, and mining engineering, where statutory requirements connected with safety demand a chartered engineer to approve design work, etc. In the manufacturing sector, while chartered engineer status is not unwelcome, it is not required by most employers. In the high-technology areas, the proportion of chartered engineers is relatively small.

One problem presented by the engineering Institutions is their conservatism, whereby they have demanded certain specific technical knowledge of those entering their particular branches. Their requirements have not always kept up-to-date with technical change in such subjects as aerospace and electronics. The result of this, in the past at least, has been an entry to those professions by scientists who in practice often work as engineers. A number of these scientists do eventually apply for, and obtain, chartered engineer status. Work appropriate to chartered engineers can, therefore, be undertaken by people who took science degrees and obtained relevant experience in industry.

The Failed Student

The variety of levels of requirement within the engineering industry (engineering technician, technician engineer, etc.) means that a student who leaves after two years of a degree course may well be able to work as a technician engineer perhaps with some further education in a technical college. The student who emerges with only an Ordinary degree has a perfectly good career as a technician engineer. This provides a flexibility of level.

There is also flexibility of subject because, for instance, a civil engineer who has learned a good deal about structures is highly employable in the aerospace industry.

Within engineering there is (despite the conservatism of some engineering institutions) considerable freedom of access, with opportunities of recruitment to even the most senior levels of the profession at many points (and by many methods) in the individual's career.

10 Access and Recruitment to Management

Ian Bruce

The conventional wisdom in business circles is that management is an art which is nurtured by experience and enhanced by character. This distrust of learning and training has been a widespread characteristic of British society but one which, in the Services at least, was exploded by Montgomery in time to save our armies in World War II. Montgomery recognized that modern warfare is a highly complex combined operation which requires the closest co-operation between the different arms of the Services. It is no arena for the amateur, however inspired. Montgomery insisted not only that his officers should be professionals in their own special field but that they should undergo training to appreciate the capabilities of other branches of the services. Business likewise is a combined operation, and those who aspire to the management of it must ensure that they have a sound understanding of the different functional activities within it, and of how they interrelate, as well as an expert knowledge of at least one function. What is our educational system doing to develop the managers our industral society requires? What is industry doing to ensure a more professional management cadre?

Is the British Manager Under-educated?

In recent years the British manager has been the target for salvoes of criticism from the pens of writers, researchers and journalists. Broadly speaking the charges against our managers are that they are an élitist group, they are under-educated, and they do not compare favourably with their counterparts in other major industrial countries. The British system of education from school — be it public, grammar or comprehensive — to university has done little to prepare its students to live in an industrial society, far less to manage one. The system has its strengths. It can build character and breed scholarship, but it was geared to an imperial past and is graded in a way which confers social status. It still produces people who want to be someone rather than do something. Martin Wiener, in his book *English Culture and the Decline of the Industrial Spirit 1850 — 1980* (1981) has provided a wealth of documentary evidence for the critical revulsion of poet and novelist, preacher, professor and politician to our industrial society. The well-bred, well-educated person would not choose to be soiled by too close an involvement with the industrial wealth-making process. Those who built up successful businesses used their wealth to escape from their industrial origins and the public schools completed the process by cleansing their sons of trade and commercial ambitions.

As a result of the attitudes which dominated our social and educational institutions, most of our industrial leaders became managers by default. They were not the most gifted intellectually of their generation and the most significant fact arising from the various studies of the British managerial class during the past forty years is the small numbers of managers who were assisted in their task by higher educational qualifications. In 1961 a survey of the Institute of Directors described the executive as a man who was trained on the job, entering business straight from school and, in the great majority of cases, from public school. As late as 1973 a survey (Institute of Directors 1973) showed that 71 per cent of our managing directors came from public schools. This need cause no surprise. Many companies were still family concerns and the sons of successful industrialists went to public schools to have conferred upon them the social status which their families sought. British business men had a strong conviction that character and experience on the job were the most important attributes of a manager and the public schools were turning out young men who were confident of their role to lead and had access to the power élite in their communities.

The Second World War greatly extended the social categories in which leadership could be found and the larger national and multinational companies began to compete for the brighter students from the universities. When the Robbins Report ushered in the great age of university expansion in the 1960s, business inevitably switched their recruitment from the schools to the universities and henceforth potential managers entered industry and banking along the path of meritocracy. In 1966 18 per cent of UK managers, who sat on company boards or carried divisional responsibilities in larger companies, had a university degree and 40 per cent had a recognized professional qualification such as chartered accountant, chartered engineer, lawyer, etc. By 1973 the comparable figures were 49 per cent and 35 per cent according to *Management Today*. In the 1980s, it can be said, it will probably be very difficult for any man or woman to get on a company board of any importance without a degree or professional qualification. In this sense

British managers of the future will be better educated than their predecessors.

However, throughout the postwar period many people inside and outside of business entertained doubts about the relevance of our educational system to an industrial society and about the contribution it has made to the professionalism of our managers. There was a call for a more business-oriented education. The polytechnics and the colleges of education were the first to answer the challenge. A wide range of business studies leading to diplomas or degrees, some of them providing exemption from parts of professional qualifications, was instituted and the polytechnics have continued to provide a valuable service to management in the private and public sector. However, those who benefit are largely functional managers and middle managers. The polytechnics have made less impact on the high flyers in industry from whom general managers are selected. They tended to come from the universities, which were slow to recognize the need for an academic discipline for business men and women. Their initial response was in the postgraduate field, when in 1963 the Franks Report recommended the introduction of business schools on the American pattern and prepared the way for a more professional approach to general management.

Business Schools to the Rescue?

With financial assistance from industry and government and the encouragement of the Federation of Management Education under Philip Nind, the business school movement soon gained momentum. London Business School and Manchester Business School were set up as 'centres of excellence'; Cranfield and Henley took on a new lease of life; several universities jumped on the band-wagon with their own Schools of Business Studies and Regional Management Centres sprang up all devoted to bringing first aid to the under-educated British manager. The major schools decided to make a Masters programme the foundation of their teaching and research effort and, on top of this, to offer a range of general management and specialist courses to middle and senior managers. Although these Master of Business Administration programmes have by and large been successful in making good some of the shortcomings of our educational system, the schools are not yet in complete harmony with the recruitment and development requirements of the companies. The early resistance to the MBA which sprang partly from the defensive attitudes of experienced managers, who felt themselves threatened by the educated newcomer, and partly from the insensitivity of the MBA, who underrated the need for experience, has given way to better understanding and mutual respect.

Dilemmas still remain, however. Companies would like their potential young managers to have the formal business training which the schools provide but they have learned to their cost that sponsored students seldom return to the companies which supported them. The majority of companies agree with the schools that candidates for the Masters programme ought to have a few years' previous business experience but then they admit to difficulties in fitting these mature graduates into their organizational and salary structures. In spite of these obstacles, the business school graduate is steadily making his mark in the upper echelons of management. Perhaps only one or two MBAs have succeeded to the most senior jobs in British Industry but time is on their side and a 1983 internal placement survey by London Business School revealed that over 50 per cent of their Masters output had reached director level within ten years. Even more significant is the urge of young men and women to secure places at business schools and acquire additional qualifications which will increase their managerial professionalism. The one- and two-year programmes are over-subscribed; the part-time MBA courses have met with an enthusiastic response; evening accounting and finance courses are fully attended. Specialists, women and minority ethnic groups are using the Masters programme to widen the career opportunities available to them. Former public schoolboys unwilling to abdicate leadership in the business world without a challenge are turning to the business schools.

In a world of rapid technological and social change the learning process is a continuous one for the manager. The business schools have a crucial role to play but once again they have not always seen eye to eye with industry in the objectives of middle management courses. The schools have been obliged to design fairly long courses because they have found that many of the participants are sadly lacking in the basic management skills. However, they have compounded their problem by building into their courses time for the individual members to reflect on their life goals, to reassess what they are doing and where they are going, and to come to terms with the mid-career crisis. These objectives are important for the manager in an individual capacity but they are unlikely to increase his effectiveness in his corporate role and they should be kept separate from company goals. Companies want shorter, business-oriented courses, which will concentrate on the skills directly applicable to the work-place. They want their managers to be better versed in financial matters, in information technology, in inter-personal skills, and in industrial relations. As a result, companies have turned increasingly to in-house training and have experimented with action learning, which Professor Revons pioneered and which attempts to draw out lessons for the manager from the work he is currently engaged in. Full advantage is not being taken of the resources of the business schools and the time is ripe for a reassessment by academics and industrialists of the business school input to middle and senior management development. A better understanding must be reached on the duration of the MBA course and the middle and senior management courses, on their content, and on the relationship between theory and practice, learning and experience.

The eighty companies which I contacted in the preparation of this paper, showed no social bias or élitism in their recruitment policies. All of them claimed that the management summit was reached by the path of meritocracy. In 1977 David Malbert, then City Editor of the *Evening Standard*, was able to entitle his study of the managing directors of thirty major companies in the FT Index *The Classless Face of Capitalism*. That title could equally well apply to my survey. Management is a career for the talents as far as the talents are available to British industry. The recruitment net is spread widely across our educational institutions. The red-brick universities, the polytechnics and technical colleges are as important to British industry as Oxbridge.

The charge which might be levelled against British management is that they display the natural weakness of being status conscious, over-interested in the fine distinctions which divide our society. This has lead our managers to avoid where possible both operational matters and contact with the workers.

The Functional Background of our Managers

The form of élitism noted above manifests itself in the functional areas from which our senior managers first emerged and to which those with high aspirations are attracted at recruitment time. Some functions are considered to have more status than others and sadly the favoured ones do not include production, manufacturing and sales. Finance was one of the first business occupations to become 'respectable'. It also became one of the more important functions as the problems of cash flow, budgeting, investment policy and taxation increased in complexity. It is not surprising that a preponderance of chief executives in the UK have a finance background. From a survey of 300 in *The Times 1000* by Korn Ferry International (1983), it was found that 30 per cent of chief executives emerged from the finance function, 20 per cent technical, 14 per cent marketing and 7 per cent sales. If chief executives with economics and accountancy training are added to those who worked in the finance function, the total rises to 38 per cent and underlines the message that a sound knowledge of finance is a key qualification for top jobs. Production, engineering, industrial relations and sales have not traditionally led to the top and the more able recruits to industry tend to avoid them or escape from them as soon as possible. After the past few

years of financial retrenchment, the vital requirement of British industry
is to open up new markets overseas and it is reasonable to predict that
marketers will supplant finance men as the chief contenders for the most
senior posts.

Although most chief executives make their initial mark in a functional
capacity, the most noticeable feature of their careers was their mobility
between functions and their exposure to general management responsibilities at an early stage. The majority of chief executives stressed their
good luck in receiving this early recognition. In the light of this it is
surprising that so many companies are apathetic to the interfunctional
development of their most promising staff.

Profile of a Successful Manager

What personal qualities and attributes are the predictors of a successful
career in management today? The answers received from eighty
companies in industry, retail and banking revealed a high level of
agreement about the personal identikit of a manager:

1 Mental agility
2 Relevant professional knowledge
3 Numeracy
4 An appreciation of technical matters
5 Familiarity with the computer
6 The ability and willingness to accept continued education
7 Analytical and problem-solving skills
8 Communication and presentation skills
9 An innovative turn of mind
10 The helicopter quality
11 Emotional stability and resilience
12 A need to achieve results
13 The courage to take risks
14 Motivation and will
15 Leadership

Although the recruiters tour the universities in pursuit of intellectual
ability, some companies have reservations about the graduate intake.
While acknowledging the analytical prowess of university-trained recruits, they find them ill-prepared for a life in industry and commerce.
They argue that time spent at university can be a disincentive to business
enthusiasm. Much of the teaching is antipathetic to business ethics and
the private enterprise system and the general environment encourages a
theoretical rather than a practical approach and inhibits decision-

making. Moreover, the companies in my survey found little correlation between academic ability and success in management.

The harsh lessons of the economic recession have underlined the importance of four of the characteristics of the good manager mentioned above — a need to achieve results, the courage to take risks, motivation and will, and leadership.

The restoration of leadership as an important attribute of management is significant. There was a time when it was played down, partly because leadership was an elusive concept which could be expressed in many different ways, partly because the theory of management was concentrating on control and co-ordination by committee. Today companies are selecting chief executives who have a pronounced leadership style, the motivation to achieve results, the courage to put their jobs at stake, and the will to break down the constraints which impede the introduction of new systems and new technologies. The days are over when companies could avoid the challenge of international competition by retreating within the colonial stockade, by sharing out markets with their rivals or by compromising with the unions to achieve the illusion of industrial peace. Managers can no longer seek refuge in numbers and collective responsibility. The management structure has been thinned out and the individual has to be judged by his results.

Conclusions

I shall now endeavour to pull together the various strands of my argument. My survey showed no evidence of social élitism in the recruitment policies of companies. It will be difficult in future to reach the boardroom without a degree or similar qualification. Meritocracy reigns, and leaves the door of opportunity open to minority ethnic groups and women. There has been a significant movement of women into senior management jobs in marketing, personnel, legal and PR, but they are less in evidence in the fields of production, distribution and engineering and in general management jobs in technically based companies. Several companies commented on the low response from minority ethnic groups at the recruitment stage, but none thought that a policy of positive discrimination was justified or necessary. Business schools had enhanced the opportunities of minority groups because recruiters found it easier to isolate the qualities of motivation and business acumen from the academic trappings of an English education at the stage of the Masters programme.

The nature of a first degree appears to have little relevance to managerial achievement, but company recruiters favour those who have graduated in scientific or technical subjects or in the more demanding disciplines such as law and classics. However, there is a feeling of disillusionment with the educational system as a whole and with its inadequacy in producing sufficient candidates of high managerial potential. The majority of employers see little merit in the narrow specialization which follows 'O' levels and which is continued into university. They are looking for recruits who are hard-headed and adaptable, who know how to communicate and work with others, who can tackle problems and commit themselves to broad objectives. They would welcome a new pattern of assessment for school-leavers which would be based only partly on formal examinations and which would provide a more convincing proof of achievement and character. In this respect they support the Education for Capability movement which stresses the importance of that part of our culture which is concerned with 'doing, making, creating and organizing'. The recommendations of the recent SRHE Leverhulme study on university courses entitled *Excellence in Diversity* (SRHE 1983) also reflect the views of many industrialists.

The reluctance of British management to become involved with operational matters and the work force has conveyed itself to candidates from universities. They believe that the preferential route to management is through finance, marketing and head office activities and those with high aspirations avoid production and industrial relations. Experience has shown that a successful career in industry depends to a great extent on the opportunity of early general management responsibility in a variety of functions. The pace of technological advance, the computer revolution, the international complexity of marketing and finance will oblige the up-and-coming manager to return to the classroom at frequent intervals, and the institutions of further learning will have to find improved methods of imparting specialized knowledge to busy executives. Moreover, those who are teaching in these institutions will require greater facilities than exist at present to return to the industrial environment if their thinking is to keep pace with the rapidity of change. The way ahead for management development in this country necessitates ever closer relationships between industry and our educational institutions.

Part 4
Curricula and Teaching Methods

11 Curricula and Teaching Methods in Medical Education

Philip Seager

The dilemma facing medical education is that facing science in general: how to attempt to keep abreast of the exponential growth in knowledge, recognizing that at least 50 per cent of it will be out of date in ten years time, with the added problem of identifying which 50 per cent. Over the past century medical training has been directed towards producing an all-round doctor who, on qualification, will step out into the world and be able to turn a hand to any branch of medicine. It was felt that the five or six-year medical course in the UK — four years in the United States — was more than sufficient to cover the ground work. In 1952 an additional compulsory pre-registration year was added following graduation so that before full registration with the General Medical Council, the doctor had to spend a period of twelve months in supervised hospital practice, divided into six months medicine and six months surgery; these two terms cover a broad range of subjects acceptable for such training. The pre-registration period is under the supervision of the Postgraduate Dean of the Medical School and is thus seen to be quite definitely part of the training process.

Following reports by Royal Commissions on Medical Education in 1968 and on the Health Services in 1979, there is recognition that changes in education and training as well as in the general philosophy of the educational process are long overdue. In the Royal Commission Report on Medical Education (the Todd Report 1968) there was recognition that the aim of medical education had to change. It was now proposed that the aim would be to produce 'an educated man (sic) who would become qualified by postgraduate training'. Thus we have to teach the medical student first of all how to learn and where to learn and secondly how to go on learning, because it cannot be assumed that the fully developed doctor is turned out at the end of the five-year medical course with his Bachelor of Medicine and Bachelor of Surgery degrees.

It is necessary, first of all, to look at the general pattern of conventional medical training in British medical schools. The majority of school-leavers are assessed on the basis of 'O' level results and a report from the head of the school, together with, at some medical schools, an interview. Final confirmation depends on 'A' level or Highers results and students are admitted, usually into the second year, to commence anatomy, physiology, biochemistry and behavioural sciences. This course lasts for about five terms, followed by examinations in each subject. The successful student enters an Introductory Course leading to clinical and para-clinical subjects over the next three years. A grand Final examination or an aggregation of separate parts results in the Bachelor of Medicine and Bachelor of Surgery degrees. Following this five-year course the compulsory pre-registration year usually takes place in the teaching hospital region although arrangements can be made for accreditation at more distant hospitals, occasionally abroad. Thus over a period of six years the school-leaver has been turned into a qualified doctor registered with the General Medical Council and licensed to begin further training.

A medical qualification offers entry into a wide range of specialist activities varying from direct live patient contact, through biochemical investigation of human products, to scientific research or administrative responsibility for populations rather than individuals. The newly qualified doctor does not simply step through one of these doors to take up a new interest. In hospital medicine there are two further stages of training, namely General Professional Training for two years, in which there is general ground work in areas related to eventual specialization, and Higher Professional Training in which concentration is directed to the specialist field. In General Practice, at first a voluntary, and now a compulsory, programme of vocational training also requires supervised training in hospital and in general practice before acceptance as a trained family doctor. Most specializations have examinations, frequently in two parts, which, while not formally necessary for acceptance into the specialty, undoubtedly are so in practice.

Furthermore, because of the ever-changing body of knowledge and concepts and the additional skills and techniques which developed, it is encumbant on all medical practitioners to exercise a process of continuing education either by attendance at formal refresher courses or at least by regular reading of current literature. Many doctors will point apologetically to a pile of journals still in their wrappers waiting to be read. There are conflicting demands on time between busy clinical practice and keeping abreast of the literature.

It is important to recognize the need for a minimum level of training for those individuals who will not be willing or able to proceed beyond that level apart from the skills learnt subsequently in the tough school of experience; the toughness is often contributed by the patients. The majority of doctors are prepared to spend more time, and of course forego some income, in order to fit themselves more adequately to deal with the difficult or uncommon problems that they may meet. Thus the aim of the medical course is to turn out a doctor trained to a level at which all day-to-day services can be provided but there is a particular ability to recognize the problems where specialist help is necessary. There is also the necessity to participate in a process of continuing education throughout professional life.

This thumbnail sketch of the process of medical training may be a distortion of the reality and unfair to the endeavours of many dedicated teachers and equally enthusiastic students. However there are issues which need to be tackled to bring realism to the process of medical education and to solve the problem of putting a quart (1.1365 litres) into a pint (0.5682 litre) pot.

Casual reference to television and radio programmes or popular newspapers would suggest that the public attitude towards doctors is tinged with doubt and distrust, sometimes full of downright hostility. The way in which doctors communicate with patients, the errors leading to law suits, the use of drugs with uncomfortable or dangerous side effects and the awareness of power, overt or covert, exercised by the doctor over the fragile and defenceless patient, suggest there is profound dissatisfaction with the present situation (Cartwright 1964; Ley 1977). It is the kind of relationship that is expressed by motor car drivers towards their garage mechanics – we only need a National Garage Service to complete the picture.

A number of studies (Helfer 1970; Ley 1982) draw attention to difficulties which develop between patients and their doctors resulting in lack of 'patient compliance' – in itself an interesting phrase to describe the patient's failure, for example, to take medication. The cliché 'they never tell you anything in hospital' also represents the patient's attitude of mind rather than reality. It has been demonstrated on a number of occasions that in spite of careful explanation by the doctor the patient recalls only about 10 per cent of the information with which he has been supplied during a consultation. Efforts have been made to improve this percentage by various techniques. This does not cater for the fact that there may be sound psychological reasons for 'forgetting' or 'rejecting' potentially frightening information. Thus on the one hand the patient needs to feel that the doctors have an interest not only in the disease but also in the person standing before them. On the other hand, the staff have to recognize that they have an obligation to be aware not only of the disease process but to recognize the anxieties, false assumptions, distortions of language and other factors interfering with communication. It must therefore be a part of the training of all staff in the medical services to appreciate these problems and to learn how to overcome them or at least to reduce them.

When is a Doctor Fully Trained?

In the relatively affluent countries of Western Europe and the United States one solution to the problem of incomplete medical training is to lengthen it to accommodate all the necessary additions, assuming that these can be identified. The topic of the trained but not fully trained doctor was discussed at a recent congress of the Association of Medical Education in Europe to be reported in *Medical Education* in 1984. It was recognized that it would be impossible to include in a 5-year training programme all possible aspects or subjects appropriate for a medical training. There would have to be some selection, and even then further training would be necessary before the individual could even be considered fully trained. The alternative view was that it would be setting an impossible goal for lately developed countries if the more developed would only accept a 7, 8 or 10-year period of training to produce fully qualified specialists. Many countries manage perfectly well with doctors who are considered qualified for any medical activity after only four or five years. There are many areas of the world making do with people trained to a very limited degree and able to cope with day-to-day medical problems, offering the best available treatment to a large geographical area.

Traditionally, the teaching in a medical school is carried out by a series of specialists teaching their specialist subjects in their specialist ways based on the specialist interests of their specialist department. One of the more revolutionary suggestions at the AMEE Conference was the abolition of separate departments in a medical school to avoid this fragmentation. Many saw the proposal as destructive and a few were prepared to man the barricades to prevent it happening. Probably of greater importance is that each department should produce a list of objectives to be considered by the Faculty of Medicine Curriculum Committee so that teaching can be integrated, constructive and purposeful.

It is usually thought advisable for the medical student to have a knowledge of human anatomy, physiology, biochemistry, genetics and, more recently, behavioural sciences before proceeding to the study of the diseased organism. This fragmentation into a pre-clinical and clinical course has stood the test of time or perhaps has thwarted all efforts of the revisionists by an appeal to tradition. It is difficult to refute two of the strongest arguments against radical revision of the curriculum: namely, it would involve closing down the medical school for a year or two to sort out the programme and avoid running two totally different courses at the same time, and integrated courses are said to be heavy in their demands on staff time. The fact that lecturers in pre-clinical subjects also devote a lot of their time to students of the science faculties may be a more cogent explanation for any lack of enthusiasm for change.

There is now an examination of the relevance for the practising doctor of the amount of detail taught in these pre-clinical subjects. It is assumed that surgeons need a good knowledge of anatomy, but should they learn it prior to their clinical course and does the future bacteriologist, medical administrator or psychiatrist need to know it to the same extent? Many doctors need to know as much anatomy as a good ambulance driver carrying out roadside resuscitation or a policeman delivering a baby on route to the hospital. There is a need for more emphasis on the teaching of principles in the first years of the course, linking detailed study of scientific subjects with the clinical conditions met with in hospital.

In the past two decades medical schools have rediscovered the interaction of mind and body as a necessary contribution to an understanding of the people and their ills. It is therefore accepted that psychology, sociology and perhaps human anthropology may be necessary subjects to be studied in order to appreciate the way in which the human being behaves, whether well or ill, alone, in groups, or in society. These subjects, too, have their general theoretical side and their practical application to the sick person. They can be studied as scientific disciplines but in the medical field need to be related to the individual, whether sick, recovering or well.

Thus there are a number of basic science concepts which need to be introduced at an early stage, perhaps before anything else in the medical curriculum. The medical student comes to the medical school to learn how to diagnose and to treat patients. Some of these are frustrated by the concentration on science during the first two years and the absence of contact with patients. Many schools offer clinical demonstrations during these early years but this is often unsatisfactory since a patient is brought in before a class of 150 or more students, allowing little or no personal contact. This process poses many problems, ethical, humane, pedagogic and perceptual.

There is a strong case for offering small groups of students opportunities to talk to individual patients about their problems during the early years of their medical training. It is said that students would not know what questions to ask as they will not be familiar with the symptoms of disease. While this may be true at first, it should be recognized that they are not learning about disease but about people and how they respond to illness – the fears, the doubts, the anxieties, the difficulties in communication and the difficulties in understanding. Furthermore, in the majority of situations the intelligent student hearing about these symptoms will be propelled towards the library or the tutor to seek further information to understand the medical problem being described. This in its turn will help in an appreciation of the need for anatomical physiological, biochemical and behavioural knowledge.

Most schools, having confronted the medical student with a dead body on the first or second day of the course, do take trouble to introduce them more gradually to the clinical demands likely to be made on them by live patients. An introductory course covers such topics as medical interviewing, clinical examination, the various systems of the body, as well as topics such as ethics, legislation and occupational health. The subject of first aid is also introduced at this stage.

At last the medical student gets to the hospital and talks to the first live patient. Students are allocated to medical and surgical firms in relatively small groups where they are taught by both senior and junior doctors about detailed history-taking, symptoms and signs of different medical conditions, management by drugs, by surgery or sometimes by masterly inactivity.

Something else is taught to the students, although many teachers are not aware of this. The students are taught, by a process of modelling, appropriate attitudes to patients under their care. The frock-coated, austere, God-like consultant with a retinue of white-coated acolytes and hand-maiden nurses is a figure of the past. The consultant who talks across the patient to his junior staff, who asks the ward sister whether Mrs. Jones is feeling better and brushes aside inconvenient questions, may still be around. Such a person provides one kind of model for the students to emulate, as does the consultant who talks directly to the patient, offers opportunities of conversation in private and certainly welcomes questions about the medical and other problems the patient may be concerned with. Such a senior doctor treats patients and staff alike, as individuals worthy of notice and discussion.

Many students are at first horrified by the rush, the apparent indifference and the callous attitudes towards patients. A few rebel against it and may even give up the medical course; most come to accept it and may even see it as the most efficient way to behave.

Some learn from the situation and promise themselves (and indeed hope to keep that promise) that they will never behave in a similar manner in the future.

In a recent questionnaire addressed to medical students at British medical schools, one of the questions asked was the amount of time devoted to teaching knowledge and concepts, skills and attitudes. In general the students identified 75 to 80 per cent of the time devoted to knowledge and concepts, 20 to 25 per cent to clinical skills (largely physical rather than psychological skills), while the rest of the time was spent on promoting the view that awareness of one's attitude and behaviour towards patients was an important clinical attribute.

In addition to basic medicine and surgery many other aspects of clinical medicine have to be taught. These include obstetrics and gynaecology, paediatrics, psychiatry, anaesthetics, and specialist branches of medicine, cardiology and neurology and surgery, such as ophthalmology and otorhinolaryngology. Time must be found for dermatology, venereology, rheumatology and many others. In addition the para-clinical subjects of pathology, microbiology, immunology, pharmacology and therapeutics are essential areas of teaching. Because these subjects are taught as separate entities there is considerable repetition and overlap while the principle underlying disease may not be as clearly formulated as is desirable.

It is noteworthy that in spite of the fact that some 60 per cent of doctors who qualify in the United Kingdom take up general practice, relatively little time is devoted to training in this field. Indeed there are arguments as to whether there is such a field as general practice. The more specialized hospital departments become, the more there is the need to recognize the specialty of general practice, concentrating on the care of the individual within the family in the context of the home and the social environment.

This is not to say that scientific measurements are not available or that specialist techniques cannot be used; rather it is to recognize that many human ailments are self-limiting and the role of the doctor is to pick out those very few which require highly specialized and sophisticated attention and to treat both the illness and the patient successfully in order to hasten recovery or to alleviate stress and suffering arising from chronic conditions. Finally there is the necessity to offer support and encouragement during a pain and anxiety-free terminal phase of life.

Throughout the five years of teaching the question has to be asked concerning the effect of such teaching on the students and means must be devised to see how well the students have absorbed their knowledge and incidentally how effective are the teachers. The General Medical Council requires an examination with an external examiner to ensure appropriate standards of training throughout the United Kingdom. Medical schools arrange examinations throughout the course of the training period although details are left to individual schools.

As a result a range of techniques is used varying from continuing assessment, multiple choice questions, short answers, essays, and clinical assessments of patients either directly or in the form of case reports and oral examinations. The more important function of examinations is their formative role, giving feedback and guidance to the students and teachers concerning the progress in understanding, knowledge and skills. For this purpose, more frequent tests with opportunity for discussion on an individual or group basis are helpful. Because of the importance that students attach to passing examinations they may be seen more as hurdles to be overcome than as learning experiences and measures of their grasp of the subject. Most small departments recognize that students pay them scant attention if there is no examination carrying weight in the final assessment.

Traditionally there is a sessional examination with external examiners for the pre-clinical science subjects, one in para-clinical subjects and another sometimes split into parts in the main clinical subjects. These may form the necessary incentives to study but it is rarely conceded that a high failure rate in the examination may reflect poor teaching rather than inadequate learning.

Over the past twenty years a number of medical schools, now linked together as a network under the sponsorship of the World Health Organization, have concentrated their attention on a different approach to medical training. They have recognized that patients present not with diseases but with problems which require a solution. The problem may be difficulty in walking to work or in producing live children or in hearing the conversation of relatives and friends. Faced with the problem, or series of problems, the doctor has to elucidate the history and accompanying features and then search out possible causes, understand the disturbance of structure and function which bring about these problems, and look for solutions to remove or alleviate them. This type of approach involves an ability to communicate with strangers, to understand the interaction between the patient and the doctor, to elicit all relevant information from the patient and those associated, and to seek help from all sources including tutors, specialists, peers, libraries and audio-visual material in order to achieve a solution. Furthermore, since such problems are not tackled by one person but by a group of students it helps to encourage a team approach to the management of such issues; on occasions the team is made up not only of medical students but also of nursing, social work and other professional groups.

After six years of hard grind one might expect subdued, anxious, exhausted and cynical doctors to emerge into their new careers. This is far from the case since the vast majority are enthusiastic, able, rigorous and forward-looking. They are embarking on a tough career where the stresses undoubtedly lead to some calamities, noteworthy amongst which are alcoholism and suicide. Some would argue that if more attention were paid to selection, to training, to support and to medical practice itself such difficulties would be reduced. It has been pointed out that some who later fell by the wayside had during their heyday contributed exceptionally valuable service, and the profession would have suffered a greater loss if they had been identified and excluded at an early stage in their careers. Undoubtedly there are increasing problems in deciding how much is essential to incorporate in the basic medical training and to evaluate the pattern of teaching for the non-specialist doctor. Fortunately, the General Medical Council has always allowed liberal local variations in the design and methods of teaching and thus offered opportunities for experiment and change. The factors which interfere with such experiments are the cumbersome organization of a large faculty of medicine and the vested interest of individual departments. These aspects are proving perhaps surprisingly less of a barrier to change than had hitherto been assumed.

12 Curricula and Teaching Methods in Engineering Education

Lee Harrisberger

Engineering education in the United States has benefited for over eight decades from the husbandry of the American Society of Engineering Education (ASEE).

This unique society of engineering educators has been responsible for a long history of unprecedented and creative innovations and experimentations in curriculum development and in the teaching process. The community of engineering educators on every campus has an impressive record of experimentation with new teaching concepts and techniques. During my own thirty-year tenure in the Society, I have seen engineering faculty learn about and try out the entire spectrum of principles and concepts in the current literature of educational psychology.

The high value industry places on the technical competency of engineers inevitably propels them into areas of huge responsibility. Engineers' roles as technical advisors to critical and enormously expensive management decisions make them early candidates for leadership and managerial assignments. Since engineering attracts students from the upper fifteen per cent of the high school classes, the individual engineering student has exceptional potential to meet both the rigours of the engineering curriculum and the demands of the profession.

The following list of issues addresses my conceptions of the unmet responsibilities of the curriculum and teaching process in engineering education. They focus on the need to individualize the education of the engineer. Specifically, the engineering education programmes of the future must address each engineering student's personal characteristics, behavioural styles, and intellectual capabilities and provide a profile of personal skills and behaviours that will meet the professional competencies required to practise engineering successfully.

Competency-based Engineering Curricula

Engineers are valued by their employers for what they are able to do –
their competencies. The skills needed to DO engineering are well known
both to the employers and to the educators of engineers. As methodical
as engineers are about their engineering, it is incongruous that the
educational process in engineering has none of the characteristics of a
methodical process to identify and develop the specific skills needed for
the student to succeed as a practising engineer. Curricula throughout
engineering education are knowledge-based (Harrisberger 1977).
Course content is almost exclusively concerned with the application of
basic principles from science and the techniques of analysis and
computation.

The notable absence of internships and competency examinations as
graduation requirements in engineering testifies to the priority of
knowledge over the ability to do. Worcester Polytechnic Institute (WPI)
is the sole pioneer in the use of faculty juries to certify competence for
graduation (Grogan 1978). The WPI Plan programme (in its second
decade) requires its students to demonstrate their engineering competency by presenting two qualifying projects – one in their engineering
major and the other in a non-engineering minor. The Co-op programmes have a long history in US engineering education. However,
although they are the nearest thing to an internship, the industrial
experience is not supervised by faculty and is not a degree requirement.
The Mechanical Engineering Design Clinic at The University of
Alabama (Harrisberger 1979A) and the programme at Harvey Mudd
College are two examples of the very few internships required for
graduation in US engineering education (Harrisberger 1975).

The medical profession is adamant about the competence of its
graduates. They expect their graduates to be competent to deal with the
highly valued health and function of human beings. Why don't
engineering educators expect their graduates to demonstrate that they
can deal competently with the highly valued health and function of
industrial products? It is NOT enough that medical students can recite
the anatomy of the human body. Why, then, is it quite enough that an
engineer can mathematically model the stress pattern in a part?

The challenge here is not to define the competencies but to develop
the delivery system to accomplish skill development and to certify that
the engineer can do what the job demands. The Alverno College
experiment demonstrated some of the operational issues that must be
addressed. The Alverno programme is the most comprehensive working
model of a competency-based degree programme in US higher
education. Each student must demonstrate competency in each of eight
areas. Different juries are convened at intervals, allowing students to

apply for certification when they feel ready. Each course must be certified to provide proficiency toward one or more of the degree competencies. The model is an intensive demand on student, faculty and administrative involvement and on managerial co-ordination. The Alverno model (Grant 1979) is a challenge to engineering educators to use their considerable creativity and technology to develop an efficient, less labour-intensive process.

A competency-based curriculum design requires the setting of outcome specifications and standards. Engineers are good at this. They can set standards and devise ways to meet them and ways to certify that they were met. It's their business! It's time they applied their engineering to the educational process.

Instructional Development through Behavioural Diagnostics

An engineer cannot design or develop an engineering process without collecting a complete profile of all the attributes and capabilities of all the materials and components involved. It therefore follows that, to develop an effective individualized teaching and learning programme, a complete data package should be obtained of the skills, abilities and behavioural styles both of teachers and of learners. There is available a large battery of proven diagnostic instruments (in particular the Myers-Briggs Type Indicator, the Manatech Personalysis profile, and the Canfield Teaching and Learning Style Indicators) that provide unusually accurate predictive indicators of the performance characteristics of both teachers and learners (Harrisberger 1983). These diagnostics identify a number of performance characteristics, including preferences for self-study, group interaction, interpersonal skills, self-management, organization, creativity, scholarship, problem-solving, tenacity, as well as preferred learning delivery systems. Clearly, the effectiveness of the teaching and learning process will not be significantly improved without accounting for the dynamics of the behaviours of the participants.

Recently a consortium of seven engineering colleges used the Myers-Briggs Type Indicators (MBTI) instrument to collect data describing the styles of behaviour of over 3700 engineering freshmen (McCaulley 1982, 1983). The data show a consistent profile of type characteristics in the engineering community. The MBTI studies have produced remarkably accurate indicators of a person's learning and teaching styles. There is considerable evidence now to show that instructors design learning activities to suit their own preferred style of learning.

The MBTI data profiles show that the majority of engineering students in a classroom have different and most often totally opposite learning styles from the professors. For example, the MBTI data shows that the majority of engineering students have an 'SJ' learning style that is essentially oriented to progress from the specific to the general. The majority of engineering professors have an 'NT' learning (hence teaching) style preferring to deal with the general concept and proceed toward limited examples. This fundamental mismatch of professor and student learning styles explains a large number of unhappy consequences found in the educational process.

A systematic collection of information about the behavioural styles of students will provide class profiles to indicate the types of teaching/learning activities that will optimize success. There is a tremendous opportunity for research and development in this area. Many useful tools are already available. Here again, data-collection and analysis is the engineer's forte. Engineering educators need to use this information to design effective instruction that accommodates the differences of learning styles among their students.

Development of Professional Skills

The host of surveys and reports of the job requirements and professional attributes demanded of the engineer in industry (Finniston 1980) indicate that engineers are more than adequately equipped to meet the technical challenges but fall far short in personal and social skills. Engineers are consultants to management and are resident problem-solving technical detectives. Eighty per cent of an engineer's workday involves the 'INGS' of professional practice: managing, communicating, listening, persuading, motivating, planning, proposing, selling, and evaluating. Only twenty per cent of an engineer's practice involves the 'ICS': physics, mathematics, statics, dynamics, fluidics, electronics, etc.(Bussard 1982; Harrisberger 1977).

It is a constant source of amazement how our seemingly irrational development of the engineering education process has managed to be 180° out-of-phase with the reality of engineering priorities. Over eighty per cent of our curriculum is devoted to the 'ICS'; yet only twenty per cent of the engineer's work involves them. Over eighty per cent of the working day of an engineer demands proficiencies in the 'INGS' and there are no'ING' courses in the curriculum. It is a considerable strain on an engineering faculty to find any activities in the curriculum that directly and rationally address these issues.

The 'INGS' are the software of engineering practice. They are best developed in a faculty-coached clinic/internship setting. All engineering curricula should include a diagnostic, practice-oriented clinic. The clinic should use a variety of diagnostic instruments to measure the students' current style of behaviour and ability in each of a selected set of the personal and interpersonal skills needed in engineering practice.

Over the past five years, I have been conducting a clinic for mechanical engineering seniors. I use eight diagnostic instruments to show each student the proficiencies he now has and to then explore the skills and attributes that best fit the job (Harrisberger 1979, 1983). Using the information openly in the clinic creates an analytical atmosphere of self-development and peer assistance. Individual and group experiences during the project activity can be debriefed and discussed against a background of explanatory diagnostic information describing each student's personality characteristics and pattern of behaviour.

The behaviourists have been busy and have produced a wealth of useful findings and tools engineering educators can use. The vast majority of engineering students are introverts who shun people-oriented situations (McCaulley 1982). They are inept at verbal communication, assertiveness, leadership, and conflict management. But when alerted to their diagnosed style of behaviour and the mismatches with the demands of engineering practice, they are remarkably serious about improving their skills.

The challenge here is to use the considerable resources available and develop learning activities that will help engineering students to meet the software competencies of practice.

Efficiency of Instruction

Industry world-wide is suffering an efficiency crisis. The 'Factory-of-the-Future' fad is preaching the salvations of productivity and energy-conservation. Likewise, the 'College of the Future' is suffering an efficiency crisis. An exponentially exploding knowledge-base, together with increasing demands for sophisticated 'high-tech' problem-solving, and the increasing professional sophistication of the engineering career add demands for more instructional time to accommodate an expanding agenda of engineering and software skills.

Clearly, there is ample rationale for the development of more efficient delivery systems in the academic process. In the past two decades, a large number of experimental learning systems have emerged, including self-paced instruction, mastery learning, Piaget methods, cassette-TV, computer-aided instruction, computer-managed testing, audio-tutorial, etc. The traditional three-credit-hour lecture class managed to survive it all. None of the above have been institutionalized into the main-line degree-programme process in engineering. How is it that engineers are the first to utilize new findings and techniques in engineering but avoid the practice like a plague in the engineering education process?

If exit competency is valued, then individualized learning activities are prerequisites. If more has to be learned and increased individual proficiency must be obtained and demonstrated, then more self-learning aids must be developed, with particular attention to computer-aided instruction. The process must be more learner-dependent than teacher-dependent. The faculty must change role from preacher/lecturer to coach and learning manager. The classroom must give way to the learning laboratory.

The challenge here is to develop the motivation for change from the traditional delivery format to computer-managed, faculty-coached, competency-based learning. We need to study how to get it done – not what to do.

Faculty Development

The development of an effective, individualized, competency-based education programme in engineering can be accomplished. There is an accumulated wealth of research, techniques, and experience in teaching/ learning and behaviour-development to draw on. The real challenge is in the implementation. The obstacles derive from the fundamental lack of experience in the use of learning techniques in the management of the learning process.

The source of the problem remains with the belief that the qualifications to enter and succeed in a university professorship must be met by a continued demonstration of frontier-level technical research competence in a post-doctoral specialization. A competent research scientist does not necessarily a competent learning manager make!

The alligator in the moat is essentially administrative. If research is rewarded – good research will be done. If teaching is rewarded – good teaching will be done. It is far easier to measure and reward research results than teaching results. More fundamentally, research will generate outside income to pay all its expenses and salaries and generate a 50 per cent income to the institution. There would be some outstanding teaching going on if every course offered was supported by an outside grant which paid the professor's salary, hired a graduate assistant to do the routine work, hired a secretary, bought all the supplies and gave the university a big overhead fee.

Aside from the motivational contingencies, there is a need for a programme to develop and recognize teaching competency. Professors must function as learning managers charged to create the instructional materials, coach the learning process, and measure accomplishment.

The ASEE was effective in the last two decades in offering workshops to teach faculty new instructional techniques. These workshops were effective agents for showing faculty how to implement new techniques. They did not, however, focus on the personal style and attributes of the instructor and the basic managerial skills associated with the employer-employee relationships of teacher-learner.

There are two challenges here: to develop administrative strategies to specify and nurture good instructional skills, and to establish mandatory in-service training programmes to identify and address the individual competencies each professor must develop or acquire to be a more efficient and effective learning manager.

Holistic Engineering Education

An inevitable consequence of a competency-based, individualized curriculum is the dilemma: How holistic is the education to be? The innovators in engineering education have explored a number of approaches: co-taught humanities courses (team-taught by engineering and humanities professors), courses in engineering ethics and public policy, 3-2 dual-degree programmes combining BA in liberal arts and BS in engineering, mandatory non-technical electives, unrestricted honours programmes, etc. Most are ways of using off-the-shelf non-engineering courses to satisfy the humanities budget of the US Accreditation Board for Engineering and Technology (ABET). ABET has a general requirement that all degree programmes must include fifteen (15) semester credits of electives in humanities and social studies.

There is a challenging opportunity to undertake a complete study of the content and objectives of the curriculum toward integrating all needed knowledge from whatever discipline into a total learning experience encompassing the entire intellectual spectrum (LeMee 1977). (There is a cadre of chauvinistic engineering professors who believe engineers are already the most broadly educated of all university graduates.)

A responsible evaluation of needed exit competencies for engineering will attend to the affective/right-brain attributes of the educated man. Florman's *The Existential Pleasure of Engineering* (Florman 1968) addressed the concepts here. Florman is an engineer who can hold his own with the philosophers (the existentialists) and humanists. He addressed the misapprehensions that exist in these camps regarding the role and responsibility engineers have in shaping the content and quality of human existence. The professional responsibilities of the engineering community include the impact of technology on our entire social system. The education of the engineer cannot ignore this demand. It cannot and should not be met by merely requiring fifteen credit hours of humanities electives.

Hence, Thus, and Therefore

The contemporary challenge to engineering educators is to develop a competency-based, efficiently individualized, holistic education programme for engineers.

13 Curricula and Teaching Methods in Management Education

John Burgoyne

The main theme of this chapter is variety. Variety in teaching methods, curriculum approaches and amongst the settings in which management education takes place. There is also variety in terms of time: education changes with such rapidity that a chapter such as this is likely to be significantly out of date by the time it is published.

Teaching Methods

Huczynski (1983a) attributes the variety in teaching methods to:

1 The heterogeneous nature of management education.
2 Market orientation.
3 The attitudes and attributes of students.

In his major work on management development methods Huczynski (1983b) briefly catalogues 300 teaching methods and attempts to construct a framework to account for the differences in nature and use between them. He concludes, probably rightly, that this latter enterprise is at the best tentative, either because of the intractability of the problem, or the limitations of our current conceptual frameworks, or both.

In this brief space, only a flavour of current methods is possible. Huczynski gives the most comprehensive available review. Teaching methods in management education reflect a remarkable degree of eclecticism. The traditional methods of education, like lectures, seminars and tutorials are in regular use. The case study, copied according to conventional wisdom from the Harvard Law School by the Harvard Business School, and disseminated to the rest of the world, being adapted to many forms on the way, is still very much in evidence. Business games are also much in evidence (usually taking the form of teams running a business as simulated by a computer, with decisions by the team fed in, and 'results', in the form of sales, profits, etc. returned by the computer). This can be portrayed as deriving from simulation itself based on a scientific tradition seeking for an alternative to the pragmatism of the case study. It has also been portrayed (Loveluck 1975) as deriving from the older tradition of war gaming, and ultimately having the same origins as the game of chess.

The notion of using 'real' managerial situations as vehicles for learning, as an alternative to the artificialities of the simulation or case, and to the abstractness of didactic approaches, has emerged in a variety of forms, projects being the most ubiquitous. Action learning, an approach or philosophy promoted by Revans (1982) in a campaign spanning at least half a lifetime, emphasizes the necessity for the learner to be a full participant in the project situation rather than a detached spectator, analyst or advisor. The approach has its origins, in this author's view, in a successful attempt to democratize operational research in its original form of multi-disciplinary problem-solving, involving the problem-sufferers with the expert problem-solvers on an equal footing.

The model of the medical profession has continually been in the mind of management educators, particularly in the sense of integrating formal training with supervised practical work in a formalized setting, like a teaching hospital, for this purpose. This has its most obvious manifestation in teaching company schemes, but is also apparent in the structure of in-company management trainee schemes. The laboratory traditions of the natural and engineering sciences can often be seen in management education, either in the form of social psychology experiments adapted as teaching vehicles, or in tell-try-review exercises in technical areas such as accounting and the use of established planning tools. The great intertwining worlds of psychotherapy, the personal growth movement, human relations training in organizations, and approaches based on eastern and western spiritual and philosophical belief systems have generated a great variety of specific approaches in management education. Possibly at the other extreme of the same dimension, principles of conditioning and behaviour modification have been applied in forms like programmed-learning or highly structured skills training. The former is enjoying a new lease of life in the form of computer-assisted learning, a medium which is also presenting the challenge to find non-conditioning applications (Boot and Boxer 1980).

Outward-bound activities and the use of the outdoors in various forms are currently areas of strong interest and experimentation. They derive in part from approaches to officer training in the military context, and partly from youth development work.

Many methods wholly or partly defined by their technology have long been a feature of management education. Films, tapes, slides and videos are well established parts of the armoury of management education. With the advent of micro-computers and their ability to interact with and control video recorders, new packages and methods based on these technologies are emerging rapidly. A combination of economic, market and technical forces seems to be making distance learning, in a great variety of forms, a particular area of expansion at the moment. Distance learning appears to range from the traditional correspondence course to high technology-based systems like interactive computer-video systems, and the use of corporate and national electronic networks for the dissemination of materials. Approaches also range from low-cost videotaping of a normal student lecture, to professionally produced packages costing hundreds of thousands of pounds. Developments in this area are particularly volatile at present, and any particular patterns of practice have yet to emerge.

Curricula

The preceding discussion on methods has touched to a small degree on the issue of curricula. In this area there are marked differences in current practice according to institutional setting, whether or not programmes are associated with certification and if so, the form that this takes.

Management education is carried out, in the broadest sense, by work organizations for their own actual or potential managerial staff, by small and large firms of consultants, by independent colleges and by further and higher education institutions, including colleges, polytechnics and universities.

Formal certification takes place through universities and polytechnics in their own right, under CNAA regulations and also under the influence of professional bodies like the Institute of Personnel Management. On the whole the certificated programmes are by many standards more conservative in terms of methods and curricula, but there are exceptions to the rule. The Postgraduate Diploma in Management by Self-Managed Learning at the North East London Polytechnic, for example, has adapted the tradition of independent studies to the management context in the form of a programme where students form a plan for their own learning, including aims and criteria for their attainment, with assessment carried out to a substantial degree by a process of peer assessment of achievement of targets set.

However, conservatism is apparent in the design of MBAs (Masters in Business Administration), which have been the standard university postgraduate programme, and which have been offered by polytechnics in growing numbers in recent years. The author of this chapter (Burgoyne 1977) found that the basic curriculum philosophy (teach concepts from cognate disciplines, integrate concepts, give exercise in application) was fairly standard in MBAs. As far as can be ascertained, the same pattern exists in America, where novel forms of MBA seem to consist of more and more varied ways of doing the same courses in different forms and venues, eg on commuter trains or in series of 'marathon' weekend study sessions.

Serious attempts have been made to implement the philosophy of action learning, as described above, in certificated programmes within the Anglian and North Western Regional Management Centres, which are also significant attempts to break with traditional patterns, though in each case there appear to be processes at work to adapt them back into the traditional form outlined above.

The issue of integration (Burgoyne 1982) is problematical in most certificated programmes. With those in the traditional pattern the problem is seen as arising from the multi-disciplinary nature of the programme content. Different disciplines tend to be seen as maps of specific areas of knowledge relevant to management, and the task of integration is construed as giving the overall map that shows the relationship between the local maps. Where this geographical metaphor gets a stranglehold on the debate the arguments are usually in terms of the rival claims of the different disciplines to be the overall map. Much variation in curricula in content terms depends on whether behavioural science, or marketing, or corporate strategy, or some concept of decision-making is used as the integrating theme.

In the polytechnic sector, management education curricula, in the formal sense, often have to satisfy multiple stakeholders, such as internal academic boards, CNAA, professional bodies, and various advisory bodies, and this can make the formal curriculum design a complex and political process. The curriculum as taught may in such cases be at variance with that spelled out in official documents.

Non-certificated programmes are much more varied in curricular terms, and are more likely to be based on a view of the problem of integration as combining new skills with old skills, or relating theory to practice, personal knowledge to public knowledge, or corporate organizational beliefs to private ones.

Independent colleges like Ashridge Management College run such programmes for mid-career general management and they are often very similar to university-based business school mid-career courses. Others, for example Roffey Park, have a distinctive approach focusing on the behavioural aspects of managing and being a manager.

Management consultancies, large and small, offer anything from general management programmes, as described above, through to highly-structured 'packages' on specific topics like decision-making, teamwork, time management, and planning. At this point the boundaries of management education shade into organization development (attempts to bring about change and learning in whole organizations or organization parts).

In-house courses are provided by numerous staff colleges and management centres, which act to some extent like internal consultancy organizations, setting up packaged or tailor-made programmes for specific groups of managers or potential managers. Such in-house colleges tend to run programmes with curricula more specific to their own organization and industry. There are also interesting examples of such colleges serving as policy think-tanks for their organizations, by having managers work on current corporate issues with both tutors and senior managers directly concerned with the policy issues. The interesting feature of the other form of in-house provision, the management development departments working from offices rather than classrooms, is that they often attempt to combine the process of education and of career planning.

Another feature of the managerial profession is its traditional maleness, and there have been various attempts in recent years to use management education to do something about the gender balance, as well as to raise the issue of the predominantly male influence on the way in which management is practised. Variety, again, characterizes the actual form of these attempts. 'Women only' programmes have been mounted in the Civil Service Staff College, for the cotton industry in and around Manchester, and in a number of other settings. Attempts at positive discrimination have been made in admission procedures for a number of programmes, and the issue appears as a substantive topic in many others.

Hidden Curricula

It can be argued that much of what goes on in management education can be interpreted as the maintenance of the ideologies that exist in management and work organizations. The hidden curriculum of much of management education (Boot and Reynolds 1983) may thus be a process of socializing. Some theorists of organization, like Mintzberg (1979), argue that such a process is necessary to achieve sufficient co-ordination and control for an organization to function.

The parallel notion of management education as an ideological arena also seems to make sense of much of some of the phenomena. Many of the processes in the planning of management education, particularly in-house ones, seem more problematical, illogical and political than they would be if only technical difficulties were at stake. There seems more reason to conclude that the arranging of management education is one of the important arenas in which differing views and values in organizations come into conflict, and reach varying degrees of reconciliation or compromise.

Patterns

The range of methods and curriculum approaches, both as they currently exist and as they appear to vary over time, seems to defy reduction to underlying dimensions, or explanation in terms of trends. The most that can be offered here are a number of observations that may indicate some of the patterns.

Research

Research on management education methods and curricula has produced little or nothing of clear-cut practical value about what methods or approaches are best for what purposes. Two reasons for this suggest themselves, the first methodological and the second that it is due to the nature of management. Studies in this area draw methodologically on educational research and the social sciences. These fields have been in turmoil methodologically in recent years, and though the weaknesses of traditional approaches were apparent, viable alternatives emerged only slowly (Hamilton *et al* 1977; Reason and Rowan 1981). The other explanation is that a clear-cut understanding of the nature of managing, and of what constitutes effectiveness in it is logically necessary to provide adequate criteria for evaluating methods and curricula. Such an understanding does not exist, and it is arguable in any case that the questions about the nature of management are ideological rather than technical.

The actual contribution of research on methods and curricula seems to have been more successful in highlighting the dilemmas in management education.

Theory

One theoretical interpretation that does make sense of much of management education, and particularly the continuous quest for new methods and approaches, is the dramaturgical analysis of Mangham (1978). Briefly, this follows a socio-psychological interpretation and suggests that people rapidly acquire habitual patterns of response, or scripts, for dealing with situations they find themselves in, and frequently categorize situations as familiar ones for which they have ready-made coping procedures. Learning and development, particularly amongst experienced managers, usually requires the breaking of such scripts. Only when people find themselves in situations which are really different for them, which they cannot force-fit into a known category, does an awareness of reliance on scripts come about. Much of the methodology of management education can be seen as attempts to put people in such situations, and the necessity for continuing change in curricula comes about because once a method has become familiar it loses its surprise value and becomes ineffective.

Tentative Conclusions

The nature of this chapter does not lend itself to strongly stateable conclusions, yet there are features in management education which are of interest in the broader context of professional education.

Firstly, management education struggles not so much with the problem of relating theory to practice, but with the recognition that there is theory in all practice. Management education is rich in methods for helping managers work on their theories in practice. Secondly, management education demonstrates ways of developing the broad professional competencies of working with and through people, and of planning and influencing complex arrangements in organizations. Thirdly, management education tends to operate in conjunction with both natural or uncontrived learning, and in the context of integrated attempts at career planning and management. Finally, management education may be a significant case study of the role of professional education both in perpetuating values and ideologies and in providing an arena in which conflict and reconciliation of such values and ideologies may take place.

Part 5

Accreditation, Validation, Evaluation and Assessment

14 Overview of Accreditation, Validation, Evaluation and Assessment in Professional Education

Roger Harrison

First I must define the terms.

Accreditation is the procedure whereby a professional body satisfies itself that a qualification granted by another institution (over which it has no direct control) meets, in part or in entirety, its requirements for admission to membership of the profession. It can apply to a qualification already gained or to a course already on offer, as well as to new or revised courses proposed by the teaching institutions, and can only be carried out by the professional bodies themselves or by a powerful employing body, such as the government in respect of teachers.

Validation is a procedure for establishing the suitability of a proposed course, in respect of content, academic standard and teaching resources, to lead to the qualification awarded on successful completion. It normally applies to future presentations of new or existing courses, but may be applied retrospectively. It may be carried out internally by the teaching institution itself, by external academic peers, by a national academic body (CNAA, TEC, BEC, etc.), by a professional body or by a combination of some of these.

Assessment is the procedure by which a student is judged to have achieved the standard required for qualification. It applies to students undergoing training (whether academic or on the job) and may be carried out by a teaching institution (with or without external examiners), by an external examining board or by a professional body.

Evaluation is any procedure by which the effectiveness of a course (of professional training) is investigated. It applies to a course which has been or is being taught and may be carried out by the teaching institution itself or by an external body.

There are considerable differences in the details by which the four procedures are carried out in different professions. In this chapter I have tried to point out the common features, at a relatively high level of generality. Some of the differences will emerge in the following chapters.

The above distinctions are not entirely clear cut because accreditation, for example, often involves a prior validation; validation is not complete until assessment has taken place; assessment is one of the most powerful and most frequently used methods of evaluation; and finally the renewal of validation depends on a satisfactory evaluation. Nevertheless, these distinctions are useful and reasonably clear. To some extent the procedures are interchangeable alternatives which may be traded off one against another. The final aim of all four is to ensure to the best of human ability that the professional accolade is awarded only to those who deserve it and have proved at least a minimum competence (which may be high or low depending on the demands and traditions of the profession), that courses are relevant and efficiently run, that resources devoted to professional education are used wisely and that students may enrol on the courses secure in the knowledge that they can gain a qualification which will be acceptable to the profession they aspire to. Thus the professions, the teaching institutions, the students, the general public, employers and the government (which pays for most of the courses) all have an interest in seeing that the four procedures, taken together, are efficient and fair.

These four procedures together also provide the machinery by which a professional body controls the training of new entrants, but they are more than just a control mechanism. They play a leading, if not predominant, role in the processes by which the profession defines itself, develops its self-image and evolves (or fails to evolve). The profession determines the training and characteristics of new entrants largely through these four procedures: the new entrants determine the future of the profession.

There are multiple channels of communication between the professional body and the teaching institutions. Most of the teachers are also members of their professional body and some play a leading role in its management. Most of the course advisers and external examiners, even when appointed by the teaching institutions, are members of the professional body. Hence there is constant two-way exchange of ideas between profession and teachers and it is often difficult to know which hat any individual is wearing at any given moment. This very close linkage ensures that the general ethos of the profession is embodied in the design and execution of the courses, often without conscious decision, where there is no controversy about the nature of the profession. This has sometimes led to suspicions of conservativism and reluctance to evolve to meet new needs. For example, the Institute of Metals retained extraction metallurgy as a major part of its syllabuses for decades after the majority of metallurgists had long since ceased to be involved in extraction processes. This particular danger has undoubtedly diminished as the rate of technological change has accelerated and as the four procedures have become more systematic, more thorough and more professional, but there is never any room for complacency. Economic pressures, for example, may in the future lead to a reduction in the effort devoted to them and thus to a failure to keep abreast of new developments.

There are also acute differences of opinion about the nature of some professions. For example, should social workers attempt to ameliorate individual problems or to change the social processes which give rise to them? The two views lead to very different types of courses for social workers. The four control procedures can do very little to resolve, and may exacerbate, such conflicts, which are not entirely under the control of the profession. Ultimately, what social work is about will be decided by the employers – central and local government – and not by the profession. Indeed, the government and other large employers are in a powerful position to determine the nature of a profession by the particular qualifications they choose to accept (or reject) and whether or not these are made a condition of employment. Such decisions may either reinforce or undermine the effects of the four procedures, which must often be carried out with an over-the-shoulder look at the requirements of the employers. In some cases the employer actually subsumes the role of professional body. For example, entry to the teaching profession is controlled by the government and not by the profession.

In other instances, however, the employers are remarkably vague about what sort of recruits they want – although they are quick to complain if they think they are offered unsuitably trained people – and are content to leave the details of professional training to the professional bodies and the teaching institutions, exerting an indirect influence on the four procedures through their own professional employees. The relationship between employers and professional training possibly needs further study.

The interests and perspectives of the professional bodies and the teaching institutions do not necessarily coincide. The latter are concerned essentially with theoretical knowledge, the former with competence on the job. This is a potential source of tension between the two, to which I will return.

A profession may seek to ensure the competence of those entering it by controlling:

– Admission standards of those accepted for training.

– Content of the accredited courses.

– Amount and type of practical experience needed for a licence to practise.

- Methods and standards of teaching.

- (Final) standards of student assessment.

The strength of these controls is greatly increased where there is a legal or quasi legal requirement for a licence to practise (as in medicine and law and some branches of engineering). In this case the professional body can exercise ongoing control of professional practitioners through prescribed professional standards, procedures and ethics. In other cases the control is much weaker and depends on the respect accorded to the professional body, since in the last resort teaching institutions could, and sometimes do, choose to ignore its requirements.

These controls may be administered by a combination of several distinct methods:

- A blanket decision to accept a particular class of qualification (eg a university degree, which until recently was a sufficient qualification to teach).

- A set of bureaucratic rules which can often be applied by lay administrators. (Eg the Institute of Physics requires a minimum of 50 per cent of the course to consist of physics or applicable mathematics for accreditation.)

- A published (core) syllabus which must be followed by any course which is accredited (eg the Chemical Engineers).

- Negotiation of the syllabus between the validating body and the teaching institution. (The professional body generally plays only an indirect role in this and accepts qualifications which it thinks have been satisfactorily validated.)

- Periodic (or even continuous) inspection of the teaching process and resources. (Professional bodies have to balance the cost of inspection against the control achieved. The present tendency seems to be to cast the net wider — to include universities as well as colleges — but less frequently.)

- Control of the assessment of the students by setting and marking or moderating the examinations or by nominating examiners. (Professional bodies appear to be opting out of direct assessment by setting their own examinations in favour of external moderation (by members of the profession) of internal examinations. This is both cheaper and more flexible when syllabuses are changing rapidly, and provides an opportunity for teachers to assess their own students and to develop their own syllabus, but it makes it more difficult to achieve comparability between teaching institutions. Visits to the institutions in connection with examinations or continuous assessment provide additional opportunities to check up on teaching standards and resources.)

– Supervision of new entrants to the profession during a probationary period. This can lead to problems when the probationer is isolated from other members of the profession. It can also lead to anomalies if students have had relevant experence prior to taking their course.

It is not necessary for a professional body to make use of all these methods, nor to carry them all out for itself. Most are prepared to accept the validations of the CNAA, etc. (on whose panels they are well represented) and the assessments of any properly constituted panel of examiners. On the other hand, when the professional body conducts its own examinations it is likely to be much less concerned about validation and accreditation.

In the past, validation and accreditation requirements have done a great deal to improve and maintain the standards of the teaching institutions, particularly new ones and those in process of upgrading. It has been difficult for LEAs to resist demands for improvement of facilities as a condition of recognition. It will be interesting to see how effective this pressure will continue to be in the present harsh economic climate.

It is worth noting that the control which most professional bodies are able to exert on their professional education is of the 'open loop' variety similar to the control exerted by a golfer on the golf ball, who sets the ball off in what seems to be the appropriate direction and hopes that it will land somewhere close to the hole. Since there is no further control over the ball some balls go wildly astray. Ideally the control should be of the 'closed loop' variety in which any deviations from the desired path are picked up by in-flight sensors so that corrective action can be taken and the golf ball becomes a guided missile. Two distinct types of correction would be needed: on the individual students or practitioners to ensure that their professional development and behaviour stays within accept-able limits, and on the type of training provided to make sure that this continues to equip novices for successful practice. One of the main functions of evaluation should be to provide precisely these types of negative feedback.

Course evaluation, as a craft, is still in its infancy and raises some fundamental problems. Should one attempt to pronounce on the relative success of the course (summative evaluation), perhaps on the basis of rather narrow and not necessarily relevant criteria, such as the course objectives, which were decided before the exercise takes place? Or should one seek to describe the course and its effects on students and teachers as one finds it with an open mind (illuminative evaluation), in the hope that this may facilitate improvements by others? Or should one seek to go deeper and try to unravel the reasons why some parts appear to be less successful than they might be and to suggest remedial action (which might be termed prescriptive evaluation)? Should the evaluation be carried out by the teachers, by the profession or by impartial, trained observers? Should it be narrowly confined to the course just completed and the students therefrom or should it attempt to follow up the graduates some way into their careers — a much more difficult and expensive exercise? Should it look only at those who successfully complete the course, or should it also follow up the subsequent careers of the rejects and failures?

There are differing views on these questions. In practice, what evaluation takes place often depends more on the resources available than on deliberate policy. In any case, before evaluation can usefully begin, its purpose must be correctly chosen and adequately defined. This brings us up against one of the fundamental dilemmas of professional education: how are the needs of the profession known? What is actually involved in successful practice? This is the first problem area for the control mechanisms.

Such questions may seem naive or irrelevant. Surely all that is necessary is to watch or consult with experienced professionals and find out what they do. This is easier said than done: even if there is no fundamental controversy about the profession it may not be easy to find typical professionals and, when found, they may not be aware of how they obtain their results. One of the hallmarks of the major professions is that they embrace a very wide range of professional expertise applied to a wide and often unforeseeable variety of problems. The best practitioners often get their results by the exercise of a personal flair which may defy analysis and may not be generalizable to fellow practitioners. The duties and methods of professionals develop rapidly in time in ways which are quite unpredictable. Even the ethos of the profession and the expectations of the clients may be changing and there may be no clear-cut picture of what a professional is. The Institute of Physics, for example, can only define a physicist by what it finds its members do, which ranges from merchant banking to electronic engineering. This poses questions both about what sort of knowledge (particularly of 'subsidiary' subjects) will be most useful and of what sort of practical experience can be accepted as qualifying for membership.

In the light of all this uncertainty how does one decide what professional training is appropriate? How long should it continue? What should it include? What is the appropriate balance between theory and practical applications? This is the second problem area. The temptation is to put the main emphasis on theory, which is justified on the grounds that a firm theoretical grounding is necessary to enable practitioners to cope with novel situations or new methods which may be developed in the future. Possibly, however, the true motivation may be first that theoretical knowledge is generally easier to assess (either the students know something or they don't – which avoids the tricky question of assessing quality of performance) and secondly because a theoretical approach is believed to give greater kudos to the teachers. Students are not infrequently very critical of what they see as unnecessary or irrelevant theory. I have, for exampe, met teachers on a part-time education course who wanted it to be based on classroom practice rather than the theoretical constructs they were getting. Is it really necessary for medical students to learn by heart all the details of the Krebs' Cycle (training in memorization?) or is this simply an initiation ritual?

The relationship between general education, theoretical training and practical experience in developing professional expertise has never been fully explored, partly because it is a very difficult area of educational investigation and partly because it varies greatly between professions. Instead, each profession has evolved a mixture of the three which it finds works in practice, but which depends upon a number of unstated and untested beliefs. There is no guarantee that a different mixture would not work as well or better.

For example, it is often assumed that a general education (in the form of so many 'O' or 'A' levels) provides both a necessary background to, and a satisfactory selection method for, entry to a profession and is written in to many accreditation and validation requirements. This certainly does not avoid a disturbingly high failure rate on some courses and one might wonder whether a more specific (aptitude) entry test might not be more appropriate. There is no way of telling how many of those excluded might, in fact, have proved very suitable for the profession.

Again, it is generally assumed that mastery of a prescribed body of knowledge, irrespective of ability to apply it, is as good a correlate of professional competence as it is necessary to find, and this is also written into some accreditation and validation schemes. Certainly large numbers of able people rise to the tops of their professions on this basis: it is uncertain how many of the impractical also get through the net or how many potentially good practitioners fail the theoretical hurdles and never get a chance.

What kind of learning is appropriate for a professional education? Superficial rote learning of the 'facts' or profound understanding of the principles? Nearly everyone will unhesitatingly reply the latter, but all too often the students get the opposite impression and respond accordingly. Reality does not accord with the aspirations of the teachers. The primary responsibility for this lies with inappropriate assessment, but the validation processes do not necessarily detect a wrong approach built into the very structure of the course and neither evaluation nor accreditation will necessarily pick it up.

The extent to which a necessarily restricted range of practical experiences on very specific topics will be generalized by the students to provide a basis for professional competence in very different fields is problematical. Such experiences are considered essential for accreditation and validation, but there is not, and often cannot be, any foolproof mechanism to ensure that they are effective. The details may be out of the control of both the professional bodies and the teaching institutions.

On the other hand, it is now recognized that the range of possibly useful knowledge is so large, and the rate of change of professional activities so high, that it is impossible to teach all that may be needed. Instead, the emphasis must be on developing the art of problem-solving, finding the necessary information from appropriate sources as and when needed. This calls for a continual reappraisal of the appropriate balance between theoretical knowledge and practical experience and hence for the continual revalidation and reaccreditation of the courses on offer. I believe that all concerned make strenuous efforts in this, but the evaluation processes which should underlie their efforts are often seriously lacking.

A third problem area arises over who decides what should be included in a professional education and what standards are appropriate? Should the ultimate power of decision rest with the teachers who have to provide the necessary training and who at least have the merit of being in touch with the students, or should it be the practitioners in the main body of the profession? If it is to be practitioners, should they be the respected leaders of the profession who may well be out of touch with normal day-to-day practice and with up and coming developments and will almost certainly be getting near the end of their active lives? Or should it be the younger men and women who do the bulk of the donkey work in any profession? How does one find such people with the appropriate experience and time to spare? All professions are in danger of adopting excessively conservative attitudes towards new methods and new needs. This danger is exacerbated if control of the training programme is vested too firmly in the older members of the profession. Institutional inertia is inevitably a barrier to innovation and fresh thinking which is only countered fitfully — if at all — by the professional pride and empire-building proclivities of the teachers. In particular, it is notoriously difficult to excise outdated material from professional syllabuses, as mentioned earlier in connection with extraction metallurgy.

Another set of problems arises with respect to the setting of standards. In many cases there is little more than tradition and rule of thumb to provide a guide. A licence to practise is, in many respects, a self-fulfilling prophecy: those who are licensed will for the most part go on to practise and do at least reasonably well — those who are failed will get no further opportunity of proving their worth. There is , therefore, certainly no safeguard against setting unnecessarily high standards and there is reason to suppose that some of the more prestigious professions may do just this. Is it really necessary for the majority of entrants to medical training to possess three As or two As and a B at 'A' level? Is it really necessary for the pass rate on some accountancy courses to be less than 30 per cent?

No doubt there are justifications for these requirements in terms of fair selection from an over-large field of would-be entrants or in terms of restricting entry to the profession in order to maintain a high standard of competence (and high remuneration for the practitioners). There is just no evidence one way or the other to show whether or not at least some of those rejected might have done as well as or better than those accepted.

By contrast are some professional standards set too low? I have heard it alleged that examiners are extremely reluctant to fail education students on the grounds that to do so would run a danger of damaging them for life not merely in the teaching profession but in any other.

Assessment of performance, as opposed to that of knowledge, poses formidable questions about how it is to be judged fairly. What constitutes good performance is a matter of professional opinion, which can vary sharply from one practitioner to another. Taking an average opinion is relatively safe but is expensive and not always possible. The necessary shift of emphasis from theory to experience and performance carries with it an increased risk of unreliability in assessment, in the sense that different assessors will give very different marks. Most teachers and examiners are aware of this possibility — whether all schemes of professional assessment have found a satisfactory way round it is more doubtful.

Finally, assessment raises questions of what to do about students who perform badly on some parts of their course? Do you allow them compensation on the strength of other parts, do you require them to repeat that part or all parts, or do you fail them outright? Practice varies widely from one profession to another. In general I suspect that assessment practices develop by rule of thumb or instinct in the first instance and thereafter remain unchanged unless there is gross evidence of inefficiency or scandal. I doubt if any professional training could prove that its standards were scientifically determined: possibly no such proof could ever be provided. It is, however, a fairly crucial matter because here particularly the interests of the profession, the interests of the students and the interests of the public do not necessarily coincide. Methods and results of assessment also deserve thorough evaluation.

The whole of the foregoing assumes that the four processes relate to a first professional education course. But professional practice now often evolves so fast that most practitioners need to update their knowledge and develop new skills from time to time. Some do so systematically on a basis of personal initiative, some have recourse to a wide variety of ad hoc refresher and updating courses, and some are content to stagnate. Only the more formal updating courses — for example, those leading to a Masters degree — so far are subject to the four processes considered in this chapter. Should the net be widened to create a new category of validated and accredited refresher courses? There is an urgent need for all such courses, whether validated or not, to be evaluated properly. More controversially, should the students on them be formally assessed, though not necessarily by examination? Most controversially of all, should the initial qualifications be time limited and expire unless renewed by an appropriate refresher? Developments on these lines may well require new techniques of accreditation, validation, assessment and evaluation.

15 Accreditation, Validation, Evaluation and Assessment in Medical Education

Don Clarke

> I have found that, perhaps because of their intimate associations with life and death, the medical, the military, and the religious professions take education (and/or training) with a degree of seriousness seldom found elsewhere. They also possess the longest, most continuous traditions for operating formal programmes. Agriculture, seamanship, and hunting, though of equal or greater antiquity, were learned on a more informal basis. Therefore, all educators have much to learn from the first three. (Rippey 1981)

Rippey's comment is unfortunately a truer description of undergraduate medical education than it is of continuing medical education, as regrettably there are some doctors, especially those in general practice, who rely mainly on the knowledge they acquired many years ago in their medical schools. The general public want, for both understandable and justifiable reasons, to have some reassurance that the doctor into whose hands they may be entrusting their life is competent to deal with their case. It is this issue of competence that, more than any other, lies behind the concern with accreditation, validation, evaluation and assessment in medical education. However, the public concern and the professional concern do not always share the same origin. Fisher (1971) is one of many people who have commented on 'the courtesy extended to a fellow member of the profession by shielding the quality of his performance as a professional from those outside the group.'

The accreditation or the licensure of physicians in the United Kingdom is a relatively straightforward procedure. Those universities with medical schools are primarily responsible for conducting their own qualifying examinations. There are still a number of organizations such as the English Conjoint Board, the Scottish Joint Board and the Society of Apothecaries which also conduct qualifying exams and which are independent of the university system. But they and the universities are in fact controlled by the General Medical Council in the sense that all qualifying examinations need to have its approval. Such examinations are made up of written papers, orals and clinicals, a pattern which has existed for about a hundred years. The pattern is therefore clearly understood by all concerned in the accreditation process and is not subect to disputes and lengthy negotiations over content and standards.

It is after the point at which the examination is taken that medicine begins to show its differences from most of the other professions. The university examination in medicine, like university exams in other faculties, sorts the candidates into those who deserve a degree and those who do not. But university graduates in medicine tend to congratulate each other on being 'qualified' rather than upon having graduated. The Medical Act of 1858 reflected the need of the public to feel that they were being cared for in their sickness by someone who was qualified, not necessarily by someone who had graduated. (It is an interesting aside that the licence to practise medicine is in fact only a licence to issue certificates such as death certificates and to prescribe certain drugs. Providing that they do neither of these two things anyone is in fact entitled to say that they are a medical practitioner and carry out all the other functions associated with being a doctor. Of course if such a person were to perform an operation on an individual then they leave themselves open, unlike the qualified, graduated doctor, to being legally charged with assault.) Thus the university examination, approved by the General Medical Council, begins to distinguish the medical profession from most others. And it can be fairly stated that, in the main, the reason is the public concern to be treated by qualified people.

It is after graduation or qualification that Fisher's (1971) comment, quoted earlier, really begins to be justified. Most professions wish to control their own membership by controlling entrance to such membership, and by controlling the maintenance of it; medicine is no exception. Up to graduation, ultimate control is indirectly in the hands of the state through the General Medical Council but thereafter it is largely in the hands of the medical profession itself. The control of what can be called, at least in the United Kingdom, postgraduate education is not centralized in one body but is dispersed amongst the various specialties that are collectively known as medicine. It is bodies such as the Royal College of Surgeons, the Royal College of Physicians, and so on that then control the qualified doctor, because it is they who are responsible for examining for their own membership. The control of the postgraduate system in the United Kingdom is in fact complex and subtle and thus far from easy for outsiders to understand. The policy of those who control is to recognize not courses but certain posts or jobs the occupation of which means that approved training is being undertaken. The great majority of the postgraduate diploma examinations can be taken some four years after the initial graduation, but entry to such examinations is not allowed unless certain specified postgraduate experience has been obtained. That specified experience takes place in the recognized training posts, so by controlling the number of training posts the control of membership can be exercised. Such a system makes for a very, very flexible system with a considerable range of variations open to individuals. This flexibility must be a bonus when judged on educational grounds because to a large extent it enables training to be tailored to individual needs. But it can also be a system that relies heavily on chance, one which makes co-ordination, and particularly co-ordination of assessment, extremely difficult.

Finally, to increase still further the complexity of the situation, there is often very little co-ordination between the undergraduate and the postgraduate systems. At the undergraduate level there is an increasing number of teachers who want their future graduates to be individuals who will want to go on learning for the rest of their lives; in other words graduates who will undertake continuing education for its own sake rather than because they have to do so to obtain specific qualifications or to remain as qualified medical practitioners.

The lack of co-ordination between undergraduate and postgraduate medical education is well illustrated by the situation appertaining to general practice. There are in fact more general practitioners than any other type of doctor, but there are still many medical schools that have no professor or chair of general practice. Not surprisingly general practitioners have been loudest amongst those who complain that the undergraduate system does not prepare them for real-life situations. Establishing a Royal College of General Practice took one hundred years but since it was founded some twenty years ago it has enabled general practitioners very largely to regulate their own area of the profession. Certainly at the postgraduate level it is general practice that has been in the vanguard of educational innovation but largely developed by themselves and for themselves. As yet in the United Kingdom there is no great movement to introduce re-accreditation. That is a system which says that obtaining an initial qualification should not be a licence to practise for a lifetime but rather that the licence requires constant renewal to see if it is still valid.

So much for a thumbnail sketch of a system that is complex and unique to medicine. It is principally the British system that has been described; there is, however, a great deal of similarity between the British medical system and that in other countries, especially if they are European in origin. The medical systems of such countries have in fact more in common than any one of them has with that of another profession. Within these systems a number of interesting experiments, investigations and developments are taking place that might well have relevance for other professions.

Two of the most interesting pieces of work are from Australia, where the system is very similar to that in the United Kingdom. Rotem *et al* (1979) carried out a study to assess the relevance of an undergraduate educational curriculum. Some 290 individuals active in either medical education or health service administration were asked to suggest five major criteria for judging the relevance of an undergraduate programme and to say how well current curricula met them. The major groupings of the criteria were as follows: consciousness of health care requirements, clinical skills, knowledge in medical school subjects, quality of interaction with patients and other health professionals, attitude towards and capacity for continuing education, and finally professional ethics and standards. The medical school professors and the senior health service administrators turned out to have remarkably similar expectations. There were frequent strong expressions of dissatisfaction with the current achievements. The authors concluded: 'The level of dissatisfaction with the present attainment of medical education in most categories should be taken very seriously.' But at the same time they were careful to point out that the respondents may have taken some of the positive aspects for granted and chosen to emphasize the critical points which require improvement. Nevertheless, in their view the research threw into question the validity of professional education. The study merits replication in the United Kingdom.

The second Australian study is that of Newble (1977). His work is a good illustration of the concern and thought that medical educators have put into the subject of evaluation, and to a large extent justifies Rippey's (1981) statement that other professions can learn a lot from medicine. However, it must be very quickly added that medical educators have had only limited success in persuading medics to change their educational practices. Newble started from the proposition that the traditional evaluation of clinical competence, which places great reliance upon the judgement by tutors as to how a student handles randomly selected patients, was highly subjective and that even more modern approaches using in-course assessment or multiple-choice questioning were still far from satisfactory. Australia and the United Kingdom are similar in that it is the job of the medical faculties to assure the state that a student has reached a specified level of clinical competence, whereas in the USA and Canada all students have to pass a national exam. The aims of Newble's project were to review the current situation in the areas of defining and evaluating clinical competence and to develop a model which would be suitable for producing a certifying examination appropriate to the conditions and needs of a medical school in Australia. Newble turned his attention to one particular method of examining clinical competence: the critical incident technique, which has been used successfully in establishing taxonomies for the subject. In one American study that he quotes the incidents are categorized into nine major areas:

1 History
2 Physical Examination
3 Tests and Procedures
4 Diagnostic Acumen
5 Treatment
6 Judgment and Skill in Implementing Care
7 Oral
8 Physician-Patient Relation
9 Responsibilities as Physician

Similarly it was possible to categorize tests used for assessing clinical competence:

1 Essay
2 Completion or Short Answer
3 Objective (Multiple Choice)
4 Paper Simulations (Patient Management Problems)
5 Computer Simulations
6 Other Simulations
   a Simulated Patients
   b Simulation Devices
   c Patient Games
7 Oral
8 Direct Observation
9 Record Audit
10 Multiple Methods
11 Outcome Measures

Newble finishes by pleading the case for the production of an examination matrix. He acknowledges that this means a lot of work for the examiners but argues that the benefits far outweigh the handicaps. The following example is of a matrix related to the problem of chest pain:

a Multiple-choice questions could be sought to test knowledge about trinitrin and betablockers, the treatment of arrhythmias, identification of risk factors, etc.
b Short Patient Management Problems could be written to test problem assessment, use of tests and procedures, other aspects of treatment, etc.
c Slides of X-rays, Electro Cardiographs monitor tracings could be projected for interpretation.

d Real or simulated patients could be available to evaluate history and examination skills and to provide a data base for a case write-up.
e Audiotapes of ausculatory findings could be combined with a PMP or a series of objective items.
f A simulation of a cardiac arrest could be arranged or a resuscitation mannequin used to observe life support skills.
g Structured orals could cover areas dealing with continuing care, effective patient education, assessing awareness of recent trends, etc.

What Newble has done is to bring together in his matrix the assessment instruments which many workers in medical education have used either singly or more often in combination with two or three others. That such work is common is demonstrated by the fact that it would be difficult randomly to select a medical education journal that did not contain some reference to at least one of the instruments.

Another good example of the way that medicine thinks about the problem of evaluation can be found in Fulop (1979). This time the context is that of continuing education. The ultimate purpose of such education is to ensure the highest possible level of preventive and curative care, but it is extremely difficult to measure whether this is being achieved. He rightly points out that 'Given the importance of evaluation it is perhaps surprising to find how little has been or is being done; how few serious attempts have been made to undertake systematic studies of the effectiveness and efficiency of continuing education and especially of its impact on the performance of health workers. While the present dearth of such studies is due in part to the complexity or difficulty of the evaluation process, it is essential that provision be made for them as an integral part of planning and implementation of programmes.'

Medicine and medics, he argues, must be responsible for putting their own house in order:

If continuing education or, more importantly, continuous learning becomes an established feature of health services, it should follow that health workers will:
– continuously monitor and assess their own and their peers' performance, and detect shortcomings in the delivery of health care
– maintain and/or improve the level of performance in, and the quality of, preventive, promotive, curative and rehabilitative health care provided by them
– introduce methods in their daily practice as soon as these are properly tested and proved to be efficient
– improve their efficiency and effectiveness in delivering health care
– work more efficiently in teams

- display a more appropriate and compassionate attitude towards the health and social problems of people for whose care they are responsible
- experience greater satisfaction in performing their tasks.

Fulop was writing in the context of a World Health Organization report. The organization has been pushing strongly for self evaluation/assessment. One of its working groups (1980) addressed itself to the question of 'The assessment of competence of students in the health field'. The group's recommendations include the reduction of emphasis on the assessment of factual knowledge and a reduction of the number of examinations in which a student is passed or failed. They conclude:

> The ultimate aim of these recommendations is to encourage educational institutions to develop a learning environment or 'milieu' in which the student acquires the will and habit constantly to review his performance against agreed standards or criteria, against his own ideals, and against those of his colleagues. In this way the importance of external assessment will be reduced, thereby encouraging creativity, self-responsibility towards a professional lifetime of learning (and assessment), and educational freedom.

An examination of the North American literature reveals the same concerns and similar approaches as they wrestled with the problems of assessment and competence. A National Board of Examiners was founded in 1915 with the clear objective of providing examinations of high quality thus permitting a licensed physician to practise throughout the USA. Objective multiple-choice tests were introduced in the early 1950s in yet another example of the readiness of medicine to experiment with the sciences, this time with the science of educational measurement. The belief according to Hubbard (1971) was that 'Objective examinations would provide valid and reliable measurements of the knowledge and clinical competence of medical students, physicians in training and physicians in practice.' The results, when analysed and studied collectively for classes of students and groups of physicians at varying points of development, would yield objective assessments of the effectiveness of the educational system. Evaluation of the product would thus provide evaluation of the process.

Yet it rapidly became apparent that objective measurements obtained by examinations were not necessarily the most appropriate or best methods of evaluating medical students or medical education. 'The continuous assessment of individual students by their own faculties had advantages that could not be superseded by formal, sporadic extra-mural examinations, no matter how good the latter might be.'

The concept of formative and summative evaluation was first enumerated in the field of curriculum studies which developed in the 1960s. The use of the concept by Leeder *et al* (1979) again illustrates the readiness of medicine to borrow from other disciplines:

> This paper describes the assessment methods developed so far to support the undergraduate education programme in the Faculty of Medicine at Newcastle, New South Wales. Formative assessment designed for frequent, informal diagnostic feedback to the student is an integral part of the various learning experiences. It requires further development to be a useful guide to the required depth of study. It aims to assist students to integrate and apply their studies. Summative assessment is required for certification and as a formal indicator of cumulative learning. A great deal of effort has been devoted to relate it to higher level intellectual competence, to keep it open to student criticism, to take account of individual rates of learning and to use it diagnostically.

The quotation neatly makes the point about medicine being prepared to adapt and adopt from other disciplines, but a point of even greater import emerges from the context in which it was being made. Leeder *et al* were in fact discussing whether assessment was a help or a hurdle: 'Assessment of student progress and achievement may support or weaken the educational goals of an institution.' This highly perceptive comment finds an echo in a statement by Harden (1979) who was giving an overview of the problem of student assessment in the UK:

> Important decisions are often taken about students as a result of the scores they achieve in examinations. It should be possible to make important decisions in relation to student counselling and course development on the basis of evaluation results, but often this is not done. All teachers are involved directly or indirectly with assessing students' competencies and should be familiar with some of the current thinking on assessment. They should ask (and answer) five questions: (1) What should be assessed? (2) How should it be assessed? (3) Why should it be assessed? (4) When should it be assessed? (5) Who should carry out the assessment?

The literature of medical education is full of examples of its concern with the topics of this chapter: accreditation, validation, evaluation and assessment. There is hardly an aspect that has not been explored by at least a dozen people in a dozen countries, and even more remarkable is the unanimity of the conclusions about the way things ought to go. The existence of many national organizations for the study of medical education, and for that matter international ones, may well be responsible for this large measure of agreement.

In spite of this vast literature and consensus among medical educators there is a tremendous gap between what is theoretically desirable and what happens in practice. Perhaps it is because Leeder's comment about the connection between assessment and institutional goals is too near the truth for the comfort of those who work in such institutions. If, as Harden suggests, everyone in an institution should be familiar with assessment then it might well lead to a radical re-appraisal of the educational goals referred to by Leeder.

Medical educators, numerous though they may be remain a small minority in a big medical profession. The younger the institution the easier it is for a minority to initiate change. Leeder works in a new medical school not yet a decade old, Harden in an ancient Scottish institution. In deference to age the last word therefore lies with Harden who, with a delightful dry Scottish sense of humour, put the whole issue into perspective with the following anecdote:

The Problem in Perspective
The following letter was written by a medical student to her mother and father.
'Dear Mum and Dad,
I am sorry for the delay in writing to you. I'll bring you up-to-date now, but before you read on please sit down. I am getting on pretty well now − the skull fracture and concussion I got when I jumped out of the window of my flat when it caught fire has pretty well healed. I only spent two weeks in hospital and can now see almost normally. Fortunately, the fire and my jump were witnessed by an attendant at the petrol station. He visited me in hospital and since I have nowhere to live now he was kind enough to invite me to share his apartment with him. It is really only a basement room, but it's kind of cute. He is a very fine boy. We have fallen deeply in love and hope to get married. We haven't set the exact date yet, but it will be before my pregnancy begins to show. Although he is of a different race and religion than ours, your often expressed tolerance will not permit you to be bothered by this fact.

'Now that I have brought you up-to-date, I want to tell you that there was no flat fire, I did not have concussion, I was not in hospital and I am not engaged. However, I have failed my anatomy examination and I wanted you to see this in proper perspective.'

16 Accreditation, Validation, Evaluation and Assessment in Engineering Education

Richard Morris and Barry Firth

With the recent more vigorous interest shown by Government in the policy and direction of education in recent years, educational institutions now have to account for themselves as not only being efficient in how they manage themselves, but also in what they teach, its relevance for the social and economic development of the nation, and how effective the academic preparation is. The effectiveness of this preparation has, wisely for the engineering profession, been left to the judgement and regulation of the professional engineering Institutions.

The Institutions have introduced, since their respective foundation dates, various systems of assessing courses appropriate to their disciplines. They are in a unique position to devise and apply independent evaluation procedures that are not possible for individual universities or polytechnics to do.

In recent years the Council of Engineering Institutions (CEI) has shown increasing concern about ensuring that every member Institution approaches this aspect of its responsibilities in a systematic, similar, and thorough way. This has also helped CEI to put its own house in order, and to demonstrate a much greater interest in the way individual Institutions conduct their work in this respect and in the recommendations they make.

The degree of co-operation shown by the Institutions has been high in an area which they have previously seen as very personal and confidential to their own membership. Both CEI and the Institutions themselves recognized the importance of being seen by an independent Engineering Council as efficient and responsible managers of this important aspect of professional qualification.

Before examining in some detail how the Institutions conduct their accreditation assessments, it is necessary to look first at how the universities and polytechnics validate their own engineering courses.

It is also important that a clear distinction be made, between the Institutions' role as accreditor, and the objective of validation sought by the academic bodies.

In its report, the National Conference on Engineering Education and Training (CONCEET) makes a clear distinction between 'validation' and 'accreditation' and it is this interpretation that is used here.

CONCEET agreed that validation is the procedure used by academic bodies to satisfy themselves that an educational course leads suitably to the qualification awarded on successful completion of the course.

In line with this definition, the universities and the Council for National Academic Awards (CNAA) validate their own degrees. Accreditation is the procedure used by professional bodies, such as the engineering Institutions, to determine by an accreditation assessment whether the course and the qualifying process meet their individual academic requirements for membership. Most courses in the various disciplines of engineering, that lead to degrees awarded by the universities and the CNAA, have also been assessed and accredited separately by at least one of the professional engineering Institutions. The number of organizations involved in the accreditation process for courses, and for industrial training programmes, has led to a considerable variation in the mode and depth of their accreditation procedure (National Conference on Engineering Education and Training 1980).

The introduction of a new course by a university department requires approval from the university only. Once obtained, no further level of approval is required, and the course is made available to those students interested and eligible. Engineering departments also depend upon 'service' courses, in such subjects as economics, industrial sociology, foreign languages for example, which are 'bought' from neighbouring departments, and are therefore subject to additional validation. If an engineering degree course, however, does not also have the recognition or accreditation of its relevant professional Institution, it is unlikely to attract students who intend to become chartered engineers. Whilst it is not mandatory to have a course recognized by an Institution, it is unrealistic to plan a course without it, or without at least involving members of the profession in its design.

From the department's submission of a detailed course proposal to the effective commencement of teaching in it, there is likely to be a lapse of at least two or three years. Graduates from the course would emerge another three or four years later. The course, as originally put forward, is then some six years old. *The Times Higher Education Supplement* (5 November 1982) reports on the planning and implementation procedure of a new course in an eminent British university, describing how the normal formality of academic planning procedure causes a time-lag. Equally disturbing was the report that there had been very little consultation with outsiders, although there was informal contact with industry through written letters and personal contact.

Within the standing committee structure of the Institutions, there is usually an Education Committee that regulates the Institution's academic interests, including the development of Model Course Syllabuses and the accreditation of degree courses. The Education Committee is generally structured to include senior practising representatives of industry and academia.

The members of such committees are carefully selected to represent various industrial specializations and academic institutions covering a good spectrum of necessarily different pedagogical practice.

Members often have excellent communication links with government departments, the Confederation of British Industries, the Science and Engineering Research Council, etc., and can therefore provide the most realistic collective view of industrial needs, while at the same time giving recognition to the academic needs and constraints of course development.

The engineering Institutions are in a position to help in the establishment of a course that is likely to be accepted by them and to be seen to reflect their perceived needs of the correct blend of academic training a student should be given. Some Institutions are willing to accredit a course at its implementation stage, whilst others prefer to reserve any assessment and subsequent recognition of a course until graduates have emerged.

Core Syllabuses

Most Institutions have now developed 'core' syllabuses that cover the essential elements as well as the complementary ones of teaching that they insist upon if accreditation is to be given, although only a few had developed this vital information prior to 1980. The core syllabuses confine themselves only to the essential minimum content of a course, which usually represents about two-thirds of its content, and aim to encourage departments to develop their own specializations, rather than to impose constraints on innovation. The core is seen to be dynamic, and is regularly reviewed and revised, to reflect new disciplinary and interdisciplinary developments.

The independence of universities in conducting their own affairs is being questioned with increasing concern by the public sector. *The Times Higher Education Supplement*, in a series of articles under the title 'In search of excellence: The Quality Game', conducted a detailed and illuminating summary of the methods of quality control applied to tertiary education. In the second article, Ngaio Crequer reported on the universities' heavy dependence on external examiners for achieving the validation objective:

University quality control is like a closed shop. To become a member you have to say 'academic excellence' three times in a voice of great confidence. There is a great deal of assumption about quality and very little objective evaluation. The Universities themselves promulgate their own standards, define them, maintain them and judge others who cannot reach them. There is nobody to judge the judges. (Crequer 1982)

She moves on to emphasize that the external examiner system is at the heart of university quality control, and is almost the only external point of influence, or of access to university courses. She also emphasizes that the word 'external' should be taken lightly as external examiners are overwhelmingly personally recruited academics from other universities. Happily, this situation is somewhat better in engineering, a point which Ms Crequer makes later in her article, as the discipline does benefit by the involvement of the Institutions.

The polytechnics have the 'benefit' of the Council of National Academic Awards' role in validation, which at least provides mandatory approval of a course before it is introduced, after a formidable visitation and assessment by its panels. These panels are representative in their composition and not unnaturally include members of relevant professional bodies, although such bodies do not have any formal right to direct representation.

A random scan of three universities and the external examiners appointed for undergraduate and postgraduate courses in engineering disciplines reveals:

Bradford: of 17 Externals 16 are academics
Sheffield: of 12 Externals 11 are academics
Exeter: of 4 Externals 4 are academics

The professional engineering Institutions have developed their procedures to complement these traditional validation methods, fully recognizing that they have a responsibility to their profession and its members to ensure that the graduate is, in the end, properly prepared for a proper role in industrial society.

The procedures require academia to accept the core material that is to be taught and to assess the academic institution's total resource and capacity to properly implement and teach the course.

Model Degrees

A review of the assessment procedure used by the Institution of

Chemical Engineers provides an insight into the general approach to accreditation by the major engineering Institutions, although emphasis and specialization are of course varied by each Institution.

The Institution of Chemical Engineers recognizes over thirty degree courses awarded by twenty-eight UK universities and polytechnics, and twenty degree courses offered by overseas academic institutions.

Without exception the same proedures and criteria are applied in assessing and accrediting each course. The Institution's experience in assessing courses began in the late 1930s. It recognized from the outset that the only way it could uniformly and fairly assess a course was by comparison with a model, and by 1944 it had published its first 'Scheme for a Degree Course in Chemical Enineering' (the Model Degree Scheme). This model, which has undergone regular revision, the most recent in 1982, defines the essential elements and formal contact time that all courses must provide if they are to meet their academic requirements.

The model also includes a mandatory design project, the objective of which is to cause the student to apply knowledge of chemical engineering principles to the design of a chemical process or part of it. In so doing, the student must demonstrate creativity and critical powers. For this reason the project requires choices and decisions to be made in some areas of uncertainty.

It is recommended that work is done in small teams, which may produce individual or joint reports provided that individual contributions can be distinguished and assessed. The resulting report must record clearly and fully all decisions, together with the calculations and other logic supporting them, in such a way as to permit evaluation of the proposal and of subsequent detailed equipment schedules.

The assessment is not only concerned with establishing that the course covers the model degree scheme's minimum prescription, but also that the remaining teaching is relevant and forms a sound and integrated programme of study.

It is expected that a high proportion of the staff responsible for teaching the course will be chartered engineers, and in this case in corporate membership of the Institution. A corporate member has achieved full membership status by satisfying the Institution's academic, training and experience requirements. This assures that those teaching the courses have had, in most cases, relevant industrial experience. A visit to the department, by both assessors, is a mandatory part of the assessment, and will include meetings with both staff and students, as well as an inspection of facilities.

The period of accreditation of a course would normally last for five years, when a complete re-assessment would be made. However, if in the interim a course or the department responsible for teaching it undergoes any substantial change in structure or philosophy, earliér re-assessment would be made. For example, there may be a substantial change in the number and qualifications of staff responsible for teaching the course, or an amalgamation with other departments. Changes in course structure might well mean less emphasis, or even over-emphasis, being given to subject matter. It is not unusual for re-assessments to be made when a department is revising its course for implementation at a future date, to ensure that the revised course still meets the core syllabus.

Whilst the external and internal examiners of courses in universities can supervise their own validation of courses, the influence of the professional body can, and does make a very significant impact.

The professional engineering Institutions' role is acknowledged in 'The Quality Game' where Ms Crequer writes:

> External accreditation of this kind is a thorough discipline and ensures that courses are kept dynamic. It would be interesting to see how many arts and social sciences courses would pass similar tests. (Crequer 1982)

The model degree scheme and its revision remains a Council responsibility. To undertake its most recent revision, a Working Party of fourteen senior members of the Institution, selected from various sections of the process industry and from tertiary institutions teaching degrees in chemical engineering, was set up in 1981. After nine meetings and seven drafts, the revised edition has finally been published in 1983. The Working Party also ensured that all departments of chemical engineering were consulted, as were the Institution's non-corporate members, before the final draft was presented to their Council.

The Institution emphasizes in the scheme that it is: 'A guide to the minimum acceptable content of a first degree course in chemical engineering which would satisfy the academic requirements for Corporate Membership. It is expected that the content of the scheme will be integrated into a balanced course of a minimum length of three academic years' (Institution of Chemical Engineers 1983).

The scheme requires a minimum of 1000 hours of formal contact time, for lectures, tutorials and practical work, to be devoted to the teaching of the essential elements and the design project, and allows each course to develop its own specialization within the remaining time. The scheme represents approximately two-thirds of a normal 3-year, full-time course. It also sets down the normal standards of entry to any course that is designed to match the model.

The application of such a model, and the assessment procedure, does ensure that graduates from any accredited course will have at least been exposed to the Institution's essential core syllabuses, and have been taught by a department considered capable of teaching the course within a university or polytechnic degree-awarding authority. The universities and polytechnics are accepted as being able to maintain the high academic standards their degree classifications describe. Whilst the academic requirements for the CEng award are normally a recognized UK first degree, there are alternatives. The CEI organizes and administers its own two-part examinations, in co-operation with its member Institutions, and the candidate has to have an entry qualification of at least two UK 'A' levels, or HNC/TEC awards. It is also possible to accept overseas entry qualifications that are considered equivalent.

The standard of the Part Two examination is generally considered to be of at least 'Pass' degree level. Successful completion of Part Two meets the academic requirements of most Institutions; however some have additional requirements that are not completely met by the examinations. For example, the Institution of Chemical Engineers requires all of its accredited courses to include a design project. Those who follow the CEI examination route are required therefore to pass a design project examination set by the Institution before they can satisfy their academic requirements for corporate membership.

Standards

A serious problem facing the candidate, who for various reasons follows the CEI examination route, is the availability of properly constructed courses that provide tuition and preparation for the examination. Traditionally, the polytechnics and the colleges of higher education were able to offer a full programme for study for each part, but due to the decreasing number of people seeking tuition on a full and part-time basis, and the regional disparity in demand, few formal courses are now available, and the candidates are very much left to their own resourcefulness in finding tuition. Some depend on private arrangements with academics in the locality, or have to travel, in some cases the breadth of the country, to attend a formal course of study. Increasing concern about this problem has led to proposals at CEI that equivalent subjects and examinations taught by universities and polytechnics as part of their degree courses should be accepted by CEI as an alternative.

The CEI has just completed a revision of its examination requirements and syllabuses and this important alternative to academic qualifications will continue to be available in the future, as the new Engineering Council has agreed that it will adopt it as a going concern. The structure, moderating and assessing of the examinations is dependent upon the professional input of the Institutions, whose members serve on the examination boards and committees.

A number of Institutions have, in recent years, reviewed their academic standards for membership. Several have decided that these should not normally be less than a Third Class Honours degree. This insistance on a standard higher than that of the CEI examination has caused some rethinking by the CEI, and it is expected that their examination will, in the future, award grades that will give some indication of the candidate's level of achievement; but this can only be relative to the performance of others in the examination.

However, the corporate efforts of the Institutions and of the CEI are generally considered to be successful in protecting and furthering the standards of their qualifications. The Council of Engineering Institutions, established under Royal Charter, awards the qualification of Chartered Engineer (CEng). The award and register of chartered engineers is the responsibility of the Engineers Registration Board (ERB) which co-ordinates more than fifty of the major British Institutions for engineers and technicians in their efforts to maintain and improve standards of qualifications in the profession.

The ERB also awards two other qualifications, TEng (CEI) for Technician Engineers and Tech (CEI) for Engineering Technicians. The professional engineer seeking the CEng qualification would normally hold an accredited degree in an engineering discipline awarded by a UK university or by the CNAA, and have at least four years of training and experience as a practising engineer. Applications for the award would normally be made through one of the relevant professional Institutions that link their professional qualifications to the CEng requirements and they would confer the title of Member. More advanced professional engineering qualifications can only be obtained if further achievement is demonstrated at a high level which could eventually qualify an Institution member for its Fellowship award. The highest award available in the profession is that of FEng, awarded by the most eminent body, the Fellowship of Engineers.

Concern about the profession's qualifications and the accreditation role of the Institutions has stimulated a lot of healthy discussion. A summary of the debate of this theme, at the National Conference on Engineering Education and Training states that:

4.5.1 The Conference was in no doubt that the significant qualification of the professional engineer should remain that of CEng, awarded by an Engineering Institution on completion of an adequate package of education, training and demonstration of capacity to accept responsibility.

At this stage the Engineer should not only have proved capable to his or her employer, but also have an understanding of the development and application of innovation to meet the needs of industry and society. It was agreed that CEng should devote the same high standard of professional competence, irrespective of which Institution awarded it. The difficulties in applying common standards across all branches of engineering were recognised, but this problem would have to be overcome, if necessary by higher qualifying standards and more thorough assessment by Institutions, if the title was to attract and retain full national and international recognition as the qualification of the professional engineer in the UK. (National Conference on Engineering Education and Training 1980)

Accreditation and Validation Procedures

Whether there should be improvements in the various systems of validation within the universities, through the establishment of a national validating body, is a matter worth considering. The establishment of the new Engineering Council with a Royal Charter that permits it to authorize nominated bodies to accredit academic courses, industrial training programmes and arrangements for experience stimulated a considerable amount of discussion by various bodies who felt they should be more involved in the accreditation process. A recent meeting of the Engineering Professors Conference produced a checklist of recommendations for improvement in the current procedures operated by most of the professional institutions. They identified the need for:

a Published statements of the standards and criteria for the education, training and experience that are determined as appropriate by the Council.
b A code of practice which requires, inter alia, that
  - accreditation procedures should be basically similar in all areas of engineering;
  - at least half the accrediting team should have current or recent experience as full-time academics;
  - the EPC should be permitted to comment on drafts of criteria and standards between the start and completion of the accreditation process;
  - there should be an established procedure for consultation over an unfavourable report before the final decision is made.
c Periodic review of the work of accreditation performed by the nominated bodies.
d Special consideration of the problems of accreditation of academic courses offered by the 'unified' departments of engineering.

e Special consideration of the problems of accreditation of academic courses in emerging technologies, eg information systems engineering, and in areas adjacent to engineering, eg computer science.

f Special consideration of the problems of assessing the adequacy of the education, training and experience of individuals who have graduated through courses other than accredited ones, eg in mathematics or physics. (Engineering Professors Conference 1982)

The Committee for Engineering in Polytechnics has also recently discussed the accreditation function, and in August 1982 issued a similar policy statement (Committee for Engineering in Polytechnics 1982).

In the wake of the Finniston Report, there has been a very welcome re-assessment of the engineering profession's qualification procedures and the status of the qualifications it confers. Such a shake-up is a healthy thing. What the Institutions must now do, however, is seek ways in which they can co-operate to a greater extent in conducting their assessments, particularly in situations where there are similar basic academic specializations. A wider use of Joint Boards of Assessors could co-ordinate their work more efficiently and benefit by a broader view than that available within the various disciplinary constraints.

Meeting the Needs of Industry

It would be wrong to give too much emphasis to the importance of the recognized degree in the qualification package. There is without doubt a clear view, accepted by both academia and industry, that the degree course should and can only teach the discipline of engineering; it cannot produce engineers. Industry and other sectors which employ engineers must provide graduate recruits with the training they see as important to their own needs and applications.

Frequently, the large companies, when asked by academia about the course and graduate they want, respond by expressing support for the 3-year, full-time degree course, and a graduate with a 2.1 Honours degree in the appropriate discipline, who can be made into 'their Company's' kind of engineer. This attitude does not encourage the student to remain in academia for a moment longer than necessary, which fact not only has a detrimental effect on the numbers studying for postgraduate qualifications, but is also draining the pool of those properly qualified to become the academics of the future. Both industry and academia must address this problem seriously and co-operatively if the quality of teaching is to be maintained in the future.

The training and experience given to the graduate by industry must, however, meet the training and experience requirements of the professional institutions. These are clearly defined, and again jealously guarded by the profession. In general, a minimum of four years in industry, practising at a responsible level, is the minimum. Each Institution has carefully specified definitions of the type of experience that is acceptable, and the sector of industry that can provide it.

Most large companies provide carefully structured training and experience programmes designed to meet the Institution's requirements, although the small company may not be in a position to do this, and it is a problem that there is always a percentage of academically qualified graduates in industry unable to obtain the proper training and experience that would allow them to become chartered engineers.

Again, the professional Institutions, with their representative membership are in the best position to specify the training and experience packages that are acceptable, and as in the case of the academic qualification, have the range of concerned professionals available and willing to maintain realistic and logical standards.

The extent to which industry influences academia in what it teaches is clearly demonstrated by the impact its representatives make on their professional bodies; by their involvement in integrated academic/industry training programmes; and by the part they play in the design and assessment of accredited courses. Market trends will also operate towards industry influence. There is no doubt that courses, or graduates, that do not fulfil the needs of the employee will in this economic climate be given little support. The professional Institutions are in a unique position to ensure that there is a proper liaison and independent view about what these needs should be.

17 Accreditation, Validation, Evaluation and Assessment in Management Education

Anthony C. Hamblin

It must first be stated that, in the narrow sense, management is not a profession, nor is it trying to become one. That is to say, there is no professional body which controls access to the occupation or lays down standards of education and conduct. The British Institute of Management, which in Britain is the nearest thing to a professional body for managers, explicitly does not try to fulfil this role. It is true that management contains, or overlaps with, certain professions or para-professions: thus, for example, the Institute of Personnel Management attempts (with only partial success) to control access to the occupation of personnel management and to perform the other functions of a professional body. But, for management as a whole, such a body does not exist.

This means that, in the strict terms in which the words have been defined by Roger Harrison in Chapter 14 of this book, the four processes of accreditation, validation, assessment and evaluation do not occur in management. Harrison says that 'the final aim of all four processes is to ensure to the best of human ability that the professional accolade is awarded only to those who deserve it and have proved at least a minimum competence'. In management these processes do not occur. There is no examination one needs to have passed, no qualification one needs to have obtained, no team of professional judges one needs to have satisfied, before taking on a managerial position: and similarly, if an educational institution wishes to set up a course to teach management to prospective managers, there is no professional body which needs to be satisfied about the suitability of the course in content and standard. The present situation (more or less) is one in which the providers of management education are selling their wares in an open market: that is to say, the 'sellers' (educational institutions) are doing their best to provide a product which satisfies the customer's expectations in terms of content and standard (and also to change those expectations by influencing the customer), while the 'buyers' (organizations employing managers) are free to decide which product to buy, or whether to buy any product at all. However this is a market which appears to be characterized by a high level of ignorance and apathy: the customer often seems to be indifferent to the content of the product that he buys, and may indeed be influenced more by the glossiness of its packaging and advertising, and by its superficial taste, than by its actual ingredients.

To many people (and especially, perhaps, to those whose background is in one of the established professions) this situation may seem deplorable. However, the difficulties of imposing a rigid professionalism on management are bound up with certain inescapable facts about the nature of management as an occupation.

In the first place, management is an extremely amorphous activity. The designation 'manager' includes everyone from an executive in a large multinational corporation (and, within this, including all levels from the managing director to the shop floor supervisor) to the manager of an individual person (an entertainer or sports star). Also the boundaries of management are unclear: for instance, the staff specialist may be regarded less as a manager than as an adviser to management, and yet he may still be a manager (and have the word 'manager' in his title) in so far as he is responsible for a number of people within his own department. Moreover, at the bottom level, the boundary between managerial and non-managerial employees is often ill-defined, and in many organizations may have more to do with remuneration and status than with job content and responsibility.

Secondly, there is the question of the actual content of managerial jobs, and of how managerial competence can be assessed. Sayles (1979, p.17) says:

> Managerial work is hectic and fragmented and requires the ability to shift continually from person to person, from one subject or problem to another. It is almost the diametric opposite of the studied, analytical, persisting work pattern of the professional who expects and demands closure: the time to do a careful and complete job that will provide pride of authorship. While the professional moves logically and sequentially to fulfil an explicit or implicit work plan, the executive responds to one unanticipated event after another and even at high levels is at the mercy of the situation — fulfilling an open-ended job.

Because of the fragmented nature of the manager's job, it is extremely difficult to assess the competence and effectiveness of individual managers. We may feel able to say that Manager A appears to be more competent and effective than Manager B, but our reasons for saying this are likely to be highly subjective and impressionistic. Often it is a question of whether an individual manager is accepted as a valued member of a management team; and this begs the question of whether the team as a whole is competent and effective. Campbell *et al* (1970, p.105) not very helpfully say:

> We define effective managerial job behaviour as any set of managerial actions believed to be optimal for identifying, assimilating, and utilizing both internal and external resources towards sustaining, over the long term, the functioning of the organizational unit for which a manager has some degree of responsibility.

But how is this to be operationalized in particular cases, and who is to do the 'believing'? There are some who believe that the problem is not too difficult. For example, Reddin (1970, p.3) says: 'There is only one realistic and unambiguous definition of managerial effectiveness. Effectiveness is the extent to which a manager achieves the actual requirements of his position.' This leads to the philosophy of Management by Objectives (MbO). But many managers believe that MbO imposes an artificial and stultifying rigidity on what should be a fluid and innovative situation, and that it is in practice impossible or undesirable to set output objectives for each individual managerial position. Certainly, if the output requirements are not met, this may well be an indication not that the manager is incompetent or ineffective, but that the goals were unrealistically set or that the situation was outside his individual control.

The other problem is that, if a manager's competence is assessed according to the extent to which he contributes to organizational effectiveness, there is no agreement about how organizational effectiveness itself should be defined and evaluated. The simpler definitions (equating, for instance, effectiveness with profitability) turn out on inspection to be inadequate. Goodman *et al* (1977) have written a book which contains a wide variety of views about organizational effectiveness: of these, the most radical is that of Weick, who says (1977, pp.193-4): 'I would suggest that the effective organization is (1) garrulous, (2) clumsy, (3) superstitious, (4) hypocritical, (5) monstrous, (6) octopoid, (7) wandering, and (8) grouchy'. We may not agree with Weick's views (although his article is well worth reading for the sake of opening up one's thinking about the problem), but we have to admit that the concept of effectiveness is not as simple as it at first appears.

If it is difficult to assess the competence of individual managers or the effectiveness of the organizations to which they contribute, it is also difficult to determine the knowledge and skills which managers need to possess (and therefore difficult to assess whether particular courses provide this knowledge and skill to an adequate standard). In Chapter 10 of this book, Ian Bruce says: 'There is... agreement on the skills a manager should acquire − finance, information technology, communication, interpersonal relationships, and inter-functional understanding.' In fact, not everyone would agree on this list; but even if it is accepted, it is difficult to translate it into an educational curriculum. To take the items on the list in turn:

− Finance: Although not all managers (at least at the middle and lower levels) need to be financial experts, it can reasonably be argued that every manager would benefit from at least a basic knowledge of the theory and practice of managerial accounting and financial management. Since this is a relatively 'hard' body of knowledge and can be relatively easily evaluated, it is tempting to lay a great deal of emphasis on it in management education. But to put an undue emphasis on finance and accounting would be dangerous at a time when it is widely argued that too many British managers have a financial background, and that it is necessary to rectify the balance in favour of other areas such as production and marketing, even though in these other areas there may be a less coherent body of knowledge and techniques to be learnt.

− Information technology: This area (including the whole field of computer literacy and numeracy) undoubtedly contains a rapidly expanding body of knowledge and techniques which is relevant (or is quickly becoming relevant) to the jobs of virtually all managers. Maybe it will soon be possible to lay down educational standards for managers in this field, but it is expanding and changing at such a rate that any curriculum will probably be out of date as soon as it is standardized.

− Communication, interpersonal relationships, inter-function understanding: This area (broadly corresponding to what academics call 'organizational behaviour') is certainly the largest area, and the one where definition of standards and evaluation of competence are most difficult. Many people believe that the skill of 'management' (as opposed to particular specialisms within management) lies entirely in this area. For example, Boyatzis (1982) lists six 'clusters of managerial competencies':
  1 Goal and Action Management
  2 Leadership
  3 Human Resource Management
  4 Directing Subordinates
  5 Focus on Others
  6 Specialized Knowledge

Of these, the first five are clearly in the 'organizational behaviour' area, while the sixth is a recognition of the fact that individual managers also need other types of knowledge and skill which are specific to their particular job or function rather than being common to all managers. The skills which are common to all managers are behavioural.

But it is far from clear that the knowledge and skills underlying these 'behavioural competencies' should be standardized into an educational curriculum and used for purposes of accreditation and validation in management education. There is, of course, a large amount of theory in this area which can be learnt; yet, even in the case of those books (eg Handy 1976) which present the theory from a management viewpoint, there is a great gap between theoretical knowledge and practical management competence. It is possible to come far closer to teaching managerial competence by teaching the subject in a more experiential way, using texts such as Kolb *et al* (1979) and using various types of management games, exercises and simulations; and in my view many educational institutions could go much further in this direction than they do at present. Just as one cannot become an engineer by book-learning alone, so one cannot acquire managerial competence other than by the experience of management-type situations.

But the problems of assessment and evaluation would remain. How can one assess whether a person has acquired managerial competence through a management course, other than by putting him into a real management job and seeing whether he sinks or swims? It is of course possible to assess a student's performance during an experiential exercise by observing his behaviour: there is inevitably some subjectivity in the assessment, but probably no greater than the subjectivity involved in marking academic examinations. Yet the assessment would still be an assessment of the student's performance within the exercise rather than within management itself. There is no artificial exercise that can completely simulate the reality of a management situation in all its fragmentation, complexity and unpredictability; and the work of people such as Mintzberg (1980) suggests that the ability to cope wih fragmentation and unpredictability is in fact the main requirement for managers. Thus, the introduction of more experiential approaches to learning is a partial, but not total, solution to the problem.

I have discussed some of the difficulties of introducing a system of professional accreditation, validation, assessment and evaluation into management education. But the question remains whether a move in this direction would be desirable, even if the difficulties could be overcome. Certainly there is a need — especially in Britain — to attract a greater proportion of high-calibre young men and women into management and away from the longer-established professions. But this does not necessarily mean the professionalization of management. Management is a different type of occupation and needs a different type of prestige, such as it already enjoys in the United States and in some European countries but to a far lesser extent in the UK. The opportunities for security, for recognition by one's peers, and for some other types of professional satisfaction are inherently less in management than in most of the traditional professions; but the opportunities for innovation, adventure and creativity are (I believe) correspondingly higher. In other words, management is inherently a risk-taking occupation, and so does not lend itself to the shackles of rigid professionalism.

In order to attract higher-quality young people into management, a shift is needed in society's attitudes as a whole. This change of attitudes has been extremely slow in coming in the UK, but there is some evidence that it is now taking place, and that educational institutions are playing an important part in promoting it. For instance, undergraduate courses in management and business administration (such as the one with which I am involved at the University of Bath) are attracting very high-quality applicants, comparable to those applying for training courses for the established professions. However, such pre-experience management courses do not constitute professional training (although they may contain elements of training for professions such as accountancy and personnel management). Essentially they are broad-based courses whose purpose is to equip students for organizational life in modern society and to teach them subjects which they may find relevant in a variety of organizational contexts. An essential part of the courses is industrial placement, during which students, though not necessarily in a managerial job, are in contact with managers and are able to relate academic theory to organizational practice. A high proportion of students from these courses are appointed after graduation either to management posts or to jobs or traineeships which will eventually lead to management; but there is of course no guarantee that success in the course will confer entry into management, nor even that students from these courses will necessarily be preferred to other students who have pursued less job-relevant courses.

It is fashionable at present to regard these courses as less important than post-experience management training and education; but I believe that pre-experience management education is playing a vital role in attracting young people into managerial careers and improving their relevant knowledge and competence. However, there is certainly room for improvement. More could be done (as I have already suggested) to move away from the traditional academic model and towards experiential learning which would be more directly relevant to managerial competence; more could be done to educate students for the organizations of tomorrow rather than those of today or yesterday, by incorporating the latest developments in information technology and other fields; and more could be done to promote dialogue between colleges and industry to maximize mutual benefit.

However, this type of pre-experience course has been, and should continue to be, only a very small part of the total effort in management education and development. By far the greater emphasis has been on post-experience education: that is on learning activities for people who are already in a managerial post and whose competence needs to be further developed. These activities are extremely varied and need not necessarily consist of 'courses' in the traditional sense: thus, the Association of Teachers of Management (1983, p.4) says:

> Much management development can be achieved without managers attending formal courses at all. Many staff members of colleges and universities are involved in assisting managers other than through formal courses. Some of these activities include:
> - advisory services for small businesses
> - assistance with project-based management development
> - provision of self-development material for managers
> - general consultancy services to organizations
> - production of case study material, learning packages, audiovisual aids, computer software
> - action research in organizations.

The evaluation of these activities is a large subject (see Hamblin 1974) which cannot be discussed here. Here we can only stress that the traditional professional model, in which the bulk of training is pre-experience and in which the satisfactory completion of pre-experience training leads to secure membership of the profession, is totally inappropriate to management. A manager needs to be continually learning throughout his career, and the aim of management education should be to facilitate this process.

Part 6
Continuing Professional Education

18 Overview of Continuing Professional Education

Cyril Houle

The founders of the complex modern professions either took continuing education for granted or were careful to include formal methods of such learning in their original plans for professionalization. To many pioneers, it seemed self-evident that advanced technical knowledge could not be acquired in a few years of schooling at the beginning of adulthood; practical necessities would require any successful physician, attorney, engineer, or other practitioner to keep on learning in order to solve the problems which appeared daily. Moreover, such pioneers, being eager activists, assumed that everybody else would be, like themselves, avid to learn anything new which would help them. Other pioneers were not as Utopian in their views and felt, for various reasons, that formal instruments and methods of learning were needed. There should be journals, conventions, local associations, and special interest groups, and the emphasis of each should be on the provision of education. The history of each profession which has managed to get itself established shows that formal means of continuing education were created early in its life and often, in fact, subsequently became the chief responsibility of the bureaucracy which maintained the organized profession.

This system of well-established study mechanisms was supplemented by new techniques of teaching as they were perfected, chief among them being the various audio-visual forms of the presentation of content. As new occupations started along the professionalizing routes of the old ones, they adopted as a matter of course the various techniques of continuing education which had apparently proved to be successful, making appropriate adaptations of form and content. Partly as a result of this continuing concern for the dissemination of knowledge, both old and new professions grew, proliferated, established rights and privileges for themselves, and generally prospered. From about 1920 to 1960 they flourished at an astounding rate (at least in the United States) and in

1963 the Fall issue of the intellectual journal *Daedalus* began with the ringing declaration: 'Everywhere in American life, the professions are triumphant.' In subsequent pages, a few dark places were noted, but the general reaction of the authors of the symposium published in that issue bore out the enthusiasm of its first sentence. The content made plain the fact that the provisions made for continuing education had had an important part in this march toward success.

But if professions took satisfaction in this and other accolades, they quickly suffered the consequences said to follow pride. Only thirteen years later, Harold Enarson, President of Ohio State University, said in a statement unconsciously paralleling that of *Daedalus*; 'Everywhere the professions are on the defensive.' All at once they found themselves caught in a rising tide of distrust, hostility, and litigiousness. Attacks came from without and within. Everyone now depends on professionals for crucial and sometimes life-maintaining services, but all too often clients began to encounter an egocentric architect, an incompetent nurse, a curt librarian, an unskilled military officer or an avaricious dentist. These individual encounters, cumulatively experienced and occasionally culminating in spectacular examples of wrongdoing, led to action by courts, legislative bodies, regulatory agencies, consumer groups, the mass media, and throngs of citizens acting in militant or vigilant ways. Devastating attacks came from within the professions themselves. The Chief Justice of the United States asserted that half the lawyers in the country were incompetent and Philip Kurland, an eminent professor of law, countercharged that judges were worse than the advocates who appear before them. Leading physicians have not been silent on the deficiencies of the health professions, including their own. ('The chief cause of malpractice suits,' said one of them, 'is malpractice.') Dissident groups have been formed in some professions to attack the alleged weaknesses of their colleagues.

The pressure induced by all these attacks has led to the proposal of many remedies, some calling for the use of a carrot and some for the sharp application of a stick. To provide rewards for outstanding performance, for example, seemed an excellent idea; professional societies blossomed forth with even more medals, plaques, and engraved citations than before. As matters turned out, however, an honour awarded to a star performer seems to do little to stimulate his or her laggard colleagues. Nor, at the other extreme, were very many people improved by harsh legislative enactments, negative judicial decisions, mass confrontations, and the virulent flow of charge and countercharge within professions, between them, or in the interactions among them and the people they profess to serve.

But continuing education seemed a direct benefit that was sure to help the situation. Professionals are not born with specialized knowledge, skills and values but learn them. To the extent, therefore, that deficiency exists, it can best be remedied by further study. Moreover, a professional who visibly puts himself or herself in a posture of learning has thereby built a defence against future attack and a profession which encourages such a posture is one which is obviously setting itself on the path of righteousness.

And so, beginning in the late 1960s the modern drive toward organized in-service education began. It might well be called a second era of continuing professional education, following the first which was part of the formal establishment of the professions themselves. Old methods of learning were vitalized; journals, conventions, and local associational meetings were redesigned. Every method of communication, from the telephone to the video disc, was warmly accepted and each was treated by its devotees as a panacea. New societies and associations were formed. Short courses had a particularly spectacular growth: on campuses and cruise ships; in convention facilities and resorts; and in such instructional centres as Miami Beach, Monte Carlo, and various world capitals, now including Beijing. New companies were formed, some for profit and others with generous fees for their sponsors. Many employment settings − in particular, hospitals − became educational centres both in their own facilities and in outreach programmes. New theories of instruction, systems of programme planning, and methods of testing were devised and put into place. A great deal of money began to be spent on all such programmes of continuing professional education.

This concern with lifelong learning has almost certainly done a great deal to re-invigorate the professions, particularly those which have been blessed with far-sighted and creative leaders. The valid but limited view that the purpose of continuing education is 'to keep up to date on the new research' has been supplemented by an increased awareness that the appropriate goals broaden out to include all the needs for the growth of a profession, beginning with an awareness of its appropriate mission and continuing through a mastery of both its knowledge base and its methods of treatment, its internal structuring, its code of ethics, its relationships with allied professions, and its responsibilities to both its clients and its society. Policy groups (or, at least, some individuals within them) are now more ready than before to take action on some matters that might earlier have seemed far-fetched. Among them are: How can a professional school choose entrants who are likely to be continuing learners all their lives? How can this trait be fostered by the basic preparatory programme of the school? What can be omitted from the pre-service curriculum and left to be learned later in life? What is the role of each of the various providers of continuing education? And, since all professions have somewhat similar problems so far as continuing education is concerned, how can they learn from one another's experience? The answers to these questions are beginning to lead to countless innovations which may in time open up into a third era.

It cannot be doubted, however, that many thoughtful people have been repelled by some of the excesses and dubious practices which have occurred as a result of the uncritical acceptance of continuing education as a panacea for all of the ills of a profession. The circus-like surrounding of some endeavours, the deadly monotony of others, and the utter inappropriateness of still others have led to a wholesale rejection of the very idea of continuing education, particularly among people who were never very enamoured of the idea in the first place. The point of view thus developed has been articulately expressed, with the result that a deep schism has appeared between some of those who support continuing education and some of those who oppose it.

The people who are interested in getting on with the task of perfecting professions by the appropriate use of continuing education are not unduly troubled by the thunderous arguments which resound about them, though sometimes actions are taken which impede progress or withhold resources. The pathway toward progress can be based on such propositions as the following, all of them basically simple, however complex their ramifications or difficult their achievement.

First, the ultimate goal of all continuing professional education is the improvement of the ongoing performance of the practitioners. The proper evaluation of any learning activity is not the degree of satisfaction of the learner, the extent to which approved procedures of teaching have been used, the length of exposure to instruction, the scores on examinations, or the demonstration of competence. These and other measures may be correlated with improvement of practice but the extent and even the direction of the correlation are unknown. (In some cases, for example, the degree of satisfaction of the students with a learning activity may be negatively correlated with its influence on what they do subsequently; a course of study in a richly equipped research center may be very stimulating but lead to a sense of despair with the meagre resources confronted on the next Monday morning.) These measures need to be used because no better ones are yet available, but results should always be interpreted with a healthy awareness of their limitations.

Steady progress is being made on the measurement of the quality of performance, though this topic remains the major challenge of those who argue the case for more continuing professional education. Systems of evaluation, many of them rough-hewn, are built into the practice of most professions. They have to do with peer ratings, progressive systems of examinations, admission to favoured practice situations, supervision by superiors, and the winning of competitions or contracts. Most of these estimates of success are too general to be related to the outcomes of specific examples of instruction, but a great deal of creative thought and action is now being devoted to the development of subtle and situation-related practice. In the United States, the organizations related to the specialty fields of medicine are probably in the forefront of such activity.

Second, most continuing professional education is carried out by the mode of instruction — the dissemination in some way of established skills, knowledge, and sensitiveness. The person who conducts the instruction already knows everything that the student will learn. Partly because this mode is already so deeply engrained in everyone's consciousness, it will probably continue to be the major formal method of conveying content, skills, and sensitiveness. It is in the development of new methods of instruction that continuing educators have excelled, but enthusiasm has sometimes led them to employ techniques without really knowing how to do so. This mode has an astonishingly large variety of techniques on which an instructor may draw and the appropriate policy is to select from among them the ones most appropriate to the achievement of the learning goal in the setting and time available and then to use the selected few, with complete mastery of each one. Any new technique is sure to be hailed as a panacea but it is doubtful whether the microchip will cause us to say farewell to Herr Gutenberg. And the experience of everyone confirms the depressing frequency with which the slide or motion picture projector (both of them available for more than sixty years) fail to perform with the infallibility suggested by their sales brochures. Much of the resentment concerning continuing professional education is a product of poor teaching. Mature and highly compensated adults will not endure what young people fatalistically accept as inevitable.

Third, insufficient attention is given in continuing professional education to the mode of reinforcement.* When a fact or concept has been mastered or a skill perfected, it does not become truly a part of continuing practice without some kind of habitual and conscientious usage. When the work life of a student is wholly contained by a professional school, he or she may be compelled by reward or punishment systems, by drill, by supervision, by peer pressure, or by many other means to conform to the standards of expected practice. The fully-qualified professional, however, working in at least a semi-autonomous way, may have only his or her own conscience as a reinforcement. Every professional develops a particular style of work, stamping even the most routine procedures with a seal of individuality and structuring the pattern and procedure of a total schedule with a distinctive style. New processes or concepts learned in a classroom are

---

*In my book, *Continuing Learning in the Professions*, I referred to this as the 'mode of performance' but now think that 'reinforcement' is a preferable term.

not merely added to old ones; a modification (sometimes profound) of an entire procedure of work is required. When continuing professional education is carried out in a work setting, with collaborators who are in continuing communication with one another, subsequent reinforcement may well be easier to achieve than in those settings where instruction is wholly divorced from practice. But it is increasingly being realized that modification of performance in desirable ways is not likely to occur without the simultaneous or sequential use of both modes.

Fourth, another mode of education, that of inquiry, is also crucial to continuing professional education. This is the process of creating some new plan of action, synthesis of thought, policy, or strategy by the use of the pooled judgement of the persons concerned with the outcome. Nobody knows in advance what that outcome will be. The professionals in a group practice, the staff members in a clinic or a welfare agency, or the policy committee of an association would use this mode to set a course of action for the future. Sometimes, in the course of such an investigation, a need for instruction may be uncovered, but that is an outcome of the process, not part of it. In the history of education, the mode of inquiry has occasionally been advanced as the only true form of learning. John Dewey, for example, in *Experience and Education*, sets forth such a view, though the simplicity of his language somewhat masks the profundity of his ideas. Without elevating this mode to primacy, I would argue for its absolute necessity in continuing professional education. A professional should be at the frontier of abstruse bodies of knowledge, combining their teachings to solve practical problems of an advanced nature. For people thus situated, no tutors may be available. As best they can, and using their highest senses of ethics, they must work together, achieving not only some formal outcome of plan or policy which would otherwise not be available but, as a by-product, a sense of that shared community which is essential to the idea of professionalism.

It will not be easy to bring into full development the third era defined by these and other general propositions, particularly since each of them is far more complex and intricate in its application than can be suggested here. But the history of the past fifty years suggests that professionals seem to relish the performance of difficult tasks and to like to tackle formidable challenges. The development of truly adequate systems of continuing professional education will continue the great tradition that has already been established.

19 Continuing Education in Medicine

David Innes-Williams

Undergraduate medical education, despite some variations between individual medical schools, follows an essentially standard course and occupies a standard length of time, agreed throughout the EEC. On obtaining the primary qualifications new graduates are accepted as members of the medical profession, but embark on a long and largely unstructured course of postgraduate education, controlled by a variety of professional bodies and financed for the most part by the NHS, until they finally obtain a career post, usually either as a consultant in the hospital service or as a principal in general medical practice. Thereafter they enter the phase long recognized in medical circles as 'continuing education', which should occupy the remainder of their careers. It is unfortunate that current university terminology applies this latter term to the whole period after graduation and entering employment in a hospital, while at the same time it confines the use of the word 'postgraduate' to study directed towards higher university degrees. In medicine, higher degrees form a very small element in the ambition of young 'doctors', and since their needs and their attitudes towards learning will inevitably change on assuming the full responsibility of a consultant post, it is convenient to distinguish the whole period up to this point as 'postgraduate'. Until they have achieved their definitive appointment the junior doctors have a powerful incentive to apply themselves to study. Afterwards their need may be as great but they are free to make their own choice on the degree of their participation.

The general pattern of postgraduate and continuing education is one accepted throughout the western world and the specifically British version has been taken up widely in Commonwealth countries. However, the organization of the National Health Service and its near monopoly of medical employment has both facilitated a broader educational system and imposed upon it certain important constraints. A profession must by definition control its own training structure and admission to its membership; the fully qualified professional must exercise considerable independent judgement in everyday decisions. All the professions, as well exemplified in medicine, have stemmed from the practice of 'self-employed' individuals tendering advice or performing a service for their clients, and the situation of a professional as a full-time salaried employee is always somewhat equivocal. In the Health Service reasonably acceptable compromises have been reached, but inevitably there are strains which can still cause controversy and may ultimately imperil the present settlement. Thus the standards of education and conduct are laid down by the General Medical Council, a professional body independent of government; undergraduate instruction and assessment are undertaken within this framework by the universities, which are undoubtedly subject to government control though to a degree currently acceptable to the profession. Postgraduate and continuing education are still largely guided by the Royal Colleges and their Faculties, performing their historic function as the arbiters of professional integrity. Furthermore the hospital consultants retain wide independence of action in determining the treatment of their patients within the constraints of the facilities available to them, while the general practitioners are still 'independent contractors' rather than salaried employees. Both groups have secured NHS financial support for education at all stages following graduation. However, the system of NHS hospital staffing is increasingly deforming the educational programme of junior doctors. In Britain, as elsewhere, the acute specialties are served by teams with consultants at the top, assisted by junior staff at various stages of training: the structure is pyramidal so that there are insufficient senior posts to accommodate all the trainees. In most European and American countries, the juniors who fail to reach the upper echelons in the public service go into private or insurance practice or, particularly in Eastern Europe, become permanent assistants who are a feature of the hierarchy. In Britain, however, we have rejected a health care system based on state insurance payments to specialists and virtually eliminated independent private practice. Furthermore our egalitarian obsession gives all consultants equal status and rejects the concept of a sub-consultant career grade, leaving the less successful juniors the option of emigration or general practice. Until recently, the system has been maintained by a cushion of overseas doctors who filled the junior posts but most of whom did not stay to compete for consultant posts. Now, however, with the steadily growing output of the UK medical schools and the closure of many avenues for emigration previously available, as well as the demands for specialized training for general practice, the junior hospital ranks are increasingly filled by frustrated British doctors unable to obtain consultant appointments. The 'training' period is consequently prolonged for many years without educational benefit and any attempts to reform the structure seem blocked by the financial cuts now being imposed by the government.

The domination of postgraduate medical education by the Royal Colleges is traditional, first formalized in 1843 when the Royal College of Surgeons of England initiated its fellowship by examination as the standard by which surgeons were to be distinguished from the profession in general. This set the pattern by which young doctors learned their craft very much as apprentices during their tenure of junior appointments in hospital and were tested by a stiff examination which many or even most candidates would fail at the first attempt. During the nineteenth century the University Medical Schools took over the undergraduate phase of medical education, based on taught courses and less stringent examination assessment, but the postgraduate phase, where the doctor must be earning his living, remained under the control of the Royal Colleges of Physicians, of Surgeons, and later of Obstetricians and Gynaecologists. Since the second world war there has been a rapid acceleration in the trend towards specialization (and an increase in the number of Colleges). The present system has evolved by an interaction between the needs of the Health Service and the standard-setting function of the professional bodies. It has been the subject of much debate, to which important contributions have been made, amongst many others, by the Todd Report (Royal Commission on Medical Education, 1968) and the Merrison Report (Committee of Enquiry into the Regulation of the Medical Profession 1975). The Medical Act of 1978 extended the role of the General Medical Council from its control of the undergraduate phase in association with the universities to the 'co-ordination of all stages of medical education' and there is currently active discussion as to how it may exercise this new statutory responsibility for the postgraduate element.

The theme which runs through all the recommendations of all the numerous authorities is that newly qualified medical graduates are still unfit to be let loose on the public: they require more training for the practice of any branch of medicine they care to enter, and very long training indeed for some branches. General practice, for long the exception to this rule, now demands a minimum of three years 'vocational' training after full registration, a requirement laid down by Act of Parliament, in contrast to the simple conventions which satisfy other branches of the profession.

It will be evident, therefore, that this short account cannot deal with all the complexities of the topic and that the evolutionary process is likely to result in significant changes during the next decade.

Pre-registration

On graduation, or on obtaining the diploma of one of the non-university licensing bodies, the young doctor is granted provisional registration by the General Medical Council and seeks house officer (intern) posts in hospitals for one year. These posts are always clinical and usually in the main disciplines of general medicine or general surgery. They are inspected by the university authority and are intended to ease the transition from student to professional status, introducing the graduate to the responsibilities of patient care. Although closely supervised by other junior staff and restricted to in-patient tasks, some pre-registration house officers find their new experience stressful and there are always a very few who are precipitated into psychiatric crisis. Long hours of duty are expected and indeed required by the system of hospital staffing, although the extent to which these hours are actually occupied by work varies greatly from one hospital to another and complaints in the press about tired and overworked junior doctors are justified only in rare instances. Stress and long hours are part of most careers in medicine, and indeed in most professions, and their introduction, although perhaps it should be gradual, should not be long delayed. Happily, most young doctors are avid for experience after six years of student life and accept their new responsibilities with pride.

General Professional or Basic Specialist Training

After the satisfactory completion of the first year, doctors are granted full registration by the GMC and are theoretically free to plan their own subsequent training. In practice the restraints are considerable, the need to earn a living being the most urgent in a hotly competitive world in which there are numerous applicants for every job. Some, especially those intending to be surgeons, psychiatrists or general practitioners, have a clear idea of their goals but do not always understand how they should reach them or what are their chances of success. Others are uncertain as to their choice of discipline and are inclined to shop around, they take a succession of posts at senior house officer level in different branches. The standard pattern of experience and achievement for many disciplines is laid down by the appropriate Royal College, although only a few doctors will be able to follow the standard in the minimum time demanded. Thus in surgery it is anticipated that, following full registration, doctors will take a senior house officer post for one year in general surgery, followed perhaps by six months in an Accident and Emergency Department, during which time they may prepare for the first part of the Fellowship of the Royal College of Surgeons examination, which is concerned with bringing up to the necessary standards for surgery their knowledge of anatomy, physiology and pathology. They will subsequently do a further eighteen months in posts giving them experience of some specialist branch of surgery or perhaps in medicine, until after a minimum of four years from graduation they are entitled to sit the final part of the FRCS. An analogous, though slightly less strictly controlled, system applies to general medicine, where the diploma is the Membership of the Royal College of Physicians. These diplomas are, however, only entry qualifications which entitle the holder to embark on higher specialist training. Somewhat similar arrangements apply in obstetrics and gynaecology and in psychiatry, with different timing of examination. Entry into the various branches of pathology, radiology or community medicine is usually a little later. General practice requires two years in a selected variety of SHO posts, followed by one year as trainee with an approved general practitioner.

There are many who feel that this first post-registration phase should constitute 'general professional training', an opportunity for the young doctor while still under supervision to practise and consolidate the ability to relate constructively with patients and particularly to acquire the skills required in consultation. This is seen as developing in relation to experience in several different branches of medicine. By contrast, many young doctors are keen to start work in their chosen specialty without delay. Moreover most consultants, when appointing their juniors, like to have someone dedicated to their own specialty and therefore most apt to benefit from their instruction. The issue remains unresolved: young doctors may well be advised to take posts in several different specialties, to improve both their education and their chances of finding an avenue which offers them the best chance of advancement, but they cannot be compelled to accept this advice.

Higher Specialist Training

The final years of postgraduate education for the hospital service are spent in the 'senior registrar' post, devoted to preparation for consultant appointments in one of the numerous specialties within medicine, surgery, psychiatry, pathology, anaesthetics or any of the many other branches. Most such appointments are undertaken in four-year programmes which involve rotation between teaching and non-teaching hospitals, often with some opportunity for research. The schemes are under the control of higher training committees based on the Colleges, with some university participation: posts and programmes are inspected and on satisfactory completion the doctor is said to be 'accredited' in the specialty and fully eligible to apply for consultant posts. The numbers of senior registrars are restricted but inevitably there are temporary imbalances between supply and demand for consultants and the four-year programme may be shortened or, as at present, very much more often prolonged.

Hospital Posts and Training

It will be clear that the basis of postgraduate medical education is experience gained in a succession of junior hospital posts with increasing responsibility under supervision for initiating and carrying out the care of patients. There is an assumption that positive training accompanies the service and apprenticeship elements involved in the duties of these posts but inevitably the educational potential of some is better than of others. All junior posts are 'inspected' by representatives of the College or their higher training committees with a view to ensuring that clinical experience is adequate, that the consultants are prepared to teach, that libraries and seminar rooms are available and used, and that living conditions are acceptable. It is admittedly difficult for some posts required for service in the NHS, for instance in geriatrics or mental handicap in 'Slagthorpe', to fulfil these criteria, but efforts are being made both by the employing and educational authorities to bring them all up to standard or eliminate them. Most Districts have a postgraduate medical centre, on which are based their seminars and short courses; all have a clinical tutor responsible to a regional postgraduate dean for overseeing training activities. Study leave with pay and expenses is available to all junior staff during their term of office.

The University Element in Postgraduate Medicine

Although the university has nominally the supervision of the pre-registration year for all doctors, participation in postgraduate medicine is largely concerned only with the small numbers who intend to seek an academic career. All teaching hospital 'firms', including the professorial department, provide training posts at the various levels. They are rather more numerous than in the non-teaching hospitals, offering more instruction and less clinical experience, but the fundamental pattern remains that laid down by the professional bodies rather than that laid down by the universities. In the professorial units there are also research fellows and lecturers with a somewhat more academic orientation, but most of these are ultimately destined for NHS consultant posts. A significant proportion of the postgraduate research work recorded in the medical schools is carried out by non-medical MSc, MPhil and PhD students, who will follow a career in science. A few medical graduates take the supervised PhD degree, rather more prepare theses for the MD or MS degrees which do not demand supervision, even though nowadays most are based upon a period of research in an academic unit or research institution.

In London, in addition to the general medical schools, there are three postgraduate medical schools. The Royal Postgraduate Medical School at Hammersmith Hospital has a fine reputation for clinical research and many of the clinical professors of medicine in the UK have spent time there. The London School of Hygiene and Tropical Medicine has a specialized role, largely related to community medicine. The British Postgraduate Medical Federation brings together the university elements of the London specialist postgraduate hospitals, such as Moorfields Eye Hospital, the Hospital for Sick Children, the Brompton, the Maudsley, the Marsden and the National Hospital for Nervous Diseases, which in the nineteenth century not only pioneered specialized medicine and surgery but were the first to put on regular postgraduate courses of instruction. All the London postgraduate schools have an important national role in the continuing education of specialists, but still account for only a relatively small proportion of postgraduate medicine as a whole.

Continuing Education

The point has already been made that the attitude of doctors settled in their careers and organizing their own practices is quite different from that of trainees still struggling to reach security, and educational courses must recognize the differing demands. Continuing education in our present sense should never be didactic. It should be essentially an exchange between equals. When it takes the form of updating on a specialist topic, the input of the expert must be matched by the generalist experience of the audience. Learning, for the established practitioner, will be closely linked to teaching and since almost all consultants in the Health Service and many general practitioners are concerned with teaching their juniors there is a very real sense in which continuing education consists of trying to keep ahead of or even keep up with the assistants.

There is commonly a view that doctors are in constant need of teaching about new drugs, new operations and newly discovered facts, so that continuing education should involve regular attendance at updating courses, usually run by a university. This model has been given an extensive trial in the United States, where in some cases re-certification of medical practitioners is dependent upon an accumulation of credited hours of study in CME programmes. The system is evidently more appropriate in the US, where most of the doctors are independent specialists in private practice, often isolated from their colleagues, than it is in Britain, where almost all consultants are members of a fairly tightly knit hospital group, always open to criticism by their juniors if not by their colleagues. Moreover, all such continuing education courses put too great an emphasis on scientific fact and too little on practice. Some medical failures may result from ignorance of recently reported facts, but many more from defects in the organization of the care provided. Continuing education should have a major concern with audit, a regular review of the outcome of patient care in any particular hospital and its comparison with results elsewhere. This will soon show up areas of ignorance or inefficiency and will teach a much better lesson than a formal lecturer.

It can in general be claimed that the consultant body within the NHS recognizes the responsibility for continuing self-education. The Colleges, and more particularly the national specialist Associations, are the major and perhaps currently the most acceptable providers of educational meetings. Membership includes a very high proportion of the specialists concerned and their annual conferences are well attended. All specialist Associations provide valuable journals which play an important part in the dissemination of new knowledge. International conferences are popular with the inveterate travellers but perhaps add relatively little to the corpus of continuing education. On the other hand, small specialist clubs, to which a considerable though unquantifiable number of consultants belong, offer exactly those informal exchanges of information within a peer group which are central to this phase of education. The university teaching hospitals and specialist centres all put on short courses on particular topics. In spite of the current concern of the universities with continuing education, it does not seem likely that the medical schools will significantly increase their participation in the field, and could scarcely do so without an important increment to their staff.

Critics of the informal system of continuing education for consultants could claim that although large sums of government money are expended in the form of study leave, expenses and tax rebates, this enables more and more meetings to be attended by the same people, leaving a substantial body of doctors uninvolved. It is true that although there are very few consultants nowadays who would deny their need for continuing education, there are many who dislike meetings and prefer private study. For them, libraries are ordinarily available in all district hospitals, as well as in medical schools, though they are not used as actively as might have been hoped. The videotape or tape-slide type of instruction for individual use is gaining popularity amongst the juniors, but very little has yet been done to provide suitable material for the senior staff, except in the rather dubious field of promotional productions by drug firms. The self-assessment tests, common enough in North America, which some find a challenge, entertaining as well as educative, have yet to obtain popularity in Britain and it is quite certain that any attempt to introduce a system of re-licensure (whether based on examination or evidence of study) as a requirement for the continued practice of medicine in Britain.would be totally rejected by the profession at large.

Continuing education for general practitioners poses more difficult problems since many work in isolation and continue in practice beyond the normal retirement stage. They may take no part in peer-group activities nor attend any instructional courses. Many studies have been made of the methods by which an interest in educational activities could be stimulated or maintained. The Royal College of General Practitioners has been active in a series of initiatives, starting with their Membership examination, relating to teaching methods and audit. There has been perhaps more innovative thinking in this area than in recent discussions of postgraduate hospital medicine, but there is still considerable difficulty in eliciting a positive response from more than a handful of practitioners. The Department of Health and Social Security makes finance available through the universities for continuing education (usually known as Section 63 funds) and courses are regularly available to general practitioners in district hospital postgraduate centres. At one time seniority payments to practitioners were dependent upon attendance at such courses. This system was discontinued in 1977. Subsequently the numbers signing on for such courses fell, though whether this actally represented lessened interest was not altogether apparent. The view is often expressed that teaching by hospital consultants is not what general practitioners need and that greater success would be achieved by courses run and taught by general practitioners themselves with minimal specialist in-put. Small group discussions, often held in practice premises and relating particularly to the psychosocial problems of patients, have attracted some interest but this trend is seen by many as accentuating the divide between general practice and hospital medicine, which joint meetings in postgraduate centres were doing something to bridge. Self-assessment programmes are being given a trial but the uptake remains small.

The best hope for effective continuing education in general practice lies in the groundwork now being laid during the vocational training period: since general practice is now the first choice for many of the best medical graduates with a strong motivation to excel in their profession, the training which they now receive should give them a commitment to continued teaching and learning.

20 Continuing Education in Engineering

John J. Sparkes

The Present Provision

Government support for continuing or lifelong education in engineering, especially at the professional level, has been slow to develop and even now it amounts to only a tiny fraction of the expenditure on primary, secondary and tertiary education. Yet it has been clear to many for some time that, with the increasing pace of change in nearly all branches of technology, a single extended period of education at the start of an engineer's working life will no longer be sufficient. The establishment of the Open University in 1969 marked an important step forward, since it provides a form of continuing education. Its student population is an adult one, and most of its students are already at work. But the motivation for its creation was to provide tertiary education for those who had, for one reason or another, missed it at the normal age of 18+. It was not initially thought of as a vehicle for the provision of continuing education for engineers, or for any other profession, although at the present time perhaps a third of its output is of this kind.

A major stimulus towards developing continuing education in engineering came with the publication of the Finniston Report 'Engineering Our Future'. Whilst the sections of this report on education are mainly concerned with the 'initial formation' of engineers, there are also some key paragraphs on 'continuing formation'. The report recommends for example:

...that the government introduce a statutory right to paid study leave for all statutorily registered engineers.

and that:

...a condition of statutory registration for engineers should be a personal commitment for them to maintain their technical knowledge.

The Report also observes that 'with a few notable exceptions, the contribution of taught Masters courses has been less than it should have been, given the resources deployed to mount them.' It envisages a continuation of the existing provision of 'short courses, seminars, workshops, lecture programmes and conferences provided mainly by private agencies, engineering and management schools and engineering Institutions'. But it also sees the need to encourage and develop 'distance learning schemes' for engineers.

As a consequence of the lack of interest in it, both in government and in most universities, continuing formation of engineers has been left mainly in the hands of the large private companies; only short specialist courses and full-time postgraduate MSc courses have been provided by universities and polytechnics. A useful report published in 1982, by R.L. Cannell entitled 'The Updating of Professional Engineers', provides data on the level of provision of updating engineering courses. He assumes that 400 student-hours of study on courses (of whatever length) amounts to one full-time student equivalent, and finds student numbers as shown in Table 20.1.

Table 20.1

	1978/79	1979/80
Universities – UK	987	741
– England & Wales	919	669
Cranfield Institute of Technology	333	383
Polytechnics – England & Wales	778	693

It is particularly noticeable that the extent of the provision declined, except at Cranfield, during the period covered, and that it amounts to an average of only about twenty students per university or polytechnic. In fact, however, as Cannell points out, eighteen universities provide no continuing education courses at all in engineering, whilst three universities provide 45 per cent of the total university provision.

A similar survey conducted by the Engineering Professors' Conference revealed similar data. In this survey it is assumed that seventy-five student-days is the equivalent of one full-time student, giving a total full-time student equivalent, for all universities, of 940. It can be argued that seventy-five days, or 400 hours, is rather a small value to put on a full-time student equivalent – double this amount might be more realistic – so that even these low figures can be thought of as rather generous.

These data do not include students who are studying with the Open University. There the picture is very different, since all its courses are a form of continuing education. The unit of 400 student-hours of study corresponds to one student-credit within the university's modular system, so it is not difficult to provide approximate equivalent figures for continuing education there.

The number per annum of adult students taking appropriate second and third-level courses at the Open University in the fields of mathematics, science and technology is about 10,000 full-time student equivalents, not far short of ten times the total attendance at all other universities and colleges put together. These however are undergraduate courses of a kind that are not usually accessible at other universities to students who are working full-time, though the figures reveal the existence of a very substantial demand for them. Indeed, in particular popular fields such as electronics and computing the demand far exceeds the Open University's ability to supply, within its limited funds.

A corresponding high demand exists for specially designed continuing education courses at professional level in popular topics, provided they are offered in convenient distance-teaching packages. One small 50-hour Open University course, on 'Microprocessors for Managers', has been studied by about 25,000 students (5,000 packages, including a micro, sold, and probably five students studying each package). This amounts to over a million student-hours; more than all the continuing engineering education offered by the other universities and polytechnics put together.

Other providers of distance-learning materials have, for some years now, been certain professional institutions. They have provided printed texts on specialist topics and a correspondence tutor for each student. They have thus enabled many students to upgrade their knowledge by private study.

At the time of writing, the government attitude to continuing education is undergoing a considerable change. For example, in the key area of information technology, the SERC has established 1,000 new postgraduate studentships (at £4,500 each) and has approved about fifty courses (not all of them new by any means), with a view to achieving a rapid influx of new graduates in the field. Earmarked funds have also been granted to the Open University for continuing education developments in general, though these funds carry the unusual condition that the money must be repaid out of fees, and interest must be paid on it meanwhile! Special grants to the Open University for courses in manufacturing and industrial application of computers have also been made by the SERC.

Concurrent with this recent increase in government interest in continuing engineering education is a corresponding growth in the provision by some universities of entrepreneurial specialist short courses. In particular, experts are commissioned to lecture in major

European cities and charge say £600 per student for 4-day courses. This is a growing activity.

The whole question of continuing education is, as the Finniston Committee pointed out, closely bound up with ensuring the continuing competence of chartered (or registered) engineers. Hitherto the educational component of qualifying for professional status has been mainly a matter for the 'initial formation' at university or elsewhere. There has been no requirement on engineers to update themselves. Equally those who wish to achieve professional status late in life have had to take exams equivalent to those set for initial graduation (or other qualification). Nowadays, however, the need to update engineers, and to open up routes to professional status that are not so closely tied to initial tertiary education is becoming clear. The government's attitude on this is set out in a letter from Sir Keith Joseph to the Chairman of the Engineering Council dated 21 December 1982:

> First, I trust that whatever new registration procedures emerge from your Council's deliberations will contain the greatest possible flexibility for people to advance from one register to another, so that the doors remain open for all who enter the profession to arrive at chartered status by different routes involving varied combinations of education, training and experience. Second, the current moves by some of the engineering institutions to impose minimum 'A' level scores – either as a requirement on individuals or on academic courses – as part of the pattern of qualifications leading to chartered status can only work in the opposite and wrong direction. 'A' level scores are an unsatisfactory indicator of future academic and professional success, particularly in a practical subject like engineering, and I therefore hope that your Council will look for more appropriate ways of achieving high standards. Third, although I am prepared to be persuaded that industry may see merit in extended engineering courses for a small minority of professional engineers, I am concerned by the current pressures in the engineering departments of many universities and polytechnics for the wide-scale and indiscriminate introduction of such courses. I therefore trust that your Council will discourage any expectation of a general extension of the length of academic courses leading to chartered professional status, and that it will take the view that any longer courses which are to be made available should be in response to the clearly identified needs of industry.

The reference in the third comment is to the suggestion by many universities that initial formation of engineers should be extended to four years in order to provide a broader initial formation.

The implication of this government view is that it envisages professional qualifications in engineering becoming available through part-time education, to those who have not taken the traditional route to university through 'A' level examinations and may wish to qualify relatively late in life. These are all features that are typical of continuing education provision whether for professional registration or simply for updating purposes in specific fields, and so can be expected to become one of the aims of continuing engineering education.

The Engineering Council and its working groups clearly have a great responsibility to the British Engineering industry to recommend an effective and viable programme for continuing education. The direction they will give it is not yet published, although some important needs are becoming apparent. The remainder of this chapter, therefore, is devoted to considering the nature of continuing education courses. Comments are based, to a large extent, on the authors' several years experience of planning and providing such courses for engineers and others.

Needs and Possibilities for the Future

The first and most urgent need is to avoid speaking and thinking of continuing education as a homogeneous educational activity that either one is involved in or one is not. Unlike undergraduate education, continuing education at professional level has to cater for a variety of types of student population; it includes a wide variety of different kinds of courses; and it may have to use one or more of a variety of different teaching methods and strategies. Indeed the variety is such that many different providers are likely to be needed, and that they may well complement each other rather than compete for students.

This variety of provision is analysed in the next few pages, and the comments apply mainly to the kinds of courses that might be offered by universities, polytechnics, colleges of further and higher education and correspondence colleges. Parts of the analyses may well, however, be applicable to the kind of in-house training provided by companies for their own employees.

Target Audiences for Continuing Engineering Education

There are two main criteria by which target audiences should be categorized; namely in terms of their ease of access to courses and in terms of their *prior* knowledge or qualifications.

As to access, it is important to distinguish between those who:

a   can attend extended full-time courses,

b   can attend courses on a day-release basis,

c   can only attend short, intensive courses,

d   cannot conveniently attend face-to-face courses of any kind, and so have need of distance-teaching courses suitable for home-based or work-based study.

Day-release courses are only appropriate for students who live locally.

Extended full-time courses are only suitable for those who are not employed or who can be released from work for long periods and who are confident that there will be a post for them to return to at the end of the course. So far, at university level, it is mainly these full-time courses (eg in information technology) that the new government initiative is supporting.

Short, intense courses continue to be favoured by industry, students and most universities alike though they have considerable limitations educationally and are usually very costly for the students. However, they undoubtedly serve a useful function.

Distance-teaching methods have the advantage that they do not directly interfere with a student's work; they allow students to study at their own pace (and in private: often a very important factor for senior personnel) and enable the best expertise on a particular subject to be brought to a large number of students however widely dispersed they are. The disadvantages of distance-teaching methods, are that they are demanding on students and teachers alike, and that they are not, in general, accompanied by the kind of social activities that residential students and staff often enjoy − though they generate other friendships.

The prior knowledge or understanding of students in continuing education is very varied. Undergraduate entry to universities and polytechnics is of a homogeneous standard, controlled by 'A' level examination, in marked contrast with the recognized entry to continuing education. Suitable applicants in engineering may have acquired their prior knowledge and expertise from industrial experience, from private study or from graduation at a university. Many, however, are likely to be changing field somewhat (from mathematics or science or even from the humanities) so that they have proven intellectual ability, but in another subject. Being aware of these differences is important since it is always essential to match courses to students' prior knowledge. In practice, this means pitching courses at a variety of different levels and explaining clearly to students what these levels are, so that they can choose the appropriate one − if necessary with guidance. Universities for some time have taken care of the postgraduate field, though, as already pointed out, this turns out to be a field where demand is limited.

There appears, however, to be a large demand for undergraduate level courses, since in most engineering fields the latest third-year undergraduate courses contain new material for a graduate of ten years' standing, and at a level he can learn from rapidly. (Postgraduate courses tend to presuppose more prior knowledge than students actually possess.) This suggests that a really helpful development would be the admission by universities, on a one-day-a-week basis, of graduate engineers of some years' standing, onto a selection of their third-year taught courses. The mixing of undergraduates with experienced engineers would be of benefit to everyone, and the costs would be minimal. Indeed a requirement that professional engineers undertake such courses of study, or their equivalent in distance-learning schemes, would go a long way towards satisfying one of the Finniston Report's recommendations.

There is also a considerable need for even lower-level courses, aimed at those who wish to change direction. There is not very much in common between one Honours degree and another. There is not even much in common between the education of a civil engineer, say, and an electronics engineer (mainly basic science and mathematics), so conversion from one field to another involves studying some topics at second-year undergraduate standard to begin with. Private study, using distance-teaching courses, may well be the right preparation to enable a student to enter third-year courses at a conventional university or polytechnic, whether full-time or on a one-day-a-week basis.

Types of Course

Unlike undergraduate courses, which are mainly academic in character, and so are concerned with teaching new concepts and understanding, continuing education courses can take a variety of forms. And since courses need to be matched to the student audience (as already indicated) and different kinds of course demand different teaching strategies, it is important to distinguish between them. The following categorization indicates the range involved.

a Awareness courses: These are mainly factual, and concerned with teaching the meanings of new vocabularies. They are intended to help engineers keep in touch with (but not become expert in) new developments outside their own field. They are non-specialist in character but not merely popular. Such a course, about microprocessors for example, should certainly include a microprocessor kit, since words alone cannot adequately explicate the meanings of such technical words.

b Updating courses: These are also mainly factual but they are specialist in character. They presuppose an advanced level of understanding and so need only deal with new techniques, processes, products, and their capabilities and limitations. Though the courses may be concerned with practical matters they may not need to include a practical element.

c Upgrading courses: Again these are specialist in character, but they are concerned with teaching understanding and with developing new concepts. Most postgraduate MSc courses are of this kind. So are undergraduate courses, but at a lower level. They are academic courses, concerned with concept development and with teaching understanding and therefore usually include several components, such as practical work, exercises, applications etc., aimed at improving understanding. With a sufficiently specialist student audience, short courses can be effective in very specialized topics. Otherwise, extended courses are necessary to allow students sufficient learning time.

d Practitioner's courses: These focus attention on the development of skills, either practical or intellectual. Examples are courses that concentrate on developing the skills of analysis, design, computing, control, etc. They are intended primarily to teach students to do things, rather than to understand or merely to know. Some understanding is of course also necessary so that the newly acquired skills can be applied to new situations. (Simply teaching skills, without also teaching understanding is a kind of training. There is an element of training in all practitioner's courses, since a good many human skills are not understood by anyone!)

Failure to be clear about which kind of course is needed, whether in student, or commissioning client, or course provider, can lead to a good deal of frustration and dissatisfaction among all concerned.

The above categorization refers to different kinds of courses. Additional variables which have to be clarified are the level involved as well as the subject matter. Under each of the above categories a brief reference has been made to the appropriate teaching strategy. The implementation of each strategy can take many forms thanks to the number of new methods or techniques now available.

Teaching Methods

Different kinds of courses and different topics require different teaching techniques. Most techniques can be used to some extent to teach most kinds of courses and most subjects; and face-to-face teaching is certainly the most adaptable. But it is by no means the best for all kinds of course, nor is it the cheapest or the most convenient method in all circumstances. Distance-teaching methods for example are obviously necessary when students cannot reach the classroom, or when a particular teacher (from industry, for example) cannot spare the time to lecture in many different locations. However, distance-teaching methods tend to be less adaptable, so that their misuse can be more unsatisfactory than the misuse of lectures, seminars or tutorials.

For example, for some kinds of specialist updating courses it is important for students to come into contact with a current expert. This might be true where the applications of new equipment such as computers or monitoring apparatus are concered. A forum is therefore needed in which question and answer is possible about how to tackle new problems. The obvious choice is a series of seminars or lectures or a short course. However this confines the course to those who are within reasonable travelling distance and can find the travelling time and expenditure. Audio telephone conferencing has however been found to be a very successful method for overcoming this difficulty, especially if the course is supported by printed notes. Quite large numbers of students from anywhere in the country (or even abroad) can be linked together and benefit from the interaction of any one of them with the expert tutor. Other updating courses, however, depend heavily upon the presentation of detailed new data, for which the spoken word is not the best medium.

Telephone conferencing is also successful for awareness courses; but it tends to be insufficiently rich in communication to be allowed to deal on its own with academic courses − though it can support them − and it can only deal with skills that are aural in character (eg musical performance).

Similarly, computers, as teaching machines, have their strengths and limitations. They are most effective (a) as aids to design, through simulation, and this capability can be adapted for educational purposes, (b) as providing means to present and assess exercises of an appropriate kind for individual students, (c) as a source of data for updating purposes. Their capabilities as teaching devices for academic courses is limited not only by the use of a VDU or keyboard at the interface between student and 'teacher', but also by the extensive demands put on the teachers who prepare the courses. Two hundred man-hours for one hour's-worth of student work is typical. All the same, the fact that distributed computer networks (including those using the public telephone network, such as Prestel) are already with us means that student accessibility is already quite good and will increase considerably in future. There is therefore much to be gained by finding effective and efficient ways of using computers in continuing education.

Similar comments can be made about the use and misuse of all kinds of teaching methods and techniques, from broadcast television to live tutorial or from interactive video discs to printed educational texts. In some cases combinations of techniques turn out to be very effective. Tutored video instruction (TVI) is one such example.

TVI simply comprises playing back televized lectures to small tutorial groups in the presence of a tutor – who is preferably not too knowledgeable himself! The advantage offered by video replay facilities, of frequently stopping a lecture in order to discuss the points being made, and ensuring that they are understood, enables the lecture to become part of an effectve teaching system. The lecture, in its normal 'live' form is best thought of as an explanatory, and often stimulating, statement of what the student audience is expected to learn. It rarely teaches much itself; the learning follows afterwards in private study, libraries, discussions, exercises and tutorials. TVI creates a much richer learning experience and is very effective in upgrading courses. It is, however, somewhat wasted on updating, awareness or practitioners courses. It also requires small groups of students; it is not effective for solitary, home-based or work-based students.

Practitioners courses, concerned as they are with teaching skills, are mainly concerned first with instruction and demonstration of the particular intellectual or practical skill involved, and then with supervised practice. Up to a certain level of achievement a good deal can be achieved (in motivated students) by self-correction, but before long interaction with a trained teacher becomes necessary, either by correspondence or through a computer, or face-to-face, depending on the nature of the skill involved. In many branches of engineering the skills involved will necessitate contact with large equipment so that distance-teaching methods of any kind are of limited use.

Conclusion

The task of matching educational methods to students, to types of courses and to course content is a complex multi-dimensional problem, in which costs inevitably play a large part. Here it has only been possible to touch on some of the principles involved, and in any case a good deal yet needs to be discovered. Each teaching method has a number of possible uses, each course can use a number of teaching methods, for each cohort of students. The mapping from one dimension to another is complex, yet for it to be useful to practising course providers it must be set out simply. Understanding of how best to do this is still in its infancy, but one prediction seems certain: that as continuing engineering education grows – as surely it will – it will change in character as understanding of how to teach it also grows. The present methods, particularly the short residential specialist courses, will surely continue to fulfil their present role. But other methods, for other kinds of courses, to reach other students and a somewhat lower price, are likely to grow up around them. The task of the next few years is to ensure that this growth is efficient and effective and that each educational institution plays its most effective role within the overall enterprise.

21 Continuing Education in Management

Christopher Higgins

The Nature and Structure of Continuing Education in Management

What do we mean by continuing education in management? Some authorities restrict this to post-experience courses which do not lead to any sort of qualification. There is a vast range of such courses. To quote Professor R.J. Ball (Ball 1983): 'Within continuing education itself there is an infinite range of different programmes, for senior managers, middle managers, specialist managers, young managers, or groups of managers in-house.' With this definition, continuing management education in Britain is characterized by considerable heterogeneity. Thus perhaps two dozen universities offer such courses, so do many establishments in the further education sector, while there are also the private management education institutions such as Ashridge and Henley. Indeed, a complete list would include consultants and industrial organizations such as Unilever and the British Steel Corporation, which have large in-house educational activities.

However, in the context of this book and of the conference 'Education for the Professions', it would appear appropriate to extend the definition of continuing education for management. We shall define continuing education as the broadening and updating educational activities carried out during an individual's professional career. In the past, the vast bulk of these activities have not led to any formal university-level qualification but recent developments in university management schools now make it appropriate to include both part-time MBA programmes (Master in Business Administration) and part-time research for higher degrees, viz. MSc, MPhil, and PhD/DPhil.

If, as many of us believe, management education should be regarded as education for a profession, then such part-time degree qualifications are part of the professionalization process. Even if one does not subscribe to this view, the qualifications have considerable merit in their own right, not only as indicators of certain levels of knowledge and skill acquisition, but also as passports to an increasing number of management posts in the public and private sectors.

The research degrees will also complement the existing output of full-time research degrees in various branches of management and, again in a professional context, will tend to be assets to those who wish to pursue careers as teachers of management, particularly in the university, and increasingly in the polytechnic, sectors. Universities are particularly well equipped to carry out the updating and broadening process in view of their particular research interests and the development of special teaching materials such as case studies, and the experience of faculty in consulting to a wide range of organizations on a variety of different management problems. The polytechnics too have made a substantial contribution, in some cases for longer periods than many university departments, through short courses and, not least, via the Diploma in Management Studies, which is available in many departments on a part-time (day-release, evenings or a combination of the two) basis.

This chapter takes for granted the existing work in university and polytechnic management and business studies schools and departments in education to first degree level (eg BSc Business Studies) and to full-time postgraduate level (eg MBA, MSc Management Studies and research degrees). But it should be noted that a substantial number of people on full-time MBA courses will have given up technical or management careers for a year in, say, their late twenties to mid-thirties, to enhance their professional abilities and prospects by this form of education.

Short Courses

Short courses in management have been on offer in Britain for the last fifty years or so, although not on the scale that they have been made available in the United States. The real growth in this country has been in the last twenty or so years, partly stimulated by the Franks Report which led to the setting up of the London and Manchester Business Schools, and by parallel developments in the universities, the polytechnic sector, companies, and some government departments and public sector agencies and nationalized industries. The Civil Service Staff College represented a specific attempt by government to establish a centre for administrative and managerial training on a post-experience basis. The Administrative Staff College at Henley (now The Management College) had also operated on a purely post-experience basis until the early 1970s when they linked up with Brunel University and began to put on part-time Masters programmes and to establish a research function.

In the university sector the post-experience market is largely catered for by London, Manchester, Aston, Bradford, Strathclyde, smaller university management schools like Oxford and Durham, and certain more specialized departments, eg Lancaster's Department of Operational Research and Imperial College's Department of Management Sciences. Indeed, the segmentation of the market reflects one of the main difficulties in 'management' as a profession, namely that managers may come from a variety of disciplines including engineering and accountancy which already have their own professional institutions. A number of other branches of management have progressively developed on a professional institutional basis, eg personnel managers and operational researchers and, although more peripheral, computer scientists. These developments are to some extent reflected in the structure of post-experience activities throughout British universities. Thus, a number of departments which would not claim to be management studies, but which are highly competent in a given branch of the field, will contribute towards the continuing education of specialists. However, it should also be noted that several of the larger university management schools offer a portfolio of short courses for the experienced manager which range from general management courses through to more specialized offerings, eg to update the financial director in the latest advances in investment appraisal or inflation accounting.

UGC statistics demonstrate that the total volume of university work on management short courses has settled down in recent years to a figure representing about 1500 full-time equivalent students, an extra 20 per cent load on the steady-state undergraduate and postgraduate loads. For example, in 1978/79 the number of full-time equivalent students in business and management studies in British universities was a little under 7550 while the full-time equivalent on continuing education short courses was just over 1450.

Notwithstanding the plateau of the past three or four years, for which the recession may be largely responsible, many of us in the university sector believe that the total market for such short courses still possesses growth potential in the longer term. The recession may have shaken out one or two more marginal activities and, of course, many topics, themes and subject areas are at the end of their product life-cycles. However, the speed of technological change and changes in the socio-political environment create new educational needs for managers at a greater rate than a decade or so ago. The obvious example in the first category is the rapid development of microcomputers. Monitoring the external environment, not only economically but socially and politically, has become more and more important. In all such cases, new knowledge and skills must be acquired by managers if they are to preserve their professional competence and to keep their organizations viable.

It seems probable too that there will continue to be a need for some post-experience courses which are at worst remedial and at best basic in the sense of overcoming sins of omission or commission earlier in some managers' education. Aspects of managerial numeracy continue to need attention in the UK.

New companies will enter the market for 'open' courses as their value is communicated to the many organizations who have never considered helping their managers to develop in this way. Not least, there may be further development of 'in-company' courses by British management schools, reflecting a general shift throughout Western Europe in the last few years from largely open market courses to a mixture of the two varieties, typically in the proportion of 30/70 in-company to open, in terms of course-weeks.

The division of the market between the universities and the further education sector, in particular the colleges grouped under the Regional Management Centres, is a little blurred, but in general the latter group are more concerned with the activities of the more regionally-based companies and with supervisory to middle levels rather than with senior levels of management.

Part-time MBA Courses

The part-time MBA is a relatively recent development, based largely on university management schools, and is now offered at a number of centres nationally including the London and Manchester Business Schools, UMIST, Glasgow, Bradford and Loughborough. A full list is shown in Table 21.1 and it may be inferred that there are a number of different patterns: two years or three years; evenings or part-time day or a combination of the two plus perhaps short blocks of full-time attendance. Moreover, although a common 'core syllabus' could probably be identified across most schools, there are considerable differences in structure, relative times devoted to different subjects, etc. Incidentally, it is because of these differences that the translation of the unexceptionable principle of transferable credits into practice may be so difficult to attain.

The experience of the author's own management school in planning and launching such a programme will be briefly cited. The school had a decade's experience of running a successful one-year full-time MBA course. Market assessment suggested an untapped demand in the Yorkshire region for a part-time version and a structure was designed (Table 21.2).

Table 21.1   Part-time Masters Degrees at University Management Schools

		Taught Master's Programme (MBA or similar) Part-time
1	University of Bath, School of Management	MSc (3 yrs)
2	Queen's University of Belfast, Department of Business Studies	MBA (DBA + 2 yrs)
3	University of Bradford, Management Centre	MBA (3 yrs)
4	Brunel University/The Management College, Henley	MSc (2 yrs)
5	City University Business School	MBA (2 yrs)
6	Cranfield School of Management	MBA (2 yrs)
7	Durham University Business School	MSc (2 yrs)
8	Glasgow University, Department of Management Studies	MBA (3 yrs) MSc (3 yrs)
9	London Business School	MBA (3 yrs)
10	Loughborough University of Technology, Department of Management Studies	MSc (2 yrs)
11	Manchester Business School	MBA (DBA + 1 yr)
12	UMIST, Department of Management Sciences	MSc (3 yrs)
13	University of Sheffield, Division of Economic Studies	MBA (2 or 3 yrs) MA (2 or 3 yrs)
14	Strathclyde Business School	MBA (3 yrs)

Table 21.2   Structure of the part-time MBA programme at Bradford

Year	Autumn School	Term 1	Term 2	Term 3
	Days			
1	1 Introduction 2 Introduction 3 Finance 4 Managerial Economics 5 Marketing	Managerial Economics Statistics 1	Marketing 1 Statistics 2 (Including Computer Programming)	Organizational Behaviour Financial Management 1
2	Production Management	Marketing 2 Financial Management 2	Industrial Relations & Personnel Management Science	Business Policy International Business
3	1 Dissertation Workshop 2 Dissertation Workshop 3 Dissertation Workshop 4 Society & Management 5 Society & Management	Dissertation ⟶ Society & Management		

Note: This schedule provides similar contact hours to the full-time programme and permits equivalent coverage of the key general management subject areas while providing time for the required short (15,000 words) dissertation in the third year.

The target intake figure of forty students was readily achieved in 1982, the first year, and the 1983 quota of thirty was met six months before the new intake. The problem is not the demand but is the resources which the parent university can provide. The profile of the successful 1982 applicants is shown in Table 21.3.

Table 21.3   Bradford part-time MBA student profile

Average Age	33 years
Age Range	25-50 years
Men/Women (%)	88/12
Private/Public Sector (%)	74/26
Sources of Finance (%)	
Self only	9
Self and Employer	24
Employer only	67

We were interested and gratified to note the following features:

i   Among the private sector group, both large 'blue-chip' multinationals and smaller, locally-based firms were well represented.
ii In both public and private sectors, the high level of employer involvement in the financing of candidates indicates strong support for the concept of the programme.
iii At the individual student level, all the major specialist functions were in evidence. Job titles ranged from Group Personnel Manager to Marketing Manager; from Works Manager to Company Secretary: from Production Engineer to Accounts Executive. Several students had board level responsibilities, including two chief executives.

We have found these students, with their fine and diverse blend of experience and skills, a lively and committed group. Teaching them is both highly demanding and very rewarding. We learn much from them too. Finally, it may be worth noting that at present the number of British MBAs emerging each year from full-time courses is of the order of 800. The author would estimate that in a couple of years' time the part-time MBA output will be of the order of a further 200 to 300 graduates per annum nationally.

Effectiveness of Continuing Education Programmes

Measurement of the effectiveness of continuing education programmes is a major problem. One method is to determine the objectives of the students and participants on such programmes and then to ask them how well the programmes met those objectives.

For example, Crotty (1974) investigated the effectiveness of North Eastern University's MBA and Management Development Programmes (MDP) via a questionnaire survey of three years' graduates. Ninety-four MBA and 117 management development programme participants responded to the questionnaire. The objectives of the people attending are shown in Table 21.4. The study included an investigation of the impact of various areas of study and it was found that both the MBA and the MDP groups rated financial management and human relations as the highest impact subject areas.

Table 21.4   Objectives of attendance* (Crotty Study)

Stated Objective	Average Scores	
	MBA	MDP
Broadened background for general management	4.6	4.6
Broadened thinking about other areas of business	4.4	4.2
Updating and rethinking of management problems and techniques	4.1	4.3
Broadened base of knowledge for decision-making and to supplement experience	4.1	4.1
Career advance through greater knowledge and responsibility	4.1	4.0
Specific subject matter: finance, economics, marketing, planning, personnel, etc.	3.8	3.7
Prestige of attending	3.9	4.5
Personal reasons of self-development, re-exposure to academic life, etc.	3.5	3.7
Reinforcement of existing knowledge	3.0	4.0

* First stated objective was ranked 5, a second objective 4, etc. to provide appropriate rank order weighting. These were then divided by the number of replies in each ranking to arrive at an average score.

An attempt was made to measure personal growth effects categorized under professional, analytical, ethical, and strictly personal, eg broadening thinking, awareness of wider problems, confidence in one's own ability, independence of thought and judgement, acceptance of other points of view. Apart from these sorts of measures, respondents were also asked what relationships existed between their attending MBA or MDP programmes and their salary increases, promotion, increased responsibilities and new career prospects. Over half the MBAs saw the programme as enhancing their prospects either of promotion within the organization or of a new career. Approximately 40 per cent saw the MBA as helping with salary increases and added job responsibilities.

It is now fairly common practice in Britain to assess the satisfaction of participants and employers with short post-experience courses in a similar fashion to the Crotty study just summarized. In other words, each participant is asked to relate his satisfaction, or otherwise, with the course to his original objectives and expectations. An interesting study carried out by R. Stuart and J. Burgoyne (1977) primarily focused on the intended and actual overall effect of management development programmes, based on research in studying and following up the participants from a sample of fifteen different programmes. Two or three-hour unstructured interviews were carried out with each of the organizers of the fifteen programmes, each organizer being asked about their goals in each of ten areas of managerial skill/quality established in earlier research. The ten skill areas are listed in Table 21.5.

Table 21.5   Relative contributions of various sources of managerial skills to the overall import of deliberate educational interventions (Stuart and Burgoyne Study)

Managerial skill/quality	Percentage of Educational Mentions					
	In-company		Non-company			
	Management courses	Other activities	School	Higher/further education	Management courses	Other activities
Situational facts	25.0	27.8	0	11.1	36.1	0
Professional knowledge	18.4	14.8	0	38.9	25.9	1.9
Sensitivity to events	20.6	8.8	0	17.6	47.1	5.9
Problem-solving/decision-making	10.3	7.7	2.6	53.8	25.6	0
Social skills	6.3	0	0	9.4	65.6	18.8
Emotional resilience	9.1	18.2	0	9.1	54.5	9.1
Proactivity	17.8	11.8	17.6	23.5	23.5	5.9
Creativity	0	0	0	44.4	55.6	0
Mental agility	14.3	4.8	9.5	52.4	4.8	14.3
Balanced learning habits	11.4	5.7	5.7	48.6	22.9	5.7

The second source of data was 157 participants on the fifteen programmes, representing a response rate of 49 per cent. The intention of the questionnaire survey to these participants was first to assess the learning outcomes in the same ten areas specified for learning goals, attributable to programme attendance, and secondly to investigate other sources of learning to which expertise in each of these ten areas was attributable. The sample of fifteen programmes was selected to give an appropriate level of heterogeneity across a number of dimensions of the educational sector; length, qualification or not, and level of participants' managerial experience. For example, six of the fifteen programmes were run in university management schools, three in the further education sector, and six by employers or private organizations. Seven provided a qualification and eight did not. For all fifteen programmes, the learning outcome ranked most highly was 'sensitivity to events', closely followed by 'situational facts' and then by 'problem-solving/decision-making'. In Table 21.6 a summary is given of the high and low ranked goals and outcomes across all fifteen management development programmes.

Table 21.6 Summary of high and low ranked goals and outcomes across 15 management development programmes (Stuart and Burgoyne Study)

Learning	High ranked	Low ranked
Goals	1 Problem-solving/ decision-making 2 Social skills 3 Balanced learning habits 4 Sensitivity to events	10 Situational facts 9 Professional knowledge 8 Proactivity 6 Creativity 6 Mental agility
Outcomes	1 Sensitivity to events 2 Situational facts 3 Problem-solving/decision-making 4 Social skills	10 Mental agility 9 Proactivity 8 Balanced learning habits 7 Creativity

The authors state that the data shown in Table 21.6 'reveal that the learning outcomes are broadly compatible with the goals set by the programme organizers. Thus, whilst positive and negative discrepancies between outcomes and goals certainly exist – that is, the outcomes are ranked greater than (eg sensitivity to events) or less than (eg mental agility) the ranks suggested by the organizers – only in the case of a learning of situational facts and a development of balanced learning habits is the expectation of a close match between outcomes and goals completely erroneous.' The authors underline the unexpectedly high learning of situational facts, which they explain in terms of the study of organization theory revealing hitherto unperceived features of the manager's situation; the value of the project phase particularly within the manager's own organization which puts the manager in contact with data that may be new to him; and the amount of learning of situational facts that comes from the interaction with other participants, particularly out of timetabled hours.

Another aspect of the whole field of assessment and effectiveness is the choice of learning and development methods. Different methods seem to be preferred by students and by teachers for different subjects. Thus, for example, case studies are a very popular method of teaching business policy. Business games are claimed to have an integrative value and are therefore useful in policy/general management learning situations.

In a study carried out by the author (Higgins 1967) of student views on a polytechnic DMS course students ranked case studies as the best of six methods of teaching operational management, whereas they felt that the economic environment and management science were best taught by formal lectures. The full rankings are shown in Table 21.7.

Table 21.7 Student preferences on learning method v. subject area (rank order) (Higgins Study)

Method	Subject Area			
	Operational Management	Personnel Management and Industrial Relations	Economic Environment	Management Science
Formal lecture	2 (3.0)	2 (3.0)	1 (2.2)	1 (1.9)
Private reading	5 (4.0)	3 = (3.2)	2 (2.3)	3 (3.4)
Tutorial/exercise classes	3 = (3.4)	5 (3.7)	3 = (3.4)	2 (2.8)
Case studies	1 (2.8)	3 = (3.2)	5 (4.4)	4 (4.0)
Seminars/discussions	3 = (3.4)	1 (2.6)	3 = (3.4)	5 (4.2)
Management games	6 (4.4)	6 (5.3)	6 (5.4)	6 (4.8)

Learning Innovations in Continuing Education

The part-time MBA, discussed earlier, represents the major programme innovation in the last two or three years in continuing management education. However, learning innovations outside normal course structures merit some discussion. Lupton (1982) recently categorized the processes of learning as shown in Table 21.8.

Table 21.8 Processes of learning (Lupton)

	PASSIVE
Lectures	
Cases	
Reading	
Tutorials	
Syndicates	
Business Games	
Role-play Exercises	
Projects (simulations)	
Projects (live)	
Action Learning	ACTIVE

Author's note: Cases may be read passively (as Lupton implies) but often form the basis for active participation in tutorials and syndicates.

Lupton went on to urge further involvement from the passive to the active modes of learning. Manchester's distinctive contribution at the active end of the scale is the Joint Development Activity (JDA) which was initially developed some fifteen years ago as 'an alternative form of management development to the 3-month full-time mid-career programme for middle managers,' as Morris (1972) put it. Very briefly the process is as follows. The school works with a given organization in which a group of six to ten middle managers, perceived as having good potential, select one or more projects from a list of six to twelve drawn up by a senior management 'steering group'. The projects must offer good development opportunities to the participants, be of definite value to the organization, financially or in other terms, and be handleable within the time constraints, eg a day a week for a year. Examples include: establishing new plant, improving the computer effectiveness, and improving the financial accounting and control systems in a food company. The three projects would be tackled sequentially by an eight-man group. As Morris summarizes it: 'The School's support takes the form of (i) help in maintaining and developing the effectiveness of the project group, taking into account the fact that it is an extremely vulnerable "temporary system", (ii) specialist information and instruction in such activities as marketing, finance, project management, R & D, organization, personnel, production, and operational research, (iii) providing wider contacts for the group where the resources of the School need to be supplemented.'

There is no one model or theory to match JDA work. In another publication Morris (1980) offers a number of models which 'have provided useful orientations to the distinctive kinds of work and learning fostered in joint development activities.' More generally, innovation in management education appears to precede rather than to follow research and the development of appropriate models.

Other management schools have developed their own variants in the live project/action learning field. Although some academics may be reluctant to enter this field out of conservatism or sheer diffidence, perhaps the major constraint on more rapid development is the resource one. Such learning methods are resource-hungry, and university and polytechnic schools with hundreds of undergraduates to teach have to look very carefully at their internal allocations of teaching resources.

Part-time research for higher degrees provides a form of post-experience development for practising managers and most university management schools register some students in this mode. Indeed the University of Bath has made this its distinctive offering rather than short courses or a part-time MBA. Where the match between employer, student and school is good, the results can be mutually rewarding. But to secure a project which is a major aspect of the student's job and will meet the academic criteria for a higher degree by research is not easy: priorities and time-spans are often at variance. In general, therefore, it is difficult to envisage this form of continuing education becoming very significant for those intending to spend their lives as managers.

A third and very different innovation is that of distance learning. Several schools have experimented in this area. Henley have invested heavily in their distance-learning project, developing audio and video-cassettes over five major strands of management: money; people; information; marketing and production; the economic environment and business policy. They are also developing a network of counsellors throughout the UK and constructing a computer data-base at Henley which will be accessible by telephone and will answer further questions about the courses and give the answers to course problems.

Research Issues

This chapter has already implied a number of possible research issues. In general, we still need to discover a good deal more about how managers learn. More particularly, in the context of this chapter, we need to establish the 'added value' of various forms of continuing education more clearly so that we can make meaningful comparisons. The cost/effectiveness of various modes of learning is at best only crudely calculable. We can compute the costs of staging say a two-day course on inflation accounting and that of producing a programmed-learning text or an audio-visual cassette on the same topic. But we cannot be nearly so accurate in our assessment of effectiveness.

If a degree is awarded then we can measure cost/effectiveness in terms of the cost per graduate. We can also attempt to assess the value of the degree in terms of the discounted future earnings of its holder. More generally, therefore, if learning elements such as certain short courses or distance-learning modules contribute towards some form of general management qualification or qualification within a management specialism, eg management accounting, then we may more readily place some sort of value on them which we can relate to their cost.

The field of continuing education also requires, some much more straightforward research, namely market research to establish the educational needs of management. Statements such as 'three-quarters of British managers have received little or no management education or training' need considerable amplification. A good example of such market research is provided by the Yorkshire and Humberside Regional Management Centre's Report (May 1981) on Management Development Needs in that region. They commissioned an outside agency to identify their potential market, surveying no fewer than 312 industrial and public sector establishments and over 15,000 managers. They extrapolated their sample for the region as a whole and estimated, for example, that only 14 per cent of the 70,000 manufacturing managers attended short courses compared with 47 per cent of the 29,000 commercial sector managers and 39 per cent of the 3000 managers in public utilities. Estimates of future business activity, numbers of managers likely to be required and the use of various categories of management development services were obtained for a three-year time horizon: figures were obtained for course-days attendance on qualification courses, external courses and internal courses respectively.

Conclusion

Successful continuing education in management will only come about if the attitudes of employers are favourable and if organizations, individual managers and schools create realistic and fruitful partnerships. To quote from the European Foundation for Management Development Report of the Committee on Educational and Training Needs of European Managers (Pocock Committee 1977):

> Corporations should see that managers are given ample opportunities for self-development. This calls for experience in different jobs and at different levels, training in line with an individual's changing needs, and education, which has a longer term objective. Throughout his working life there should be developed, in discussion and by agreement with him, a phased programme of training and development opportunities extending from recruitment well into his fifties, in the form of 'education permanente'.

It is also very relevant to quote a major conclusion of this report that 'Schools should involve themselves even more with the real, messy world where managers operate, where the ideal solution is a theoretical luxury, where the important thing is to make decisions which are right enough (and right often enough) to get effective results, all within the time available.' By developing an active and substantial continuing education activity the schools benefit themselves, particularly if part of that activity involves them working closely with individual managers and companies, whether on co-operative taught course programmes, on part-time MBA programmes, or on joint development activities of the Manchester sort.

Part 7
Reforms and Innovations

22 Sources and Types of Reform

David Warren Piper

In general terms there are two possible sources of impetus for change in professional education: changes in the profession itself and associated bodies, and changes in the theory and practice of education. It is tempting to assume that the first gives rise to changes in the content and the second to changes in the form of education. In fact that is not so. Apart from form and content often being indivisible (for instance, an instructor is necessarily a role model for some kinds of personnel management), professional bodies can be influential on the form of education (discussions over dinner with senior council at Inns of Court) and educationalists have power to decide the content of their courses. However, for the sake of orderliness the two sources may be considered in turn.

Changes in the Profession

Earlier chapters of this book pondered the definition of a profession. Without re-treading that ground, three distinguishing characteristics of a profession need highlighting to reveal possible areas of reform in training and education. They are: receipt of payment, reliance on a body of theory, and independence. Indeed, these three provide an hierarchy which distinguishes the more from the less noble professions. At the lower end only the matter of payment — and what follows from it — distinguishes the professional from the amateur. Sports, the stage, music and prostitution are examples of activities which, if it were not for payment, would be regarded as recreation. At the middle level the professional is characterized by having to deal with unique and at least partially unforseeable circumstances. Thus she or he cannot work by rote but must first analyse or diagnose, then either summon up or create possible courses of action or treatment and choose one, and thirdly, either execute, or ensure that others execute, the chosen course of action. Managers, officers in the armed forces, administrative-grade civil servants, school-teachers, nurses and most engineers fall into this category. All of those people work within an organization, serve its ends and are responsible to those senior to them. At the 'noble' end of the professional scale the individual has a third distinction added to the other two. That is, their first allegiance is to their calling rather than to their employer. Often they work outside organizations, either as individuals or as colleagues in a practice. The purpose of such groupings of professionals is to enhance the support each individual has without detracting from their individual freedom or responsibility. When a professional in this league is employed within a commercial or a public organization (a ship's doctor, a company's lawyer) he or she does not form part of the line management and nobody in the company can do more than to seek their advice or administration.

Typically, the noble professions rely very heavily on the individual working to a code of ethics backed up by a professional body that takes corporate responsibility for protecting the public against incompetent or dishonest practice. The two main means by which they seek to maintain confidence and trustworthiness is by control of training, and by the right of the individual to practise, using the appropriate epithet. Into this group of professions falls medicine, the law, architecture, and recently, speech therapists.

In reality things are not quite as neat as the three stage hierarchy would suggest. For example, nurses may not operate as independent agents but do carry a personal responsibility for ethical judgements and, on occasion, independence of action is granted as a personal right (as when a nurse refuses to administer certain prescriptions or declines to assist at an abortion). Despite untidinesses, however, these three defining characteristics exist and each has a direct implication for education and training.

The simple fact of being paid, for instance, requires the professional sportsman or actor, however much they love the play and need adulation, to continue even when the fun has faded. This calls for technique and emotional protection less necessary for the amateur, and gives rise, among other things, to the 'professional foul'.

The second key characteristic of the profession is that action is not guided by precept but rather by a body of theory. A typical sequence is as follows. First the professional is faced with a highly complex situation and calls upon theory to make an interpretation. This usually involves giving greater significance to some information above some other, and the searching out of other important but not immediately apparent information which the theory suggests is both possible and critical. The theory makes sense of what otherwise would be a mass of unconnected observations. The second step is either to create possible responses or solutions to the problems or to choose from a stock of unoriginal solutions. Either way, judgement is required which may be technical, ethical, political, commercial, aesthetic or whatever else is seen as appropriate to the profession or desirable by the individual. This second step implies an element of evaluation; or rather two elements. The first is of the solution chosen, judgement of which entails reference to the theory used to perceive the nature of the original problem. The second is of the process by which the solution was arrived at (the strategies used to generate solutions and the way in which the choice was made). The third step concerns the implementation of the solution or treatment or course of action chosen. This may or may not be undertaken personally by the professional. The surgeon does his own knife-work, but an architect supervises a builder. Steps two and three imply the acquisition of a repertoire as part of the training and step three implies skills either of execution or supervision.

This analysis of the stages in work typical of the professions reveals various areas of possible change which would call for appropriate reforms in education. Before moving on to that, however, we have the third characteristic of the noble professions, that is of being responsible to no one except fellow professionals. In particular we must pay attention to those professions which set up professional bodies to ensure monopoly of practice and control of access in exchange for guaranteeing proper training and competent ethical practice.

We are now in a position to identify the types of reform that might arise from changes in the profession. A change from amateur (unpaid) to professional status (paid) may call for changes in the content of training or indeed lead to the initiation of training courses, but it is at the 'higher' level within professions that the most interesting possibilities for change exist. There can be changes in each of the steps in professional problem-solving described above.

First, there can be shifts in the types of problem. Not only do new technologies bring forward new problems requiring professional expertise (designing computer systems) but they can also eradicate problems: for instance dental caries are largely a product of western diet; if we applied all we knew now about their prevention, fewer dentists (at least as we know and love them) would be required. Second, without there being a change in the actual problem there can be a change in its perception. Such a shift is occurring in nursing training for developing countries. A person who is perhaps the sole provider of medical treatment in one thousand square miles of Africa containing only rural communities not only needs to know different things from a European nurse but is going to act by different ethical standards and undertake tasks which in Europe would constitute trespass into the doctors' areas of practice. Such shifts of perception can be slow in coming. Third, theory can reveal situations amenable to treatment where before no problem was percieved or was simply regarded as bad luck. For instance, greater theoretical knowledge in recent years in the field of psychology has given rise to student counsellors.

Other changes, while not affecting the problem, do affect the solutions available. Technical developments are the most obvious, widening the potential repertoire of doctors, managers, engineers, teachers — in fact, just about everybody. Social changes however can also affect the repertoire. General medical practitioners, for example, have to adapt their treatment to patients as they become more sophisticated, richer, and more socially secure; not only can the treatments change but the treated can change too.

If the solutions available change, so do the bases upon which they are chosen. Ethical changes lead to different treatments of difficult prisoners, to new solutions to the accumulation of nuclear waste or the demand for ambergris. On a more personal level, the general political and aesthetic climate affects individual professionals' everyday choices.

Yet other changes can occur in the execution of solutions. There may be a change in a profession's monopoly in administering a particular treatment: for instance it has been suggested that as drilling and filling teeth is more a skilled craft than a true professional activity, dentists could delegate that kind of treatment to dental assistants — much as most dentists now delegate the making of false teeth to specialist technicians (although some dental courses still teach all students how to do it). Changes in the scale of solutions — semi-detached houses to tower blocks, estates to new towns — can quite alter the management problems involved in their execution and if these remain under the control of the professional then scale too has obvious implications for training.

The possible changes listed in the last four paragraphs relate progressively to stages in the problem-solving process. In so far as professional education trains students in each of the stages in problem-solving, any of the changes described above would call for reform of the curriculum.

Changes in the end-product of education, in this case the qualified professional, are seldom achieved by changes in the syllabus alone. Chapters in this book have examined access (recruitment and selection) curricula, teaching methods, accreditation, validation and evaluation. Professional bodies usually concern themselves with all these elements of education, but as they are all interdependent, interference with any one of them usually necessitates change to all. A charming example of recruitment policy directly affecting the syllabus occurred when the British army started to enlist in its officer corps people other than from the nobility and landed gentry; they found they had to teach them how to behave like gentlemen (Dixon 1976).

One noticeable trend in professional training is what might be called 'academicization'. Not only do professions drift towards the higher education system (nursing and speech therapy are recent recruits to the degree-giving professions), but within a profession emphasis gets placed on the high status, abstract and academic parts of the syllabus, often to the detriment of competent professional practice. Two engineering examples will illustrate the point.

The first example concerns an undergraudate course in polymer science. The lecturer responsible had written a list of forty-one objectives. A preliminary analysis of the key verbs used revealed the frequency distribution shown in Table 22.1.

Table 22.1

Verb	Frequency
describe	15
outline	9
DERIVE	6
define	4
DISTINGUISH	2
PREDICT	2
list	1
state	1
ESTIMATE	1

The verbs in lower case suggest a theoretical or academic task. Of these there are thirty. The verbs in capitals could be applied skills although not necessarily so. Of these there are eleven. Such a frequency count gives the first hint of a drift to abstract academic conceptions even on a course that is basically a professional and practical one. A closer analysis of two of the objectives will illustrate the drift. Two read as follows:

a   Outline quantitatively, and with examples, why polymers based on different nominers have different physical and other properties.

b   Describe the amorphous and partially crystalline states for polymers and their significance in terms of mechanical processing and other properties.

Discussion with the lecturer concerned produced more precise objectives subsumed within these two. Students should, the lecturer explained, be able to choose an appropriate polymer with which to make some mechanical part, provided the performance specification for that part were pre-determined. This is a statement of a practical skill; when designing a complicated piece of machinery the engineer must be able to choose the appropriate materials from which to make the various parts, taking into account such factors as weight, stress, elasticity and so on. In the course, however, this objective had been made rather more abstract. A student, the lecturer went on, should, given a nominer, be able to speculate on its properties and the properties of its derivatives. Pushed further, he suggested that students should be able to say by heart the properties of ten common polymers. However, further discussion revealed that the properties of any polymer could be discovered by using a catalogue, possibly with guidance from a chemist, and indeed, that these were the circumstances under which the students would operate, once qualified. This led to a further defining of objectives. The students should perhaps learn how to ask a chemist appropriate questions and get answers in a usable form. They should also be able to use any given catalogue. Discussion of this point suggested that students should know the weaknesses of the catalogue and should be able to relate the weaknesses of any catalogue to the category system upon which it was based. The final statement of this objective was that 'a student should be able to take any catalogue, deduce the category system upon which it was based and identify any inherent weaknesses in that category of system.' It will be noted that this last formulation is a highly intellectual educational objective, calling for a good deal of abstract thought and analysis on the part of the student. In one way this discussion led to that part of the course becoming more academic or at least to the intellectual level being raised. Yet the primary practical objective of increasing the student's abilty to design, had been retained; further, this practical objective could be built specifically into both the teaching and the assessment of student progress.

The first example illustrates how a key skill, designing, had been omitted in favour of listing information which it was felt an individual should be able to recall. Perhaps in the first instance the knowledge was regarded as a prerequisite to developing the skill. Yet gaining knowledge (rather than developing a skill) came to be seen as a more prestigious form of learning; it is unlikely to be confused with that undertaken by tradesmen. With the burgeoning of electronic information systems must come a radical reappraisal of what it is worth teaching people in order that they might use the unique features of the human brain to best advantage. Clearly, trying to use the brain as a substitute for vast data banks is not one of those features (see for instance Pritchard 1982). Technological changes of this kind cannot take away from human beings responsibility for the three basic stages of problem-solving — perceiving the problem, creating or choosing the solution, and implementing the solution. The teaching of problem-solving or designing (for they are much the same) as a process therefore comes to the fore. This is becoming a growing practice, first in industrial design, then in architecture, now in engineering. Such professional training concentrates on competence in the process of analysis, creation of solutions, evaluation of solutions, and management.

The second example, illustrating such an approach, is provided by the Department of Chemical Engineering at Imperial College in which each of the steps listed above is practised and evaluated separately. Thus the course focuses on the process of problem-solving and its attendant skills, rather than on the solution of a range of common engineering problems. The students are evaluated on the skills they develop, not simply on the merit of the engineering solution they present. Students are first taken stage-by-stage through a relatively simple design problem. They then work in teams on projects, again taking the task a stage at a time. They first explore differing ways in which a problem might be cast and are introduced to a scheme by which various ways of posing the same problem can be arranged in order of their generality. The students are led to an understanding of how the terms in which a problem is set influences both the range of solutions admissible and the criteria of success to be applied to the final solution. This leads directly to an exercise in negotiating a design-brief with a client and writing a brief that will form a feasible basis for a contract.

The students then move on to creativity exercises designed to widen the range of solutions they devise; their work at this stage carries marks for the diversity of solutions they can outline. Next, the students are required to present a written rationale for selecting from among their possible solutions. In so doing they have to make explicit their view of the relationship between measurable criteria (eg financial costs) and value judgements (eg political acceptability).

When the teams present their solutions in the conventional way they also have to present an analysis of how their group members have worked together. This report picks up from some earlier exercises on group dynamics and marks are awarded to groups which have improved the effectiveness and efficiency of their team work.

The educational strategy is to concentrate attention on a number of professional skills which are crucial to the practitioner but which do not appear in the conventional engineering syllabus (the strategy's subject matter being the engineer rather than the engine.)

Changes in Education and Training

Educational institutions are, of course, as subject as any part of society to general changes in social values. In both employment and education there has been a longer-term shift in the relationship between manager and worker, teacher and taught. It is a move towards a kind of egalitarianism which, if it does not dismantle hierarchies, at least does more to preserve the esteem of those lower in the order. Partly this change is ideological, closely related, no doubt, to improvements in communication and the widespread education which followed, but it is also technical, in the sense that the early studies of industrial psychology showed how production could be raised by giving employees greater freedom to decide their goals and methods of work (eg Koch and French 1947). These lessons were not lost on education, and much modern theory, even of the most mechanistic kind of psychology, recognizes the importance of the learner's emotional identification with a desired goal. For the behaviourists this means ensuring that both staff and students foresee and describe the goal, thus first allowing it to be shared, and second, allowing goal attainment to be associated with immediate reward. Thus Fred Keller, one of the pioneers of independent learning, in which students work alone at their own pace through a highly organized and pre-packaged course, wrote: '(The course designers) had the goal of maximising rewards for educational behaviour, minimising chances of extinction (forgetting) and frustration, eliminating punishment and fear' (Keller 1968).

This concern with the emotional as well as the intellectual aspects of learning was, as one might expect, emphasized even more by those psychologists whose professional work centred on counselling. Carl Rogers claimed: 'Learning is facilitated when the student participates responsibly in the learning process. When he chooses his own directions, helps to discover his own learning resources, formulates his own problems, decides his own course of action, lives with the consequences of each of these choices, then significant learning is maximised' (Rogers 1969).

A large ethical shift of this kind, which concerns who is responsible for what, has considerable impact not only on the way in which education is conducted, but on how the very nature of education is conceived and so, in turn, on which research questions seem interesting. It also presents, four square, a challenge to any profession which perceives professional training as a process of passing on 'the mysteries' and whose courses consequently grow ever more cumbersome and unmanageable as they attempt the impossible and futile task of 'covering the ground'.

Take first the impact on education and its close cousin, research: the ethical shift to greater independence coincides with a greater economic need to reduce staff/student ratios, not only because more people are entering higher and professional education, but because education in technologically advanced countries gets relatively more costly unless it too replaces increasingly expensive manpower with machinery; thus the development of 'education-at-a-distance', private-study packages, computer-assisted learning and automatic marking. If such systems are cheaper per student to run than chalk-and-talk, they are more expensive to set up in the first place. Fewer people are needed to write the courses and they can be the best people available; but to capitalize on the outlay, the material must be used by as many students as possible. This has at least two implications for professional training. First, the political control and the financing of courses change considerably. Second, there is pressure to write common core courses for related professions. This pressure runs counter to the tendency for every branch of engineering, or medicine, or social service to have its own professional body demanding discrete courses. As it were, the Oxbridge rather than the Imperial College approach to the engineering curriculum is indicated: that is, concentration on generally applicable theory and higher level skills rather than early specialization in a particular branch of engineering.

The second impact of the ethical shift in the relative responsibilities of teacher and taught is on the very conception of education. If students are to work more on their own (or if they are to·be given greater powers to negotiate their courses) then more needs to be known about the process of learning. The behaviourism of the nineteen-sixties and early seventies really gave rise to theories of instruction rather than of learning. Success was reflected in measures of how much a student learned (expressed in objectives), and the teacher's task was that of a manager of situations creating those conditions under which the objectives were most quickly achieved: that is, with frequent feed-back, minimization of error, over-practice, active use of all students' sense modalities, and so on. The 'Keller Plan' of self-study packages (adopted for instance at the University of Surrey) is a rigorous application of all these principles (Elton, Boud and Nutall 1973).

In the seventies educational theory became interested in how students learn rather than the conditions which produce learning, and in what students learn rather than how much is learned. Four interwoven strands of theory may be identified: cognitive processes, intellectual development, creativity and personality theory. All of these have implications for the way professional education is undertaken, how the progress of students is reckoned, and what relative importance is given to various parts of the curriculum.

In this country, Gordon Pask (1976) has studied cognitive strategies which people adopt when faced with the complex intellectual task of putting discrete and incomplete data into some form of organized pattern so as to make sense of it. He identifies various strategies and he points to the difficulties which occur when there is a mis-match between the strategies adopted by teacher and taught. He describes, for instance, people who habitually collect information, relating each new piece to what they possess already. In this way, detail by detail, they build up a complete picture. Others hypothesize on the nature of the overall picture and try sketching in its main features early on. Information thereafter is used either to fill out the scheme or to reject the first grand conception.

In Sweden, Marton and his colleagues (Marton and Saljo 1976; Svensson 1977) have studied the ways in which students make sense of the material they read, distinguishing those who try to memorize from those who try to reorganize information. Those who struggle to reproduce what authors say, and similarly try to learn by heart their lecture notes, tend to do poorly in examinations (although not necessarily in short answer or multiple choice questions). It may seem blindingly obvious; but if so, why is so little done to identify and correct this common crippling condition? How does the notion of such ineffective study habits come to be so firmly implanted in students' minds; could it be that they have actually learned to do it that way as a direct result of experience in the educational regimes provided for them? Kolb (1976, 1981), in America, has studied learning styles. He and his colleagues have developed a descriptive scheme based on two basic dimensions of abstract-concrete thought and active-reflective experience. These two parameters, when set one against the other, produce four quadrants which are typifed by 'convergent' and 'divergent' learners, 'assimilators' and 'accommodators'.

All this work suggests at least two points important for higher level education: first, the need to accommodate to individual differences which, if ignored, result in some people appearing less clever than they are; second, the fact that learning is a skill, itself open to training.

One reason why educational theory has seemed irrelevant to professional educators is that it was concerned with children (and seemingly based on the study of rats). In the seventies there was a significant move towards paralleling pedagogy ('leading boys') with andragogy ('leading men'). Intellectual development is no longer assumed to stop somewhere in the mid-teens. William Perry (1970), for instance, has described nine levels of intellectual sophistication, moving from a belief in absolute truth, through a grasp of relativism and of the importance of context to knowledge, to a dynamic ethical commitment to a system of knowledge. Perry's description of this journey from dualism to commitment, is summarized in Table 22.2. Not all make the journey smoothly: some never start, some waver midway, some escape, others retreat.

Knowles (1978) has identified distinct differences between the assumptions made about the ways in which children and adults learn (Table 22.3) and the educational regimes which are appropriate (Table 22.4). It is also significant that a book of such wide scope as *The Modern American College* (Chickering 1981), a review of all the current major

Table 22.2   Scheme of cognitive and ethnical development

Position 1	Authorities know, and if we work hard, read every word, and learn Right Answers, all will be well.
Transition	But what about those Others I hear about? And different opinions? And Uncertainties? Some of our own Authorities disagree with each other or don't seem to know, and some give us problems instead of Answers.
Position 2	True Authorities must be Right, the others are frauds, We remain Right. Others must be different and Wrong. Good Authorities give us problems so we can learn to find the Right Answer by our own independent thought.
Transition	But even Good Authorities admit they don't know all the answers yet!
Position 3	Then some uncertainties and different opinions are real and legitimate temporarily, even for Authorities. They're working on them to get to the Truth.
Transition	But there are so many things they don't know the Answers to! And they won't for a long time.
Position 4a	Where Authorities don't know the Right Answers, everyone has a right to his own opinion; no one is wrong!
Transition (and/or)	But some of my friends ask me to support my opinions with facts and reasons.
Transition	Then what right have They to grade us? About what?
Position 4b	In certain courses Authorities are not asking for the Right Answer; They want us to think about things in a certain way, supporting opinion with data. That's what they grade us on.
Transition	But this 'way' seems to work in most courses, and even outside them.
Position 5	Then all thinking must be like this, even for Them, Everything is relative but equally valid. You have to understand how each context works. Theories are not Truth but metaphors to interpret data with. You have to think about your thinking.
Transition	But if everything is relative, am I relative too? How can I know I'm making the Right Choice?
Position 6	I see I'm going to make my own decisions in an uncertain world with no one to tell me I'm Right.
Transition	I'm lost if I don't. When I decide on my career (or marriage or values) everything will straighten out.
Position 7	Well, I've made my first Commitment!
Transition	Why didn't that settle everything?
Position 8	I've made several commitments, I've got to balance them – how many, how deep? How certain, how tentative?
Transition	Things are getting contradictory. I can't make logical sense out of life's dilemmas.
Position 9	This is how life will be. I must be wholehearted while tentative, fight for my values yet respect others, believe my deepest values right yet be ready to learn. I see that I shall be retracing this whole journey over and over – but, I hope, more wisely.

Source: Perry 1981

advances in thinking about higher education, should take as its unifying theme a model of the human life-cycle focusing on maturation and ageing.

Table 22.3   Comparison of assumptions made in the education of children (pedagogy) and the education of adults (andragogy)

Characteristics of the Student	Pedagogy	Andragogy
Expectation of own role	Dependency	Increasing self-directiveness
Previous experience	Of little worth as resource for learning	Learners are a rich resource
Readiness to learn	Principally dependent on biological development and the tasks involved	Greatly determined by changing social roles in them
Time perspective	Postponed application	Immediate application
Orientation to learning	Subject centred	Problem centred

Source: Knowles 1978, p.110

Table 22.4   Comparison of educational regimes associated with pedagogy and andragogy

Aspects of Regime	Pedagogy	Andragogy
Climate	Autocratic, formal, competitive	Mutual, respectful, collaborative, informal
Planning	By teacher	Some form of negotiation
Diagnosis of learning needs	By teacher	Mutual self-diagnosis
Formulation of learning of	By teacher	By negotiation
Course design	Based on an internal rationale of subject matter, with the course divided into sections according to subject content	Course sequenced to reflect the readiness and immediate needs of learner, and divided into units organized around problems

Table 22.4 Cont.

Learning/Teaching methods	Transmittal techniques of teaching	Experiential learning and techniques of inquiry
Evaluation	Assessment of student by teacher	Mutual re-diagnosis of needs and evaluation of programme

Source: Knowles 1978, p.110

The implications of cognitive and developmental theories are immense. They all bring attention back to the intellectual structure of the subject matter being taught at the higher education level. Whereas in the common view of professional training the roots of rationality might perhaps too easily be seen as grounded in the nature of the subject itself, this psychological view of learning reminds us that the intellectual foundations of all subjects are the cognitive processes of the human brain and that it is these very processes which need to be trained. This insight has two immediate effects. First, it relieves us of the need to think of courses in terms of facts that have to be known, and thus gives an escape from the ever-expanding syllabus designed to cover an ever-increasing field of knowledge. Second, it provides a quite different set of criteria by which to reckon educational progress. For instance, Perry's nine stages of development can equally well be applied in an engineering and in a medical course. What is even more striking is that the scheme necessarily faces teacher and student alike with the need to come to grips with those ethical decisions of professional practice which are absolutely central to the life of the practitioner but so often peripheral to the 'academicized' university course. (For instance, students may be asked to choose the quickest and most 'efficient' procedure for decontaminating a chemical plant without including consideration of the risks to personnel.)

Similarly, theories of creativity and problem-solving focus attention on the central activity of all professions; that is, devising responses to unique situations. The problem-solving models allow a separation of the various stages — problem definition, solution, solution implementation and evaluation — so that the weak links in the chain may be identified and strengthened as individual students progress. Again, the evaluation of students' solutions to problems raises ethical questions and matters of social value not always amenable to the slide-rule. The theory of creativity points to tricky educational problems in devising courses in which both discipline and creativeness must be fostered but each thrives in almost diametrically opposed and seemingly incompatible educational regimes. Just how poorly educators have identified and tackled this problem is reflected in the fact that, taken as a whole, science teaching favours the introverted, conforming, and often anxious students above the independently minded, sensitive and aesthetically aware (Entwistle and Wilson 1977). There is no evidence that the latter make poor scientists; in fact anecdote would suggest the opposite. Yet they apparently make unsuccessful science students. The inference hardly needs pointing out.

If creativity is related to cognitive processes on one side, on the other side it touches closely on personality theory. The effective manager, army commander or engineer typically has those attributes summed up by the term 'creative personality'. It is an effectiveness which goes beyond mere technical competence. It is essentially a matter of personality rather than intellect. That is not to say that it is inborn and immutable. Most of the basic and persistent personality traits are formed in early childhood but later training can help individuals to overcome incapacitating psychopathology, or at least avoid situations in which their judgements or behaviour become suspect. It is to say, however, that the key to success in professional life lies not only in the intellect and in knowledge but, just as importantly, in the perceptual predilections and emotional responses of the individual.

Incompetence is not always easy to study as its effects are often undramatic: new projects do not flourish; routines carry daily business forward. Initiatives may not be taken, but by the same token the opportunity for taking them may not be made evident by the uncreative person. Things may stagnate and wither. In one area of human endeavour however, incompetence has a very dramatic, historically important and usually high public effect. That is in the armed forces. Projects do not just wither; people die, often in their thousands.

Norman Dixon (1976, p.287) in his book *On the Psychology of Military Incompetence*, draws an important distinction between irrational authoritarianism and rational authoritarianism. By the latter is meant the readiness to accept and obey the dictates of rational authority. An irrational antipathy towards all authority, as evidenced in some cases of student militancy, may be just as neurotic and non-adaptive as a predisposition towards irrational authoritarianism. The common denominator of irrational authoritarianism and blind anarchy is that both states of mind are compulsive and derive from underlying ego-pathology. So-called rational authoritarianism is better referred to as 'autocratic behaviour'. Whereas the autocrat exercises tight control when the situation demands it, the authoritarian is himself tightly controlled no matter what the external situation.

This distinction has direct relevance to all professions and to professional education. The authoritarian personality is the antithesis of the creative one, its most consistent characteristics being as follows:

1 Authoritarians are comfortable in (rather than at the top of) an hierarchy; they obey those above and demand to be obeyed by those below.

2 They are socially conforming, often with a rigid conformity to some idealized moral authority.

3 They are aggressive, and ready to condemn, reject or punish people who violate convention. They are thus very chauvinistic and apt to be racially, sexually and class discriminatory.

4 They are opposed to the subjective and suspicious of imaginative and tender-minded people.

5 They have a well-developed sense of fate and destiny and confuse belief with fact; they tend to believe that wild and dangerous things go on in the world.

6 They are disposed to think in rigid categories.

7 They are preoccupied with power and shows of toughness.

8 Their destructiveness and cynicism leads easily to vilification of human beings and, although sometimes courting popularity through their manner, in the final analysis they do not care for the people in their charge and will neglect their needs and blame them when things go wrong.

9 They often show a prurient interest in sexual 'goings-on'.

Dixon points out that on the whole authoritarians are more dishonest, more irresponsible, more untrustworthy, more suspicious and more conforming than non-authoritarians. They also tend to promote sycophants rather than competent juniors. It follows that they are unlikely to make successful leaders (and teachers). However, they are likely to rise in organizations which value conformity, reward obedience and admire toughness. Possibly the armed services are not the only organizations which do just that.

We must consider personality and its effect on competence in two areas. First, in the professions themselves. What can be done to spot authoritarians and prevent them from taking high command? At an earlier stage what can be done in their training to help ameliorate the worst effects of their psychopathology? Second, within the teaching organizations, What can be done to promote the creative teacher and keep the authoritarian from becoming the director of courses?

Conclusion

I began this chapter by looking to the professions themselves for the impetus for change in professional education. I described the professional, in effect, as a paid problem-solver and I listed developments which could change various stages in the process of understanding problems, thinking up solutions and putting them into effect. I described and illustrated the idea of 'academic drift' applied to designing professional courses. I then gave a second example which illustrated an attempt to come to grips with some of the professional skills of being an engineer which are shouldered out of courses which concentrate solely on the study of the materials and products of engineering.

I then looked for impetus for change in the field of education. Here I traced a shift in concern from the conditions of learning to the intellectual and emotional processes of learning. This corresponds exactly with developments in theory changing a profession's perception of a problem, as described in the first section. I suggested four areas of research and theory in psychology which have a direct impact on both the conception and conduct of education. This brought together studies of thinking, maturation, creativeness and personality. I intimated that all four bear directly on an understanding of problem-solving and how to teach it.

With problem-solving as the binding theme I might allow myself a final observation. Education is also a profession. Educationalists try to solve the problems inherent in helping people to learn. To do so they call on theory, as do other professionals, develop a wide repertoire of skills for producing solutions, as do other professionals. But, unlike other professionals, they have, as yet, little influence on those who actually execute the solutions. The working relationship that actually exists between the person who crafts and delivers a course of professional education and he who studies the process and designs educational procedures is the equivalent neither of the relationship between architect and constructor, nor between biochemist and physician. In theory it is somewhat the same; in practice it is virtually non-existent.

23 Problem-based Professional Education in Medicine

Victor Neufeld and John P. Chong

Problem-based learning is an approach to professional education that represents a clear alternative to subject-based education. It involves the student in the process of defining, analysing and managing problems in order to acquire the competencies required to provide effective, efficient and humane patient care. Here we will briefly review the history of problem-based professional education in medicine, present a rationale for its use, and describe the experience of one programme which has used this approach since its beginnings in 1969: the MD Programme at McMaster University in Hamilton, Ontario, Canada.

History

The notion of using problems or cases as the basis of professional education is not new. Glimpses of it can be detected in the writings and educational practices of great teachers in medicine through the ages. An example is Sir William Osler who maintained that the secret of lifelong learning for medical practitioners was to ask questions about the patients they saw every day, find the answers, and apply this new-found knowledge to the management of patient problems.

The 'case method' pioneered at the Harvard Business School is an example of the concept expressed in basic curricular form. In his description of the method, Christensen says that it is a device to bridge the classroom and the realistics of practice (Christensen 1981):

> Business men have to deal with a daily succession of problem (cases). Why not bring those case problems to the classroom for an apprentice manager's use? What better preparation for business? So was the case method developed first by having businessmen come to the school to talk about their companies' problems, later by sending case researchers into the field to write up these situations.

In medical education, the first institution to use this approach as the basis for an entire curriculum was the MD Programme at McMaster, which admitted its first students in 1969. At that time there were several other medical schools where certain courses were problem-based: for example the 'focal problems' course at Michigan State University's College of Human Medicine (Ways 1973). As described by Dr. Howard Barrows in his well-known treatise on problem-based learning (Barrows and Tamblyn 1980), the founding members of McMaster's programme were committed to providing students with access to patients and their problems. It was realized that packaged problems ('problem boxes') could complement contacts with actual patients or simulated patients (Barrows and Mitchell 1975).

The common-sense decision to use clinical problems as the basis for designing a medical education curriculum was strengthened by other developments. In the general education literature there was some evidence that 'discovery learning' was effective (Katona 1940; Hilgard 1953). In addition, groups of researchers were refining the understanding of how clinicians were thinking when confronted with a clinical problem (see below). At McMaster University, the result was that an entire curriculum was based on the study of a series of clinical cases or problems (Neufeld and Barrows 1974).

Within the next several years, other new medical schools adopted the approach, including the University of Limburg at Maastricht in the Netherlands, the Faculty of Medicine at Newcastle, Australia (Maddison 1980; Neame 1981), and the Faculty of Medicine at the Suez Canal University in Egypt. Other institutions have adopted problem-based learning as the structure for special tracks within a medical curriculum; for example the Primary Care programme at the University of New Mexico (Kaufman 1982). The approach has also been adopted by other health professional programmes such as nursing, occupational therapy and physiotherapy (Dardier 1973).

Rationale

The theoretical basis for a problem-based approach in medical education is derived from two general sources. There is a body of writing and research in the general educational literature which supports the concept. Additionally, in the last decade or so insights into the clinical reasoning process have been derived from a specific line of research.

The general rationale is quite simple. It is assumed that the task of medical doctors is ultimately to identify, analyse and manage (or 'solve' in some instances) the medical problems of their patients, and to do so effectively, efficiently and with compassion. If dealing with the problems of health and illness is at the heart of the matter, the argument goes, why not use problem situations as the basis for designing a medical curriculum? But assumptions need to be questioned and analysed. We shall address two questions. First, are doctors problem-solvers; what goes on in the mind of a clinician when confronted with a clinical problem? Second, is it sensible to use problems as a basis for structuring a medical curriculum, rather than subjects or courses?

In his essay *Scientific Method in Science and Medicine*, Sir Peter Medawar contrasted inductive and deductive ('Popperian') thinking:

> Confronted with a sick patient the clinician is not observing passively, he is exploring, forming tentative hypotheses which guide further observations and which in the light of that observation have often to be discarded: a typical process of hypothesis formation corrected by negative feedback. (Medawar 1975)

In the last decade, systemic research into how physicians think has substantiated Sir Peter's assertion. Several groups of researchers in the United States, Canada and Britain have conducted studies into the clinical reasoning process (Elstein 1978; Barrows 1982). It has been found that when doctors are confronted by a clinical challenge, a remarkably consistent pattern of thinking occurs. Usually in the first minute of the doctor-patient encounter, the doctor's mind identifies a problem focus, and several possible explanations (hypotheses) for this problem come to his mind. These hypotheses are usually three or four in number. They are not easily rank-ordered, but a clinician can identify the most likely explanation. Most importantly, these hypotheses strongly influence the subsequent clinical data collected when the physician takes the medical history and examines the patient. The hypotheses are more influential than any data-gathering sub-routines, although these are used. It has also been found that most of the important information is obtained within the first few minutes of the encounter − that is, the physician in many cases has already decided what the problem (diagnosis) is within ten minutes or so. During the rest of the encounter, the physician is collecting confirming (and less commonly refuting) data, building his confidence in the initial problem-formulation, developing rapport with the patient, and collecting information which will be useful in developing a plan of investigation and management.

Of particular interest is the discovery that medical students, even very early in their education, have patterns of clinical reasoning that are remarkably similar to those of seasoned clinicians (Neufeld 1982; Vu 1980). They also generate hypotheses early in the clinical encounter, and use these hypotheses to collect further information. The key difference is in the quality and accuracy of the hypotheses, which are dependent on increasing knowledge and experience. These findings lend weight to the argument that a medical curriculum can be designed which encourages medical students to use problem situations as the basis for learning.

From a more general perspective there is a large and long-standing literature on the nature of human problem-solving and its application to teaching and learning (Conley-Hill 1979). Several arguments have been marshalled to support the use of problems as a basis for a medical curriculum. Problem-based learning encourages students to acquire and use information in the context of problem analysis and solution, thus increasing the likelihood of retention of information (Miller 1978). Students are more able to transfer knowledge and skills to other problems (Schmidt 1965). There is potentially a higher level of intrinsic motivation and interest as students see themselves engaged in a relevant learning task, 'discovering' the knowledge they need to analyse and solve the problem at hand (Knowles 1975).

Having reviewed some of the theoretical background for problem-based learning, it should be noted that in most instances medical schools using this approach have usually done so on the basis of more practical and less theoretical arguments. In Egypt, for example, the founders of the Faculty of Medicine in the Suez Canal University have considered the major health problems of the country. They have then analysed the tasks of physicians in contributing to the solution of these problems. The problems and tasks have then been incorporated into a curriculum which is structured accordingly. Practical experience with problem-based medical education has accrued over the past decade. One institutional example is described in more detail in the following section.

The McMaster Experience and Future Directions

The purpose of a medical undergraduate programme is to impart to the student the skills of 'learning to learn', as well as to guide the student in indepth explorations of knowledge areas thought to be important to the future practising physician. The evaluation of a student's clinical competence encompasses not only specific clinical and learning skills but also mastery of concepts in a defined area of clinical practice (General Guide 1983; Engel 1979).

The scope of knowledge required for a student to understand the biological basis of disease, determinants of health and illness and function of the health care system is constantly changing and expanding (Barondess 1983; McDermott 1978). The MD Programme at McMaster University has established a problem-oriented method as its fundamental educational approach so that the student will be equipped to cope with changes in medical knowledge in future practice.

Since its inception in 1969, the MD Programme at McMaster University has pioneered certain innovations in its educational approach. Key features are the analysis of problems as the principal method of acquiring and applying information, the fostering of independent learning by students, and the use of small groups as the main educational forum. The duration of the programme is thirty-three months, and consists of a series of interdisciplinary curriculum units, several elective blocks, and a year-long clerkship. There are no discipline-specific courses. The 'basic sciences' are learned in the context of clinical cases (Leeder 1976; Pallie 1978). There are no examinations; evaluation of student progress occurs informally and continuously in the tutorial groups, supplemented by performance in a variety of individual problem-based exercises (Simpson 1976; Painvin 1979). An intensive selection process admits students from a variety of academic and experiential backgrounds, whose learning habits are compatible with the style of the programme, and who demonstrate both academic ability and desirable personal qualities (Ferrier 1978). The MD Programme is seen as the responsibility of the faculty as a whole. Its operation is entrusted to a programme committee, rather than to departments or disciplines. Departments supply the human resources for several defined educational roles within the programme (Evans 1970).

In general terms, the programme has been successful. Close to 1000 graduates are engaged in postgraduate training, or have entered professional practice. It appears that McMaster graduates are going into academic or research positions at a rate higher than the national average. The attrition rate is low (less than one per cent). Reports from supervisors of McMaster graduates in postgraduate training across the country are very favourable (Woodward 1981). Graduates surveyed at two and five years after graduation are generally supportive of the programme's approach to learning (Woodward 1982). The programme has attracted considerable national and international attention (Fraenkel 1978). Several new medical schools in various parts of the world have adopted a similar approach (Neufeld 1978). One Canadian school, making a major curriculum change, has been considerably influenced by McMaster's experience.

Over the past two years, the MD Programme education committee has conducted a major review of the programme. This initiative arose out of the recognition that there has been much new knowledge in human biology, health care and health-related societal developments that needed to be incorporated into the programme. Certain persistent criticisms of the curriculum required a thoroughly integrated review. There was a sense that the programme could become trapped in its own neo-orthodoxy, and it was felt that the process of review could be a stimulus for institutional renewal.

Consistent with the faculty's commitment to problem-based learning, we have embarked on a major review of all health-care problems (HCPs) used in the MD Programme. This has involved the steps of problem-selection, and problem-design.

Problem Selection

The questions addressed regarding problem selection are: Can knowledge-objectives, stated as priority problems and conditions, be defined for the medical undergraduate curriculum? What is the level of agreement among faculty on the definition of priority knowledge? What are the appropriate criteria for selection of priority problems and conditions?

The clerkship committee has conducted a series of surveys as part of this problem-review project. All academic clinicians across the city have been asked to indicate which problems and conditions have the highest priority for our students, and to give justification for their responses. The justification criteria include prevalence, clinical logic, prototype value, life-threatening, treatability, and interdisciplinary input.

Priority problems and conditions, once specified to students, tutors, and clinical supervisors, serve the following functions:

1 To provide clearer guidance to students in self-directed learning.

2 To direct the assignment of patients to students on a clinical teaching unit.

3 To guide the selection of patients for analysis in tutorial sessions, both in the clerkship and in the pre-clerkship part of the programme.

4 To give a baseline for student evaluation, clarifying what is expected of a student.

5 To enable the construction of self-assessment packages facilitating feedback with regard to students' strengths and weaknesses.

6 To identify important resources for review and critical appraisal.

Each respondent was asked to rate potential clinical problems and conditions using the following categories:

a Problems or conditions that the student will be expected to have covered during the clerkship rotation.

b Problems or conditions that the student should take every reasonable opportunity to cover during the clerkship rotation.

c Problems or conditions that the student may not find it absolutely necessary to cover during the clerkship.

The potential problem and condition list generated by each clerkship committee was sufficiently comprehensive to cover the wide range of clinical situations likely to arise during the clerkship's rotation. The weighting assigned to a particular problem or condition was then justified according to the above justification-criteria. Whether each criterion was an important factor in the selection of the weighting given was indicated on a scale from high to low. A participation rate of greater than 80 per cent was deemed acceptable. The complete list of potential problems and conditions was given to clinicians with generalist-practice patterns while those faculty with specific disciplines received all problems but only those specific conditions which pertained to their specialty area.

Problems and conditions were classified according to the distribution of weighting assigned, allowing for a definition to be made of priority-knowledge. The level of agreement among faculty on ratings of educational priority are reflected in the distributions of weightings. The relative importance of various criteria for the selection of priority-knowledge was then examined.

Problems were displayed by categories reflecting educational priority; which has been very useful in planning the curriculum revision. Similar displays were prepared for the sub-specialties showing priority-ratings for conditions.

By this questionnaire method, clerkship priority-knowledge, problems and conditions can be defined for a unit within the MD Programme. The level of agreement among faculty respondents was reasonably high, with only a few problems and conditions showing considerable disagreement. The justification criteria for each problem and condition varied considerably and, hence, no single criterion could be used alone to justify educational priority. Further analyses are in progress: for example, comparing generalist and sub-specialist choices. These results will be compiled in various ways and used by faculty planners in the development of various case materials. In particular, we expect this systematic process of problem-selection to facilitate linkage between the interests of clerkship and pre-clerkship faculty planners, and between discipline groups and the chairmen of our interdisciplinary curriculum units. The survey results may also be of considerable interest to other institutions who are wrestling with the question of determining priority-objectives for their medical students.

Health Care Problem Design

The case study materials in preparation have two components: the Case Protocol itself and a Problem Guide for faculty tutors in the form of printed handouts of a few pages. There is considerable variation in the way the clinical information is presented to students. As several examples are available there has not been a sustained effort to use other formats for the problems. These include card decks and booklets, audio-visual and computer-based formats, and simulated patients (Barrows 1975, 1980). We plan to develop a much wider variety of case-presentations, using these various formats.

The case protocol consists of an opening scenario, clinical history, physical examination, and diagnostic tests. A problem-guide provides the clinical summary, problem-formulation, key-question list, a listing of problem-specific learning resources and various self-assessment materials. Although the problem-guide is intended primarily for faculty tutors, it may be shared with students as appropriate, after the student groups have completed their problem analysis.

We are particularly interested in helping our students to develop critical appraisal skills. Rather than providing separate courses or events, we intend to incorporate critical appraisal-guidelines and materials in an integrated fashion as part of the basic analysis of health problems. A comprehensive inventory of the health-care problems will be developed to display all priority problems and conditions, key concepts covered, and linkages to the various disciplines within the Faculty of Health Sciences.

Summary

The history and rationale for problem-based professional education in medicine has been reviewed and the experience and future directions of the MD Programme at McMaster University highlighted. McMaster has offered a course with problem-based learning as its central theme since its inception in 1969. The response has been very positive, but as in any new initiative, constant refinement and revisions are required due to internal changes in the medical school (in people and philosophy) as well as to changing forms of health-care issues in our contemporary society. The major challenge for professional educators is to create an efficient and comprehensive curriculum that will prepare the future practising physician for a career of lifelong learning. The major challenge for our students is to acquire the ability to identify, analyse, and manage clinical problems in order to provide effective, efficient, and humane patient care.

24 The MIT Undergraduate Research Opportunities Programme

Margaret MacVicar and Norma McGavern

The Undergraduate Research Opportunities Programme (UROP) is a twelve-month-a-year undergraduate academic programme at the Massachusetts Institute of Technology (MIT) which fosters, encourages, and financially supports project-based intellectual collaborations of undergraduates with faculty members across all of its academic departments and many of its interdisciplinary laboratories and administrative offices. More simply, UROP provides the way for any MIT undergraduate student, starting in his or her first year, to join as a junior colleague in research inquiries at knowledge frontiers. Approximately three-quarters of the 4500-person undergraduate student body joins with almost two-thirds of MIT's 1000-odd faculty in research ventures of mutual fascination.

A majority of student participants earn academic credit for their efforts; half as many again receive instead a modest stipend; the latter being the preferred circumstance during summer collaborations. At least as many again, motivated by love for the subject, undertake research for neither pay nor credit. A typical UROP student research commitment extends over two semesters but quite often continues for two years or more. Time spent on research during the semester varies from appoximately six to twenty hours per week; during the summer, a full-time immersion is the norm.

Tangible student achievements include patents, publications in leading journals, professional society prizes for research presentations, invitations to appear on radio and television programmes, job offers from industry, visibility in the professional world (such as adoption of student recommendations by government agencies), grants from funding agencies, and invitations to lecture.

When it is mutually desirable, some of the research collaborations between faculty and undergraduates also incorporate third parties – professionals from industrial, governmental, and medical establishments.

Members of faculty state with force and enthusiasm that the opportunity to work with bright, creative undergraduates is a major reason they choose to come to, and stay at, MIT. Students comment that the unique opportunity MIT offers them in UROP is a vital consideration in their decisions to attend MIT and in the value they retrospectively ascribe to their undergraduate educational experience after graduation. Senior administrators of the Institute regard UROP as the ideal vehicle for bringing students and faculty together in the arena where discovery and knowledge-generation occur, overcoming the remoteness of the classroom and the tendency of normal professional research activity to be an otherwise centrifugal campus force.

The Seed

In 1957, Dr. Edwin H. Land, founder of the Polaroid Corporation, gave an invited lecture at MIT which struck a deeply-recessed chord in the audience composed of faculty and administrators (Land 1957). He reminded them of the heritage of MIT as a special undergraduate institution, a tradition which had grown faint during the rapid growth of graduate and postgraduate education following World War II. Students entering our universities, Land said, ought to be entering a world in which their dreams were encouraged, their creativity given full rein. It was not an environment for genius alone that he envisioned, but an atmosphere which allowed each student to bring to fruition his or her own unique way of thinking and seeing and which nurtured his or her private dreams of greatness. An early association with an experienced preceptor could usher the young student into the world of scientific investigation with a degree of wonder and guidance not plentiful in classrooms and textbooks, he asserted.

Objectives, History and Philosophy

Following Dr. Land's address, MIT experimented very modestly, beginning by inviting a few first-year students into research and by establishing a format of first-year seminar programmes. Although the seminar programme later grew to be a staple of the first-year experience, the research programme was abandoned by 1961 as unsuccessful. Nonetheless, a climate of curriculum overhaul and innovation persisted, and by the middle of the 1960s substantial changes in the MIT undergraduate 'core' degree requirements were made. Events of social turmoil preoccupied the campus for the next few years, particularly during 1968-1970. A gift from Dr. Land to MIT for the initiation of educational innovation starting with the 1969/1970 academic year coincided with a campus in ferment over the United States involvement in the Vietnam conflict.

It was at this time that discussions at the level of provost and of chairman of faculty were focusing on just what kind of academic programme might encourage individual student achievement and faculty-undergraduate colleagueship. Strikingly to the authors, at this time of widespread estrangement and suspicion between faculty and students, MIT prepared to undertake a risky new form of faculty-student partnership on a wide scale.

No model existed for a faculty-undergraduate research collaboration programme as broad and sophisticated as the one envisioned, nor for an undergraduate MIT academic programme spanning all departments at MIT from humanities to electrical engineering, and even those not offering undergraduate degrees. A thorough and totally new invention was called for. All policy and procedures were devised from scratch. No advisory oversight-committee was established. No time limit was pre-scribed as a probationary interval for programme performance. No formal programme proposal was made to the faculty by its customary committee process; nor was the faculty's approval obtained in a formal way. UROP began as an academic initiative by the MIT administration, with a junior faculty member as director. To this director were given modest funding resources ($50,000 initially) and solid backing by the senior administrators. A climate of faculty and departmental goodwill was a crucial great asset: in many MIT offices and departments were people who wanted UROP to succeed and who were willing to break most bureaucratic rules to encourage that to happen.

Each semester of its first decade, UROP gathered together approx-imately twenty-five to forty people to meet for an evening with the president, the provost, or the chancellor. The composition of the group was different each time and deliberately included the strong and diverse viewpoints of students, faculty and administrators so as to afford broad discussion about, and participation in, UROP's evolution.

UROP was established in such a way that it was accessible to all faculty and all students in every area of academic activity. Each department designated a faculty member as liaison to UROP, to be called a UROP Co-ordinator. The network of Co-ordinators established at the outset, proved a keystone in the evolution and success of the programme. Administration was not excessively centralized. A small UROP staff was set in place to work with Co-ordinators and with students and faculty directly. This staff cajoles, hand-holds, inspires, and chides where appropriate. The strategy at the programme's beginning was first to establish a nine-month academic year, credit-based programme in all of the academic departments. First-year as well as second-, third-, and fourth-year students are eligible participants. Next were added summer research activity, a stipend option, and opportunities to interact with off-campus organizations.

The major aspects of UROP were largely in place within five years: philosophy; award-procedures for Institute-wide accreditation, stipend, and proposals: linkages of UROP to federal government research contract policy regarding overhead recovery and to MIT's student financial aid policies; and a legal framework for formal research collaborations with off-campus organizations. Then began an enlarging of UROP's scope to include formal opportunites for students to present their research work to bona fide audiences, to receive coaching in writing and oral presentation, and to learn from one another in research seminars. UROP also undertook to serve as an institutional link with alumni.

The programme has been supported throughout by a steady and substantial budget from MIT internal general funds. With the growth of summer research participation, as well as increases in UROPer academic year requests, this budget has been hard pressed and inflation has cut its buying power. Outside gifts to UROP and faculty willingness to absorb undergraduate research costs on sponsored research contracts more than offset this loss.

The objectives of the programme at the outset were just what they are today: to allow the seed of individual promise room to grow and to flourish; to join students and faculty as professional allies; to give students the benefit of 'real world' experience under the guidance of experienced hands; to afford faculty members the inspiration of young creative intelligence, unbounded by knowledge of what cannot be done.

Academic Content, Mentors, Evaluation

All research undertaken is expected to be substantive research, that is, deserving and worthy of MIT academic credit whether or not credit is actually book-kept by the registrar. A student must compose a structured description of proposed work, have it approved by the faculty supervisor, and pass on this description to the faculty member's departmental UROP Co-ordinator for oversight and early feedback. When the research work is to be undertaken for pay, a well thought-out and justified financial request must be included. Each department via its Co-ordinator, determines what it will approve of as substantive undergraduate research to be supervised by its faculty. Funding for student wages and research expenses comes from faculty members' sponsored research grants and from departmental funds as well as from MIT's own internal general funds. Negotiation with faculty and students with regard to funding a specific student's research proposal is done by the UROP staff directly and on a case-by-case basis. Approximately 1000 financial requests are reviewed each academic year, of which almost ninety per cent receive part or all of the amounts requested — sometimes by creative and unconventional means.

All MIT undergraduates are eligible to participate in UROP, as are Wellesley College students via a formal MIT-Wellesley exchange programme. Students are informed warmly and repeatedly within their first week at MIT that they are welcome to become involved in UROP: right away, or at any time in their next four years. Participation in UROP is voluntary. It is not an 'honours' programme. No grade-average threshold must be met. Faculty say they look for persistence, a gleam in the student's eye, conscientiousness, and intellectual aggressiveness. Our almost fifteen-years experience with the programme tell us that the weak students, the strong ones, the international ones, the timid ones, the brash ones — all find something in UROP. The only requirement for entry is that students have enough courage to try, not a trivial requirement for talented students who are often unaccustomed to risking an open-ended opportunity to succeed or fail.

At the heart of each UROP project lies the personal relationship of the faculty supervisor and the individual student. The supervisor must be a regular faculty member. (Occasionally, individual departments extend the privilege of serving as a research supervisor to lecturers or professional research staff affiliated with the department.) Each faculty member supervising a student serves as a mentor and is expert in the particular area in which he or she and the student are jointly working. A student is not generally expected to have had previous experience in the area of study. Although certain subjects may be desirable pre-requisites for UROP work in some fields, a few days or weeks of background reading are all that are commonly required in preparation. Like faculty and all professionals, students start new interests in the middle, not systematically from an ideal beginning point.

It is expected that the student will do all the necessary footwork required to arrange a research undertaking. Encouragement is given by UROP staff and faculty advisors to those faint of heart. The faculty member who will become the student's research supervisor discusses arrangements with the student. A faculty member may invite the student to work on a project in progress, or a student may provide an original idea and plan which interests a faculty member. Student and faculty together discuss the number of hours planned for the student's commitment, and arrangements for attaining pay or credit. Most UROP students remain with a given research undertaking for anywhere from one and a half semesters to more than two years. During intense periods of term-time research, twenty hours or more sometimes may be spent at research by students in addition to their regular studies.

There is no built-in formal reward system for faculty who participate in UROP as supervisors. Although undergraduate mentorship and teaching are usually noted in tenure decisions, it is the personal satisfaction of colleagueship and the real professional contribution of the undergraduate researcher as a collaborator that are the faculty member's rewards. For students, the tangible reward may take the form of a grade when credit is chosen, or a paycheck; a letter of recommendation from a faculty member is most prized. The intangible rewards are increased self-confidence, learning to structure time and set priorities, and genuine citizenship in the scholarly community.

Evaluation letters are written at the end of each term and summer period by each research partner: the faculty member evaluates the student's progress, and the student evaluates the research experience and comments on the partnership with the faculty member as a supervisor. These evaluations alert Co-ordinators and the UROP staff to particular achievements or problems. All are carefully read by the UROP staff and followed up when necessary. Good news and bad news alike are discussed with the writers. Evaluations serve as early warnings on emerging issues or trends and aid in assessing 'track records' of particular students and faculty supervisors, for consideration when subsequent proposals for financial support are submitted.

Participants

Out of an undergraduate student body of about 4500, almost three-quarters are involved in undergraduate research each year. More than half of each graduating class is participating by the end of its second year. Students routinely carry out research in all of MIT's twenty-two departments and in most of its many interdisciplinary laboratories.

Approximately 650 of a total faculty of 1000 are involved in supervising UROP work in any one year. About eighty per cent of the entire faculty have served as research supervisors to UROPers at one time or other. MIT faculty are impatient and demanding. To have sustained their goodwill for the fourteen-plus years of UROP's existence is powerful witness to the quality and attraction of undergraduate research colleagues. Faculty research proposals to federal funding agencies now budget for undergraduate researchers as a matter of routine. There is a willingness on the part of faculty to support students, to find them laboratory space, and to count them as part of their research teams. Former UROP students have, in the past few years, begun to reappear: as UROP faculty supervisors.

Perhaps the following descriptions of three students and their research will illustrate the kinds of enterprises UROP students become involved in and the experiences UROP gives them.

The first student was in her first semester when she became involved in UROP last year. UROP staff introduced her into the circle of the Cambridge area's eminent faculty with interests in nuclear weapons and disarmament. She joined with a physicist active in the area of international security issues. As a freshman and a research beginner she found herself nearly overwhelmed at her first assignment: to calculate the recovery time of the United States economy after nuclear attack. Using available data she eventually made her calculations, having first discovered that widely-employed current statistics are based upon incorrect or highly questionable data. As a second-year student, she is now constructing an original economic model of the United States in order to obtain more realistic input for future calculations. As a result of her explorations, she has learned not only an amount of nuclear physics but also economics, political science, and systems dynamics. She presented her work at a physics department symposium while still a first-year student and recently was asked to present her analysis to an alumni conference. She is now arranging a lecture tour to address audiences who have invited her to Northeastern University and MIT alumni clubs in Los Angeles and New Jersey.

The second student conceived of an ambitious team undertaking and then laboured in the spring of his third year – and now into the following year – to design, build, and eventually launch a small orbital vehicle to place a one-kilogram payload into orbit as a private venture. As one of four student members of his engineering team, his activities started with the construction of a test stand for a chosen rocket-engine of twenty-five pounds thrust and included conducting theoretical studies into rocket performance. He is now involved in long-range systems analysis. The team is supervised by two faculty members and has recruited graduate student colleagues. The undergraduate team has had to pursue funding diligently. With department backing and advice from the UROP staff, they have received UROP stipend support and significant research expenses support, which were awarded to the udergraduates as an engineering design prize. One team member has presented the group's work to a Boston meeting of the Model Rocket Society. Launch is scheduled for 1988 and has garnered considerable interest from industry.

A slow-to-heal knee injury to the third student while he was still in high school led him to develop a deep interest in the healing properties of bone and tissue. Subjecting himself to controversial electric field treatments, he was impressed to see his leg heal. At graduation, he chose MIT, where such an interest could be pursued seriously at the undergraduate level. He had not been in the Institute long before he discovered a faculty member in electrical engineering who shared his curiosity about healing mechanisms of bone and tissue. Mounting an investigation of how individual cells perceive change in their environment, this student seeks to specify roles which mechanical and electrical forces play in cartilage cell-synthesis. Currently his work focuses on developing a system which can provide an appropriate environment for a piece of excised living cartilage. A published paper as co-author is one result of his work. Another is an invitation to present his results to a national professional electrical engineering conference this winter.

UROP and MIT: Institutional Fit

For students and faculty, UROP has created a new alliance. As a member of a research team a student has the opportunity to observe more senior professional scientists at work. There is involvement in the entire research process: from dealing with the funding agencies and other research sponsors, to reporting on a project's scientific and technical progress to business or government representatives as the investigation leaps forward or hits snags.

For a faculty member, there is identification with the young person working with him or her, a *déja vu*, a positive reminder of what being at a university means as compared with being at a non-academic research laboratory. It brings out the uncle or aunt in each faculty member. As one faculty member recently put it:

> ...there is a peculiar personal satisfaction for a faculty member who's been involved in UROP. You almost become your own little college. That is to say, I can now see UROP students all over the country in different kinds of jobs who went through my laboratory. We keep in touch, they come back, we have get togethers, and so on. There is a tremendous feeling of satisfaction which is different from the kind of satisfaction you get from classroom teaching...

Another faculty member adds:

> I have very much enjoyed helping with their development in understanding the 'real' world of physical investigation. The close personal contact under UROP makes possible a kind of instruction which seldom occurs in the formal classroom, ... They have joined me at my home for lunches, and my wife and I have been invited to dinner at their dormitory.

An item of the hidden agenda of UROP is that the programme is in actuality a major faculty professional-development programme that is congenial to, and enhances, the educational mission of MIT. It is not solely a programme of student benefit and primary focus. This has proven to be a key element in continued support from the faculty as a whole. UROP is also a seeding vehicle for risky and venturesome research ideas, with undergraduate zeal providing the impetus. Taking on a student researcher is a way for a junior faculty member to begin building a research team. In certain instances, taking on UROP students may be the only way to build a multi-disciplinary research team, since the graduate student and postdoctoral team-members are usually specialists in the faculty member's field. One faculty member working in water chemistry put it this way:

> What you get (with UROP students) is an enormous range of talent: I've had architects, chemical engineers, food scientists, chemists, physicists, and even a mathematician. What you have when you put all these elements together is something no other faculty member whose professional interests lie in one area could possibly gather together.

Similarly, the collegial role played by undergraduates has affected graduate students, who frequently find themselves in 'big brother' or 'big sister' roles. Visiting scientists, technicians, and postdoctoral fellows are also brought together with the undergraduates. As a result, undergraduates have unusual opportunities to become aware of their own special qualities. Importantly, undergraduates learn of the context and format in which research is carried out. According to survey studies, UROPers identify with their research group more often than they do with either their academic department or field of major study. (It has been asserted by some that UROP is functioning as an organic advising system.)

In general, the close fit the programme has with the style, demands, and traditions of MIT has been its strongest cohesive force. The programme has remained flexible and responsive, and retains the ability and credibility to adapt to different needs at different times. Policies consistently have been set together with, rather than at odds with, academic departments, faculty, and the students themselves. Decisions are made by personal interaction whenever possible. The close faculty tie to the student is insisted upon as being at the very heart of the programme. Policies enjoy broad goodwill. (It was once remarked by Dr. Malcolm Parlett, then of the University of Edinburgh, that UROP is an example of benign collusion on a grand scale.) In day-to-day operations, paperwork and bureaucracy are minimized. The annual financial cost of UROP to MIT has hardly changed in more than ten years, and UROP's staff and office-space sizes are approximately the same as in 1972. No finances reimburse faculty time; no operations monies are expended on meals for meetings or fancy furniture. This lean image has been invaluable.

Effect on Undergraduate Education at MIT

Two years afer UROP began, in the spring of 1971, a survey of UROP students and non-participants was conducted. In spring 1981, exactly ten years later, almost the same questionnaire was administered again to a sample of 900 students: some who had done UROP work and a group which had not. A comparison of the responses to both surveys revealed that: the majority of UROP students continue in their research for two or more semesters; most become involved early (in their first or second undergraduate years); the proportion of students receiving pay as compared to credit remains relatively unchanged; the prime motivating factors for becoming involved were and remain 'the desire to build career experience' and 'the desire to work with a particular professor'. The initiation of the programme met an enthusiastic audience of participants, whose ardour remains intense. The first semester of UROP saw 150 participants. In the third year, 800 students joined into research with faculty. By the five-year mark, participation approached current levels: three-quarters of the undergraduate student body.

Before UROP was established, a fourth-year special project (required as a Bachelors thesis) in the spring term was likely to be a student's only independent research effort. Quality was generally thought to be low and enthusiasm on both faculty and student sides was lacking. Today departments note that undergraduate research quality is noticeably higher; a number of awards presented to students at commencement derive from UROP work. Companies which recruit for Co-operative programme positions remark on the increasing quality and experience of MIT applicants (who apply at the end of their second year) due to UROP experiences as underclassmen. Some graduate schools, eg the physics department at Princeton University, request that MIT seniors specify on their applications existent UROP experience because it so beneficially influences their subsequent performance in graduate school.

In 1977, the MIT Graduate Student Association voted UROP the Sizer Award, given for the Most Significant Contribution to MIT Education. 'UROP', said a senior faculty member, 'is without question the most significant modification in undergraduate education that I have seen in almost fifteen years at MIT. It has provided for many students the direction and motivation they have needed to allow them productive and rewarding careers.'

In 1974, 1975, and 1976 the main faculty governing committee, the Committee on Educational Policy (CEP), took a hard look at undergraduate research, forming several subcommittees to examine different aspects of it. The result was a list of CEP-issued Guidelines for Undergraduate Research, applicable to all individualized project work at MIT. These derived in the main from UROP's particular procedures and policies now to be extended to all independent study, internship, and generically-related unstructured educational experiences.

Besides having deeply affected the relationship between faculty and undergraduates, UROP has had a rather dramatic effect upon how undergraduates learn. The cumulative effect of student involvement in research has enabled them to be more realistic about professional demands and standards. They are more likely to have honed their problem-solving techniques and to be less frightened by situations that do not exist in textbooks. They know more about the working lives of faculty and technical staff; they have more balance than those subject to the hard grind of regular coursework. The UROP staff monitors nearly continuous feedback from students about their research experiences via evaluation letters, written reports, staff site visits, and student interviews, correspondence with faculty and students, and oral presentations.

The comments below are taken directly from current evaluation letters which the UROP office received while this report was in preparation. Such letters have come by the hundreds for fourteen years, three times a year:

- Without my 'nuts and bolts' UROP exposure, I may have continued with my engineering studies and would have discovered – much too late – that I was a misplaced economist.

- I was fortunate to find a UROP project that matched my interests in several areas. My major is electrical engineering and I wanted to get some experience in digital electronic design and in actually making that paper design work. But I am also very interested in psychology and cognitive science; this UROP has given me a doorway into the field.

- I was allowed to take an idea from its very conception – research it, toy with it, form a hypothesis about it – then design an experiment to test it out. That involved specifying test criteria, selecting controls, formulating stimuli and testing all possible combinations, finding the best format to present the stimuli, trying to keep the subject's attention, trying not to let the subject be able to figure out what exactly is being tested for, and so on.
  Next was the tedious and time-consuming task of gathering data and sorting it all out, finally analysing it on the computer. Eventually the end was in sight...or perhaps the beginning once

again. The most frustrating, but also most exciting, aspect of the project was in the final interpretation. Was I right? What's going on here? Where do we go now? Sometimes it seemed like a vicious circle, or an exercise in futility, but sometimes something useful came out of it. I suppose that's what research is all about.

– One hour out of every four in the lab is spent washing glassware. Another hour is spent mixing up solutions or finding reagent bottles, or giving up and buying a fresh supply. Another hour is spent processing samples and repairing broken machinery. Another 45 minutes is spent discussing how one person can evaporate an acetone solution and another person can heat samples over an open flame, when the lab has only one hood and explosions are frowned upon. This leaves only fifteen minutes in which to do the actual experiment before your next class. If you skip lunch.

– I have never done serious experimental work before, and I have enjoyed the break from routine in learning to use my hands and in facing problems to which there is no one answer. I have learned simple things like a methodical approach to research; the need to check and recheck results; to do the experiments so that they can be easily repeated; to record results so that they are clear and understandable two weeks later; to plot graphs of meaningful quantities on proper scales, and to learn to interpret them. And, most important, to learn to deal with my own mistakes.

– There is usually one brief moment of glory which is preceded by a long series of frustrations and plenty of hard work.

– I developed an appreciation for what I am learning in textbooks, because I can see that each line represents somebody else's summer, graduate years, or even lifetime.

– UROP has served as a superb introduction to the astrophysics community and has provided me with an invaluable link to astronomical and astrophysical research. It has reawakened a strong interest in these two areas, an interest that had been suppressed as a result of a heavy workload and a hectic schedule.

– I have learned what the equations and phase diagrams in my books really mean when I can see the results in the material with the scanning electron microscope. My work has influenced me to major in materials science and archaeology because I realize how much information the study of materials reveals, and that the material tells something about the culture from which it came.

Standing Back

Requests for information about UROP occur almost daily and correspondence about UROP fills several file drawers. Inquiries come not only from colleges and universities, but also from teachers and counsellors at high schools and junior high schools, and from individual students at other colleges. UROP has been the subject of national public radio and national public television features (eg the *NOVA* series), and magazine and newspaper articles, for example in *The New York Times* and *Change Magazine*. UROP is listed in the recent report by the United States Department of Education's National Commission on Excellence in Education as an example of the quality the Commission is seeking for the nation as a whole (US Department of Education 1983).

Can UROP be exported? There are several university programmes in existence now which are directly modelled on UROP: eg at the University of Delaware, Stanford University, Utah State University, Imperial College of Science and Technology, Johns Hopkins University, and Harvard University. Serious inquiry from, and consultation with, other institutions occurs with some regularity. Many of the virtues of UROP as an educational innovation certainly are transportable; they are matters of attitude and style which can be employed as a philosophy and strategy even for innovations quite different from undergraduate research. Our experience suggests that specific mechanisms, specific reward systems, and operational guidelines for a programme should reflect the peculiarities of the particular host institution. They and the innovative idea itself must fit the heritage and spirit of the institution, and the programme's resulting rituals and customs should reflect the personality of the organization in which it is housed.

At MIT, this means no prescribed limit on the student's time-commitment to the research; availability of desks and door keys and coffee mugs; twenty-four-hour-a-day access to facilities; funds for research awards to students; emphasis on research collaboration sited on the campus but with opportunities for off-campus collaboration where mutual motivation is sufficient; procedures for accrediting the research work flexibly and according to departmental preferences; eligibility of all undergraduates irrespective of grade point average, class year, or major; accommodation of a new indirect-cost recovery-scheme to encourage faculty support of student expenses; co-operation of media, resource development, counselling, scholarship aid, legal, and provost offices in the development of policy; and establishment of a small administrative office, reporting directly to the chancellor in UROP's formative days. This office, now reporting to the provost, is empowered to 'make things happen' for would-be undergraduate researchers.

25 Innovations in Management Education

Nancy Foy

A long-haired young man who had been a leader in the student movement in the sixties turned up, soberly dressed but no less revolutionary, in a Regional Management Centre in the early eighties. I asked him how he'd been able to make the transition to pin stripes.

'This is where the action really is in education,' said the student-turned-teacher. 'Management education is the frontier. If it isn't happening here, it isn't happening anywhere.'

He was right, of course. Perhaps this is because managers, as authority figures themselves, seem to expect to be treated as adults slightly more than any other educable segment of the population. Or perhaps it is some happy accident that has created a 'critical mass' of excellence within this single slice of British education, to the extent that I can still claim Britain has the best management education in the world.

Whatever the reason, this picture of British management education leading the world, and management education as the most advanced place in British education generally, is particularly poignant when you consider how little impact it still has on British business.

We still suffer a seemingly impregnable wall between the haves and the have-nots. The favoured few firms are still whirling their A-list élites through a handful of the world's finest management education institutions, while the mass of management is left to the tender mercies of the Sunday business news, a bookkeeping course at the local tech, a brush with the son's computer games, or a twice-yearly outing to a BIM meeting.

Looking Back Optimistically

About five years ago I published findings of a major survey into British management education. *Missing Links* (Foy 1979) homed in on Britain's lead in project-oriented approaches, and highlighted the need for clusters and networks to help managers cross boundaries within organizations and to the outside world. It proposed that more management teachers should be encouraged to have sabbatical terms as managers, and that more managers shoud be enticed into management education.

The Foundation for Management Education also encouraged these ideas. They and I believed that the gulf between the purveyors and users of this fine management education could be bridged by people who had experienced both cultures.

This was not to be. I tried it myself, and now I know why. The gulf between the world of education and the world of management is virtually unbridgeable within today's culture. A few can speak the languages of both worlds, but it is not possible to create a cadre of people who are truly mobile between them.

The basic behaviours as well as values are different. In education, including the best of management education, people value owning themselves and their ideas. They value their long holidays. (A few even use them to pursue research interests, but that wasn't as common as I had expected.) Money isn't terribly important (though I found quite a few who were active in academic unions on behalf of downtrodden brethren). They like working terribly hard on occasion, but most of them sleep in their own beds every night.

The management culture, on the other hand, is fuelled by anxiety. If you don't have current crises to worry about, you can find new perks to aspire to, or your company will create some new myth about what upstairs does or doesn't want, to keep you anxiously endeavouring into the small hours, or rushing off to meetings in some Godforsaken place without time in the schedule to enjoy your jet lag. Very few managers use all their holiday entitlement. Money is a counter in a game, perhaps, but getting and spending it matters a great deal. Not many managers have savings, or own their own cars.

These are cartoons, and stereotypes, but I spent three years in each camp, and I am now convinced that the twain will seldom understand each other. And it may be important, in the future, to understand how we could have the finest management education in the world, less-than-the-finest management, and some important innovations in management development springing up almost without benefit of academic clergy.

Let me stop and try to recreate a snapshot of the management education world at the end of the seventies:

 - Action learning was begining to emerge, along with cousins of it like joint development activities or project-oriented management development (AL, JDA, and PMD, respectively − of course).

— The Regional Management Centres were full of energy, albeit having trouble managing former competitors (like any other agglomeration put together after a too-hasty courtship).
— People were worrying about how to improve the teaching of industrial relations.
— Courses (or 'learning activities') for small firms or would-be entrepreneurs were beginning to be talked about, and Durham had already combined with the Teesside Poly people to build and maintain a 700-member small business club in the Northeast.
— Elitist MBA programmes aroused complaints that they turned out people whose expectations were too high.
— Most good management education institutions that had weathered earlier storms were doing more tailored activities for firms.

Looking back, I think I evaded the industrial relations (IR) question — and it was a crucial one — but so did everyone else, including the abortive 'IR Training Resource Centre' set up to improve the overall training of managers in this realm. On the other hand, I highlighted the need for networks, and helped a few get started, and I started needling my colleagues in companies that used management education to send their managers in clusters, rather than singly, or from far-flung lonely corners of the corps, so they could go back with shared energy, to fight down the awful re-entry blues that characterized so many excellent courses, workshops and seminars.

Today's Pragmatic View

The reality today still seems a long way from the models. One great achievement, I think, is the wide advance of action learning, once the province of GEC and a few others alone. The management educators and consultants have helped in this process, almost as they do in America, adapting action learning ideas (eg that one learns best by working through a real problem with a group of peers who are similarly engaged, on their own or shared projects) to the circumstances of many different kinds of organizations. Like MBO before it (and hopefully employee involvement after it), the name 'action learning' may fade from fad, but the principles, processes, and resulting effects will be long-lasting. Most organizations today have some form of objective-setting, and thus somewhat more rational ways of measuring progress against those objectives.

Action learning doesn't take place in the classroom, and this has been one of the greatest advances in management education. The action learning 'set advisor' doesn't need to be more expert than the managers in the group he helps. Often, he just has to shut up and learn from their living cases, just as the other members do. Sometimes he has to bring them back to reflect on the experience they are sharing, to make sure they wring from it all the learning each member can stand.

The concept of the regional management centre has faded a bit, except for the few that were lucky or wise enough to start before the seventies had their slump, much less the eighties. In my own focus, the lowly 'local tech' is much more important now. If 'British management' is to be influenced, even marginally, by 'management education', it will happen here, not at the London Business School, or the Oxford Management Centre – though the excellence at the top of the market creates an ambience in which excellence can also flourish in some local colleges lucky enough to attract and develop a cluster of good, enthusiastic, pragmatic tutors or teachers or whatever they want to call themselves.

Most local technical colleges have been under siege for years. On the other hand, they have learned how to keep out of the firing line, and get on with their business – and quite a few have developed small business programmes, or 'courses' for our increasing army of extruded, redundant, or early-retired managers who are sent out to pasture before they view their own usefulness as finished. At Luton College, for example, the 'LEAP' programme is based on a room with coffee, phones, meeting facilites for self-help groups, and projects in which the focus is starting a new venture.

This outflux of managers from larger firms, still full of energy and activity, may be one of the most profound influences on management education when we look back a few years hence. They are demanding activities that are more individually driven. They may want qualifications, but they aren't blindly taking courses. Both the distance learning programme at Henley and the management education innovations in the Open University were much more heavily subscribed than their founders expected. A large proportion of today's management education is funded by the manager himself, for his own development. The indentured servants from large firms are necessarily rubbing shoulders with larger populations of these free agents, and I think management education is playing its role here quite responsibly in moving ideas and values across a wide population.

The action learning trend, and the rising numbers of individuals recycling themselves merge in today's great fad for entrepreneurship and small business courses. One of my colleagues who set up a small business last year found the army of people (mainly recycled from large firms) who wanted to come and 'advise' him on everything from marketing to 'product strategy' to grantsmanship were actually costing him time he needed out in the shop, in shirtsleeves, to help the two other executives of the company run metal-bashing machines to meet a deadline for their first product. Small businesses have a range of needs, and some of these are now being met by offerings from management education – for which we may all be duly grateful. But I think 'entrepreneurship' is best left to the entrepreneurs – and with the exception of most of the managers of management education institutions, I don't think there are many of those in business school faculties.

'Japan' is to the eighties as 'Sweden' was to the seventies, and the business schools of Britain owe their lives to the 'United States' bugaboo of the sixties. In physics or sociology, it takes energy to bridge a gap, but in British behaviour I think 'gaps' like these are sources of energy. In the sixties we all read 'Defi Americain' (or *The American Challenge* (Servan Schreiber 1967) by any other name), and decided we had to have national computer companies and our own versions of the Harvard Business School. Like the Germans with TV, by starting later we were able to take advantage of all the pioneering that had gone before at Harvard and others, and were able to leapfrog over the straitjacket of 'the case method', while avoiding too much typecasting ourselves. We have that gap to thank for the prevalence as well as the excellence of management education today.

In the seventies, Sweden's turn, we argued about autonomous work groups, and co-determination, and 'Participation' (which, with a little help from governments and non-business institutions, took on connotations of workers on the board rather than problem-solving on the shop floor). With all the argument over Lord Bullock's recommendation for workers on the board, it grew increasingly easy to find firms setting up real shop-floor participation in Britain as the seventies progressed – and a few people in management education helped this process immeasurably.

Today, in the wake of the Japanese gap, we have quality circles in strange places where no one could ever have expected real participation to flourish. Here, again, it is the local tech rather than the top of the market institution that has done a great deal to move circles into a wide variety of companies. The training is fairly rigid, and hasn't been invented by British management educators, but some of the adaptations in more lowbrow locales have been brilliant. I spent three recent years in a large company as manager in charge of employee communications, and in the process managed to mother a quality circle programme. We were able to find excellent consulting, and good research as well, to help us move the idea from place to place. Hundreds of shop-floor people are now having weekly meetings, and their supervisors are finding their roles more central, and their managers are pleased to see what good ideas people have when they are encouraged to contribute to the quality of the product or their work environment.

These are useful phenomena. But the mainstream of British management education has a tremendous flywheel effect (by which I really mean 'inertia'). IR training? Very little progress is evident here. And still we have the favoured few, with their A lists, reinforcing their advanced views to each other. Courses are evaluated (by insiders) by their ICI-worthiness, or IBM-ness, or regular attendance by a few other household name managers.

Looking Ahead – Optimistically?

We will keep on having élites. MBA programmes are useful because they attract excellent people, usually with at least a couple of years' experience (which is not always the case in the US – and perhaps why ours are really better). They learn well, from each other as well as from their courses. As a result the accountant is able to become a finance man; the computer expert can exit the sterile dead end and get into more general management. Most MBAs are still fed too much expectation-raising 'corporate strategy' nonsense, and too few British companies know how to rub off their overpolished shine to find the gems underneath. (A juicy project with a chance to gain visibility, and partnership or membership with other recent MBA types is as good a recipe as any, courtesy of the US banks who siphon off our best MBA products.)

I can picture a time when the mainstream of management might 'consume' education in new ways. In Norway and Denmark, for example, 'management centres' act as brokers, pulling out of universities, consultancies, other firms, and across national boundaries expertise their members have decided they want. In Denmark an industry-specific programme for a few computer-related firms, for example, included a 'going-to-work'-club for young managers, with projects and lectures from 8-10 am. A 'going-home-from-work' club for senior executives had a strong project content, and dealt with more strategic problems. The groups met together frequently, and managers from a single company in the programme had their own separate meetings to review progress and plan further activities.

This is 'user driven' in the corporate sense. I can foresee more audio cassettes for self-improving managers who want to use the time driving to and from work (and indeed, we already have Personnel Training Bulletin on Tape in Britain, started in 1983). Video cassettes are presently fairly expensive, and markets are small, but I expect that will change fairly rapidly as we head towards the nineties. 'Self-managed learning' will certainly make further inroads, whatever the medium.

But managers will go on needing each other, to learn from and with. More than half the benefit of any course for practising managers is in rubbing shoulders with other practising managers. The coffee breaks, or residential periods, or lunchtimes are crucial – and will certainly remain so.

I think we will also see 'management' ideas extended beyond the narrow definition of corporate management in which they are embedded today. That army of people who retire early, voluntarily or otherwise, is turning up on local councils, and doing good works, and starting new leisure activities – and all of these thrive on good management.

The transitions between corporation and small firm may become more graceful, helped by such examples as Rank-Xerox's 'networking', in which individuals or even groups go outside the corporate walls, but go on providing it with necessary services under their own banners. The help they get from each other by means of a club (or 'the network') is considerable, and their usage of management education (sometimes from each other) is higher than average among new firms.

Finally, the incurable optimist in me still hopes to see British management educators in the future emulating their American counterparts throughout all time – acting more as consultants, peripatetic carriers of good ideas and good practice, earning, learning and teaching, all at once. It may take a real shift in the culture of education itself before that can happen gracefully.

26 Biomedical Engineering: a Nascent Profession

Colin Roberts

Doctors have drawn on the physical sciences ever since the time of Da Vinci. However, only relatively recently has the physical scientist become an important member of the health care team. The contribution of the physical scientist today is perhaps most commonly associated, at least in the public's eye, with problems of radiation and X-ray technology. Medical physicists, brought into our hospitals to ensure the safety of X-ray equipment in the 1940s, are now an established part of our health care system. More recently, however, the appreciation that the skills of the conventional radiation physicist are limited, and that the industry which supports medical technology has requirements of its own, has led to a demand for other skills. These include those of the computer specialist and the materials scientist, together with those of the electronics and mechanical engineers. This composite demand has led to the creation of the biomedical engineer, and this chapter will describe how biomedical engineers have evolved from interested enthusiasts to professionals in their own right.

Terminology

Firstly, what is meant by biomedical engineering? An examination of the literature today will reveal a confusing array of terms such as bioengineering, clinical engineering, biomechanics, medical electronics and rehabilitation engineering. All come within the general umbrella of biomedical engineering. In 1972 (bio)medical engineering was defined (obviously by a committee) as being:

> ...the application of all forms of physical science and engineering, or fabrication, or assembly, to the production and manufacture of

equipment or instruments for use in the diagnosis of illness, or treatment or care of patients, or research into the causation of illness or methods of alleviating the effects of illness or injury.

Since then, although retaining the basic emphasis suggested by that definition, the field has broadened to include material sciences (which are often chemically based) and a need to provide a technology management function. Thus a more recently issued (equally obviously by a committee) definition of clinical engineering states that:

Clinical engineering is taken to mean the application of medical and biological engineering within the clinical environment, for the enhancement of health care. Such application is undertaken by ... clinical engineers who bring to health care facilities a level of education, experience and accomplishments which enable them to ... manage and interface with medical devices, instruments and systems, and the use thereof, during patient care ... in collaboration with other health care professionals.

Role of the Biomedical Engineer

Biomedical engineers are found throughout our health care system. Many are established in isolated clinical departments: some are found in large medical physics and biomedical engineering departments at regional level, some are found in research institutions, and others are found in industry. Often supported by technicians, the professional biomedical engineer is responsible for areas extending from design, manufacture and maintenance of hardware to quality control and the interpretation of signals from medical instrumentation. Some of the principal activities are outlined in the following paragraphs.

An Advisory Service on Available Technology

The range of technological devices and systems available to improve health care is vast, extending from the simplest aid intended for use by a disabled patient in a domicilary setting, through the variety of medical equipment standard in many hospitals, to the most complex electronic diagnostic and therapeutic equipment available as yet to few. With every passing year, technological advances in areas such as instrumentation, materials science, computer manufacture and nuclear engineering have significant impact on what it is feasible to implement for the benefit of the patient. The biomedical engineer whether based in industry or hospital will often advise on the applicability of such technology in the clinic, either in direct response to the presentation of a clinical problem, or by taking the initiative to introduce new products and methods as appropriate.

Equipment Management

Biomedical engineers are involved in the evaluation, purchase and installation of equipment within our hospitals. This includes the evaluation of equipment, taking into account cost-effectiveness as well as running and manning costs and subsidiary expenses, assuring the suitability of equipment to perform the desired task in the proposed environment, and checking on its safety. Planned maintenance of equipment is also vital to ensure safety and efficiency, and planned obsolescence and replacement of older equipment ensures continuity of service.

Biomedical Measurement and General Technical Support

Increased objectivity and scientific investigation in health care has led to a proliferation of biomedical measurement techniques. Many of the measurement devices require controlled operation by scientific and technical staff, and many require the services of a biomedical engineer to interpret the raw data into a relevant summary for clinical use. The biomedical engineer can also contribute to a higher quality of care by providing engineering competence in many day-to-day problems in our hospitals: supervision of workshops providing special purpose equipment, modification of existing facilities to meet new demands or upgrade performance, computer programming and extension of computer facilities, are examples of such a contribution. Equally, the industrially based biomedical engineer can provide similar services, though on a contract basis.

Education and Training

Biomedical engineers have a responsibility to educate not only the next generation of their own kind, but also their medical and industrial colleagues and the consumers of health care. This educational responsibility can embrace the provision for engineering personnel who have completed adequate formal education of in-job training (perhaps in collaboration with industry), including a range of clinical experience and responsibilities; the provision of instructional lectures/courses/ workshops aimed at giving medical staff, from student to qualified practitioner, the clearest view of what technology can offer the patient; and the provision where appropriate of advice to consumer representative groups on availability of hardware, effective use of resources and new developments.

Research and Development

Ideally, the involvement of a biomedical engineer with a proposed technological solution to a health care problem begins at the point of problem definition. In the clinic, problem formulation may require extensive measurements and analysis followed by a survey of similar cases before the design stage can properly be started. After design, adequately controlled trials of the resultant system and a close working relationship with the medical engineering industry will be necessary, for the introduction of the new system into common use is vital for effective carry-over of research into practice.

The National Scene

Having examined the types of activities in which biomedical engineers are currently engaged, let us now examine how biomedical engineering has developed within the United Kingdom. In 1958, a small international conference was held in Paris. The common interest of the delegates was the application of electronics to medicine and the objective of the meeting was to foster worldwide collaboration. A second conference was held the following year, and it was then that an International Federation for Medical Electronics and Biomedical Engineering was founded. The initial intention of the Federation was to encourage the formation of coherent national groups.

In the UK this led in 1960 to the founding of the Biological Engineering Society (BES), whose aims were to further co-operation between workers in the fields spanning the physical and life sciences. For most of its life the Society has functioned exclusively as a learned society, arranging regular scientific meetings and visits to institutions. Initially an élite 'club,' the membership, though open to all disciplines including surgeons, engineers and industrialists, was largely drawn from people who were fully established in their own field and for whom biomedical engineering was an activity of interest rather than a profession. The last decade has seen, with the growing membership, a need to encompass professional aspects of the field.

With the growth of interest in the subject came an appreciation that there was a need for schemes of postgraduate education. This reflected an awareness that for biomedical engineering to succeed clinicians needed to be taught something of the physical sciences and engineers needed a knowledge of the biological. With this further training communication between the two disciplines becomes possible and achievement of the common goal is reached through mutual understanding. The first such course was started in 1962 at Imperial College, London, within the Electrical Engineering Department. Further courses followed in 1966 at the Universities of Surrey and Strathclyde (both oriented towards biomechanics, or mechanical engineering applied to medicine) and others followed at St. Bartholomew's Hospital (medical electronics) and Chelsea College, London (biophysics and bioengineering). These courses were all postgraduate and served to train their students to be useful not only in their primary discipline, but in the necessary art of building bridges to another. A few other courses have followed, but the expansion of job prospects within the field anticipated in the late sixties has not occurred and as a consequence there has been little growth in new MSc courses. Despite this, many other biomedical engineers are trained by pursuing research towards PhDs in a number of institutions throughout the United Kingdom. There is as a consequence no real lack of suitably educated professionals to suit the job opportunities of our health care system, though arguably more opportunities are needed.

In pursuing its support of the educational process, the BES launched its own *Journal of Biomedical Engineering* in 1979. By this time membership of the Society had grown to around 600 and many of the founder members were reaching retirement age. With the passing years and the increasing awareness of the importance of the field the Society has come under greater pressure to help in the professional development of biomedical engineers. In responding to the pressure it successfully applied for affiliation to the Council of Engineering Institutions in 1981, and the first biomedical engineers to be chartered through the Society were registered the following year.

In defining what was necessary for the chartering process the Society quite deliberately set a standard which was higher than that required by any of the existing engineering Institutions. In addition to the requirement for basic training in the candidate's primary discipline (viz electrical engineering or mechanical engineering), the Society also requires evidence of training in biomedical engineering. The Society stipulates that this higher training is carried out at, or sponsored by, one of a network of National Training Centres. These are as yet few in number, and are rigidly examined by a team of experts drawn from several different disciplines before being designated. Each centre must be able to provide training in at least two of the major subject areas of biomedical engineering and with the growth in the number of centres it will become progressively easier for an aspiring professional biomedical engineer to become chartered. At present the professional biomedical engineer is one of a small élite. As an indication, the current edition of Who's Who of British Engineers lists only eleven biomedical engineers out of more than 2000 associated with engineering in general, and of that eleven only four are to be found within our hospitals.

The International Scene

The role of the International Federation for Medical Electronics and Biological Engineering has to a degree paralleled that of the BES. Initially conceived as an international co-ordinating group for scientific activity, it has grown steadily and now comprises twenty-five national societies, representing more than 9000 members. In the mid sixties the word electronics was dropped from the title in recognition of the fact that other professionals such as mechanical engineers and materials scientists were developing an equally important role in the general field of biomedical engineering. As a vehicle for communication the Federation established its journal *Medical and Biological Engineering* in 1962. As the Federation has grown its constituency and objectives have changed and in the mid seventies the words 'and Computing' were added to the journal's title. Considered to be the prime scientific publication in the field, the journal has always been edited and published in the United Kingdom.

Table 26.1   Year of actual affiliation to the IFMBE

1961	GDR, Netherlands
1962	Japan
1963	United Kingdom
1964	Belgium, Israel, Sweden
1965	Canada
1966	FRG
1967	Australia, Italy, Norway
1969	Finland
1971	USA, Yugoslavia
1973	Hungary
1974	France
1976	Austria, Denmark, South Africa
1979	Mexico, Spain
1981	Brazil
1982	Argentina, Cuba

During the last decade clinical engineering has become a viable sub-discipline with an increasing number of the Federation's members employed directly in health care. These now represent almost half the total membership of the Federation, and in 1979 the IFMBE established a special Working Group on Clinical Engineering. This group has recently established criteria for professional qualifications in the field of clinical engineering throughout the world (Roberts *et al* 1982). As a relatively young profession it has been possible to stimulate international agreement on criteria for registration before too many divisive national barriers have been erected. As a consequence the working group's activities have already stimulated governmental action in some countries within Europe directed at the establishment of legislative control of those allowed to practise.

In formulating its criteria, the IFMBE has taken due note of registration schemes already in existence (such as those in Canada, the UK and the USA), as well as those in an advanced stage of preparation. As a consequence, its recommendations represent, to a degree, the lowest common denominator of the existing national schemes. Thus the IFMBE is establishing the minimum standards which are acceptable for a professional clinical engineer, though these will inevitably be exceeded as each clinical engineer develops his own career. It is the belief of the IFMBE, like the BES within the United Kingdom, that qualifications and experience beyond those normally accepted for registration as a professional engineer are a necessary requirement for those wishing to practise in the field of clinical engineering and, furthermore, that such additional qualifications should be subject to certification through a similar review process. This scheme of mutual recognition will be administered by an International Clinical Engineering Board which will operate through an international network of national examining authorities all working to common standards. The peer review process on which all of the national schemes are based is already well recognized as an essential ingredient in maintaining the quality of professional registration throughout the world.

The Future

It will be apparent that the scope of biomedical engineering is very wide but that those considered to be professionally competent are relatively few. This problem is compounded in the UK by the fact that our health care system is presently outstripping the resources available to it. This reflects in part the failure of the physical scientists properly to advise their clinical and administrative colleagues on the cost consequences of applying technology, and in part their inability, because of their number and placing within our health care structure, to advise how and where it should be applied. The ever increasing awareness of the benefits of technology has not been matched by an informed appreciation of either its true costs or the achievable benefits. This in turn is producing, and not only in the UK but elsewhere, an anti-technology backlash. However, this problem is not peculiar to medicine.

So, at the very time when medicine most needs the help of the engineer to sustain and improve the effectiveness of resource deployment there are too few professionals around who are able to give such help. Why are there so few? It is partly because until very recently most physical scientists working inside our health care system saw no need, or indeed incentive, to establish professional working standards. Furthermore, the DHSS has been content to accept the lack of professionalism. Low (and often uninformed) expectation on behalf of clinicians and administrators of what the technologist can offer has been matched by poor salaries and career expectations. This inevitably has affected the calibre of personnel recruited to the hospital scientific service.

It has been interesting to see that the drive towards professionalism has been mainly fuelled not by those recruited into hospitals straight from university but by those who have come in at a later date and at a more senior level. It is also interesting that of the biomedical engineers working for the NHS only 12 per cent are chartered engineers while of those working outside 52 per cent are chartered engineers. If it is accepted that chartering is synonymous with professional competence then something clearly is wrong. In other countries, particularly in Canada and North America, hospital administrators have been quick to realize the enormous benefits to be gained from recruiting highly trained professional biomedical engineers. Many of these now have responsibilities far in excess of most of their clinical colleagues and the salaries to match. It is also interesting to see that many of the top jobs are now being taken by biomedical engineers additionally qualified in business administration.

The other problem which faces the emerging profession is its size. Couple limited finance with a small profession and the hurdles to be jumped in order to establish it become very real indeed. Professional secretariats, journals, examination and registration schemes all cost a disproportionate amount of money for the few who can benefit in the short term. For example, the costs of establishing a credible examination and registration procedure have almost bankrupted the Canadian Biomedical Engineering Society and yet no more than a handful of people have been professionally registered out of a total membership of hundreds. Fortunately the UK does not cover quite the same area as Canada and lower travelling costs are incurred both by candidates and by examining boards. The problems, however, are no less real.

One solution could be to piggy-back an existing professional body, but how would the Institution of Electrical Engineers look after the professional interests of the mechanical engineers designing limb orthoses? Or the Institution of Mechanical Engineers the interests of electronic engineers designing implanted nerve stimulators? Both of these professionals will be working together in rehabilitation engineering and both will have common problems beyond the experience of either of the large institutions. Inevitably, to establish a new profession which touches so many others demands that it is independent and as a consequence a few people have to make a very substantial financial sacrifice in order to ensure that this independence is successful.

Until relatively recently biomedical engineers have had neither the stature nor the professional competence to stand as equals (in every sense) alongside their clinical colleagues. The situation is changing and as the profession emerges it will be as natural for the biomedical engineer as the surgeon to assume full responsibility for those areas of direct and indirect patient care in which he and he alone is competent. This transition will take time for it will inevitably be viewed with scepticism and alarm by some clinicians as a potential threat to the concept of clinical responsibility for the individual patient.

However, the transition is taking place throughout the world as the value of professional biomedical engineers is becoming more widely appreciated and in some countries matched by both job responsibility and salary. Health care in the UK would unquestionably be enhanced by the accelerated development of the profession of biomedical engineering for there is no doubt that it has a major role to play in the deployment and development of health care resources.

Part 8
Issues, Research, Action

27 Education for Management outside Business

Charles Handy

How should you educate managers for the professions? The question seems simple enough, but it conceals enough assumptions, confusions and distorted traditions to have kept argument alive for generations, as we shall see.

Should the professions be 'managed' at all? The professions shun the word. Hospitals have administrators, schools have heads and deputy heads, universities have deans and provosts, professional institutions have clerks; there are bursars, wardens, governors and principals, but no managers. Is this all semantics or is there some meaning in this imagery? Do the professions have a point?

Let us concede however that, use what words we may, professional groups and institutions do have to be managed. Who, then, should those managers be? If management is a profession in its own right then presumably you would use a trained manager, preferably certificated in a properly professional way. After all, doctors don't do their own legal work or even staff the kitchens, why then should they bother with management? To a degree, they don't. There is the hospital administrator and a respectable career linked to this post. But teachers do not call in managers to run their schools, nor do professors, nor architects or accountants. Engineers would perhaps prefer to be managed by engineers but cannot always have it that way. Should we, in other words, be concerned to teach managers to run professions, or should we be teaching professionals to manage?

Is there anything intrinsically different about professional groups which makes them exempt from the rules and practices of management as they apply in industry and commerce? Does the discipline of management need to develop sub-disciplines not only for the professions, but for government bodies, for voluntary societies and political groupings? If so, where is this happening and who should be doing it? Or, conversely, has management been over-inflated into an independent discipline or quasi-profession? Perhaps it is better to see it as a necessary ancillary of professionalism, like codes of good practice. In which case each profession ought to be establishing its own theory and tradition of management and training its people in management as part of their professional duty. This, for instance, is the route that is being followed, rather tentatively and slowly, by the teaching profession.

The simple question with which we started is therefore the gate into a quagmire. It is however an important gate to open so that the confusions and the possibilities can be discussed. Because that discussion has not taken place each profession has adapted in its own way to the need to run its institutions, with the inevitable result that the education for management in the professions is a patchy affair at best, low in status and impoverished in concept. It has been a peculiarly British conceit that great men and great works need neither management nor marketing, or that if these things have to be done they can be done by anyone of reasonable competence in their spare time. It is an approach that has let us down in other areas before now, it would be a pity if it were to continue to prevail in the professions where, arguably, Britain's distinctive competence is to be found in the future. The education of the managers of our professions is crucial, but first we have to be clear <u>what</u> it is that needs to be taught, <u>who</u> it is that should be educated, as well as <u>when</u> in their careers and in what environment, <u>where</u>. Before we attempt to answer these questions it is important to be clear about the tradition which we inherit of management in the professions, and to unravel some critical confusions in the thinking about the institutions of professionals. It will, or should, become clear that professionals are right in their instinctive feeling that 'management' as practised in industry and commerce is not right for them without some major modifications.

The Tradition

Professionals are individualists, trained and licensed to practise as individuals. They grouped themselves together, first for mutual convenience as in a doctor's practice or a lawyer's chambers, then in institutions so that they might better combine their individual specialities in a service to the public. Once qualified, professionals have no master or boss. They may respect the greater wisdom, experience or expertise of a fellow-professional but that does not carry any right to issue commands or employ sanctions. Professional groups are meant to be partnerships not hierarchies, partnerships of autonomous competent individuals.

This pure tradition has become adulterated, but the core of it remains in the hearts and minds of the professionals themselves. It has become adulterated because it is impossible to run institutions of fifty or more professionals without hierarchies of responsibility, which means setting one man or one woman over another. Yet professional partnerships are meant to be self-governing communities serviced by people who do the paperwork, the appointments and the book-keeping. Thus it is that the professional firm would have Senior Partners, and secretaries or clerks or administrators — the managers serve the professionals, administration is a chore and something of which the professionals are glad to be relieved.

Institutions of any size, however, require their element of formal organization. There have to be roles set upon roles and authority emanating from those roles. Management is then controlling rather than servicing. This confuses the professional tradition and a variety of compromises have been worked out to try to retain the autonomy and the dignity of the professional while recognizing the needs of the institution. The most important of these compromises concerns territory, both psychological territory and physical territory. The teacher is king or queen of the classroom, a professional entitled to exercise professional discretion and autonomy, the doctor has his patients, the consultant his beds (a quasi-physical territory), the lawyer his clients and the engineer his plans, projects or plant. Within these territories the professional is supreme if not always unchallenged. The institution, through its managers who are still not called managers, will always try to gain more control of these professional territories or to redraw and tighten their boundaries by prescribing rules for treatment or curriculum, by requiring information and reports, by regulating time of access. The result will be a shifting compromise.

The professionals will also seek to capture the managerial role for themselves, preferring to be ordered around, if they have to be, by one of their own kind than by an outsider. The senior partner, therefore, in effect becomes the chief executive, even though he may or may not be a good manager. Professionals, after all, rise in the professional hierarchy because of their professional not because of their managerial competence. There is no guarantee that a good teacher will be a good manager, indeed rather the reverse. Sometimes, as in universities, the management role is shared out, on a rotating basis, between the leading professionals, which again seems to be a recipe for not getting the best management available. Hospitals, on the other hand, have tried to build up the role of the administrator, but this has inevitably put the potential conflict between the institution's requirements and the professionals' autonomy into higher profile, requiring diplomatic and political skills of a high order from people who still have a relatively low status role.

In other words, the traditions of professionalism, which are necessary and right whenever individual skill or talent is at a premium, cut across the requirements of large institutions, which is where most professionals now work. The problem is difficult and perhaps intractable. It is not made easier by the unthinking confusion that can be caused by the superficial application of management principles to professional organizations.

The Confusions

There are two principal confusions which bedevil management outside business: the confusion between Leadership and Administration and the allied confusion between Policy and Execution. In business the word management and the role of manager neatly combine the two. In professional organizations this is not possible because the proper traditions of professionalism do not permit such a handing over of power.

In professional organizations the leadership function has to be carried out by the senior professionals — to hand it over to an outsider would be an abrogation of their responsibilities. The administrative function, on the other hand, can be delegated to outsiders or to junior professionals because it is under the direction of professionals. The mistake is to imagine that leadership also entails administration. It does in business because there is no separate professional function of businessman. The engineers have long ago sunk their professional pride by joining business organizations and settling for a place in one of the functions, rather like doctors in pharmaceutical firms. 'Management' then became a word used to bond the two ideas of leadership and adminstration in one. Professional organizations need to separate them out, which is why they are right to be suspicious of the word management and fonder of its two more traditional component parts.

There is a similar confusion between policy and execution. In proper professional partnerships policy-making is a joint activity, led by the senior professionals but in which all the professionals can participate — it is a collegiate activity, based on consensus. The executive side of things, on the other hand, requires hierarchy and a formal structure of oversight. Professionals are more likely to accept an executive hierarchy if it is part of an agreed policy in which they participated. The managerial model tends to be oligarchical in that the executive also decides the policy. That is because business organizations are not collegial, they are usually owned by outsiders and rely on an instrumental contract with their staff; that is the staff are there to do a job for money. If the job is interesting and rewarding and status-providing so much the better, but they are there to work for the organization, whereas, in its present form, the organization is there to serve the professionals.

Participation and involvement in business organizations is put into the executive function, not the policy function. It is true that, at present, there is considerable discussion about the nature of the policy function. Japanese corporations, for instance, encourage full participation in the policy function and demand obedience (or dutiful respect) in the executive side of things − but then their workers are lifelong members of the institution, with what amounts to tenure in professional language. Foreigners claim to be frustrated by the length of time it takes Japanese corporations to reach a decision and amazed by the speed with which they can carry it out. In Germany and Scandinavia there is provision for formal representation by the workforce in policy decisions, but this does not come near to the collegial concept required by professionals. Because the word management includes both policy and executive functions the debate about participation is blurred in Britain. You can 'participate' at either the executive stage or the policy stage and be held to be participating in management. Too often it is participation in the executive function which can seem to amount to arguing about the menus while the ship is heading for the rocks.

Professional organizations have often shunned the word management but bought its substance, to their detriment in this instance. Too few of our professional institutions have separate policy and executive functions. The managers have mostly captured the policy system, with appropriate genuflections to consultation, usually through the executive function, and have then allowed the professionals to quibble about the details. The result can seem to be a muddled inefficient business trying to be a hospital or a school or a consultancy. Inevitably, as the Japanese know, participation in policy takes time. It is no part of corporate virility to take quick decisions. Time is the price one pays for consensus, which then allows one to execute with consent.

The difference between consensus and consent is a crucial one. Consensus implies that everyone is agreed and committed − active participation is therefore required. Consent implies acquiescence, or passive participation. If you want consensus, everyone's opinion has to be sought, but you can manage by consent if you allow time for people to express dissent before you act. No comment is therefore no dissent. Professionals, on the whole, like to be allowed to get on with their job, provided they are involved in the big decisions and know about the small decisions in time to object if they want to. Policy is management by consensus, execution is management by consent. To sum up:

− Professional institutions are different from business organizations because they are still, at heart, colleges of autonomous licensed individuals, not hired hands.

 — Professional institutions need therefore to distinguish between leadership and administration, between policy and execution.
 — Leadership belongs to the professionals, administration can be delegated to outsiders or to junior professionals.
 — Policy needs to be participative, execution formal, but with space for dissent.

I have stressed the differences of professional institutions at some length because, if these differences are real, it makes it unlikely that a person qualified and experienced in the management of a business will necessarily be properly equipped to run a professional institution. This may change, not because professional institutions will become more like businesses but because businesses will become more like professional institutions, but we are a long way from that yet in Britain. In the meantime, professional institutions, including schools, colleges, hospitals, social service departments, architectural practices and legal firms need to formulate their own organizational theory and practice, borrowing where appropriate from the tools and techniques of business but not slavishly imitating the structures and philosophies, complaining about them the while.

We can now more sensibly turn to the questions of who, what, when and where in education for the management of the professions.

The Questions

Who?

If the previous argument is accepted, it is the leading professionals who need to be educated for leadership. It would be highly unusual to bring in an outsider to preside over a professional institution, although there will be enough exceptions, in the shape of unusually talented and committed individuals, to prove the rule.

Administration is different. There is no reason why each profession should not develop its own cadre of administrators, as the health service has done. The more this is done, the more this will be a career in its own right with a quasi-professional status. The alternative, of using junior professionals part-time or on secondment, is acceptable if they are chosen for their administrative skills, not because they 'can be spared' or 'need the experience' — that is to sacrifice the institution to the individual. It is unnecessary and expensive to use senior professionals as administrators. Many schools who use a deputy or even a head as administrator end up by having the most highly-paid (and untrained) bursars in the business.

What?

Professor Katz long ago (Harvard Business Review 1958) listed the three skills that managers need: Conceptual, Human, Technical. He went on to point out that as you rise higher in an organization you increasingly need more conceptual skills and less technical skills. He also pointed out that whereas technical skills (counting, timetabling, running machines, etc.) can be taught, human skills can only be learnt and conceptual skills developed (if you haven't got them to start with you are unlikely to acquire them).

The implications are that administration (with a high proportion of technical and human skills) can be taught in the classroom and learnt by planned experience, ie one can have a programme for administrators, but that leadership (being conceptual with human skills) is more difficult to develop in a formal way. It remains crucial however, particularly because leadership in professional organizations is not confined to the top but is spread all over; professional organizations tend to be flat and wide, rather than tall and thin. There will be more pockets of leadership than in a tightly controlled structure.

When?

The easy answer to 'when?' is 'constantly'. It is not appropriate to rely on the 'banking' theory of education, in which you put away all that you need at the start of your career and draw on it thereafter. The technical skills of administration, for one thing, are likely to change rapidly and continually for as far ahead as one can see. The administrator trained today will be out-of-date in five years' time. Human skills and conceptual skills depend on practice and experience. To them the old adage applies that 'education is experience recollected in tranquillity', particularly if you add understanding to recollection.

In other words some version of continuing education or in-service training is essential. Unfortunately, professionalism is tied to the banking concept, because of the need for lengthy training as a prelude to certification. Therefore any later, non-certificated, education is seen very much as top-up or second-level education. Ways need to be found to make continuing education for professionals more prestigious, as the Armed Forces have succeeded in doing, partly by linking promotion to attendance at Staff Colleges or the National Defence College.

Where?

The need for more prestige for education for leaders and administrators would suggest one or more centres of excellence. Preferably, again following the Armed Forces, there would be separate centres for each profession, with one or more where the various professions would meet. Perhaps at the senior level this principle could with advantage be extended to include business and government, for the comparison of differences can be one of the best paths to conceptual learning. Furthermore, professionally insulated centres and courses are dangerous in that they can act as barriers to the introduction of new ideas and new ways of thinking.

Such centres are necessary to provide places for recollection and understanding as well as focal points for the development and recording of new theory and practice. But by themselves they would be useless. Within the organizations there needs to be constant debate and experimentation so that all professionals have the opportunity to develop their conceptual and human skills as a prelude to the leadership roles that many of them, at different levels, will be required to assume. Learning has to be a constant endeavour.

This means that each professional institution has to become a learning organization. That phrase is pregnant with implications. It means that the organization has positively to encourage people to ask questions, to search for answers and to test out those answers. It must promote curiosity, discovery and experiment: because that is how people learn. Most organizations, however, actively discourage such inclinations. Questions are seen as insubordinate at worst, as time-wasting at best. 'Because I say so', the irritated parental response, is also the irritated organizational response. Organizations want routine and predictability. They do not want discovery and experiment, particularly if the experiment goes wrong. They punish failure and mistakes, instead of regarding them as an initiative which didn't succeed. Organizations on the whole are inimical to learning. Only enlightened leadership can change that.

Conclusion

It is time that the professions paid serious heed to the problems of managing their institutions and educating their managers, or rather, their leaders and administrators. It is not enough to hope that any competent person can do it, nor is it enough to look to business for concepts, techniques and training methods. The professions must develop their own theories, train their own people and enliven their own organizations, whilst remaining aware of the dangers of insularity and of group-think. Some professions have made a start. More momentum is needed.

28 Review

Sinclair Goodlad

It is neither possible nor desirable to offer recommendations for education for the professions which could or should apply to all professions. By way of review, however, this chapter lists some questions (arising from the issues reviewed in the preceding chapters) which may serve as an initial agenda for discussion both for those attending the conference for which this book was written and for other groups.

Even the choice of questions for an agenda, however, implies a perspective, or a 'position'. In this selection of questions, the emphasis is a 'liberal-democratic' one stressing facilitation rather than control as a primary motive. The underlying assumption is that education for the professions is not, and indeed should not be (even if, politically, it could be), dominated by any one agency in society. Rather, education for a profession is the product of several competing interests which act as checks and balances on one another. If any one agency comes to dominate at the expense of the others, then the rich, pluralist (and therefore potentially democratic) texture of education will be diminished.

The questions are grouped under those with which the Introduction of the book opened and around which the discussion has been articulated.

Questions 1-5 are pragmatic: answers to them may point to specific action to be taken. Questions 6-8 are more complex (arising from some of the issues raised in chapters 1,2 and 3); it may be more difficult to give clear or decisive answers to them.

Agenda for Discussion

1. How may a greater flexibility of access to the professions be achieved compatible with efficiency and effectiveness in the education to be given and the maintenance of public confidence in professional services?

1.1 Is there at present an equitable distribution by sex, social class, ethnicity, etc. of those who are admitted to education for the professions and to subsequent practice?

1.2 If access is inequitable, is there a case for positive discrimination, and, if so, of what sort? Is there, for example, a case for ensuring that grade-for-grade, more applicants from working-class or ethnic minority backgrounds are admitted than applicants from those groups at present over-represented (cf Fulton, p.88 above)?

1.3 Do those with mixed GCE 'A' Levels (science and non-science), who may more often come from comprehensive schools with smaller curricular choice, deserve special treatment?

1.4 How valid or fair is the use of GCE 'A' Levels at all in selection for education to the professions? Should we encourage a wider choice of entry criteria?

1.5 Would a 'self-denying ordinance' by institutions of higher education and by professional bodies in terms of entry requirements permit and encourage changes in the school curriculum — towards, for example, a broader syllabus?

1.6 Is 'manpower planning' for the professions possible or desirable? If it is, who should do the planning? Should those responsible for recruitment to the professions seek to provide an 'over-supply' of potential entrants (in terms of numbers of practitioners required) to ensure that appropriately educated people are diffused through society not only as practitioners, but also as 'critics' of professional practice (through work in consumer organizations, mass media of communication, etc.) (cf Smith, p.111 above)?

2. How, through the design of curricula and the use of appropriate teaching methods, may intending professionals be encouraged to learn-how-to learn and simultaneously to receive a liberal education?

2.1 How may courses be designed to accommodate students having widely differing backgrounds (for example, if policies of 'positive discrimination' are adopted)?

2.2 How may curricula and teaching methods best accommodate the ever-increasing volume of material which it is desirable for professionals to know?

2.3 What are the relative attractions (or disadvantages) of taught options, projects and dissertations, and undergraduate research opportunities (cf MacVicar and McGavern, Chapter 24 above) as methods of bringing students into contact with the advancing edge of knowledge?

2.4 What obstacles (if any) prevent problem-based learning (cf Neufeld and Chong, Chapter 23 above) from being more widely used in education for the professions? For example, how can autonomous departments in a professional school be enabled to collaborate effectively (particularly if departmental headships rotate on a three-yearly basis)?

2.5 What have been found to be the most effective ways of linking theory and practice in education for the professions? How, for example, is informal (or 'osmotic') learning from placements, sandwich courses, internships, study service, etc. assimilated into the curriculum? How is it assessed?

2.6 How do institutions of higher education and/or professional bodies prevent the 'academicization' of learning (cf Warren-Piper, Chapter 22 above)?

2.7 If appropriate arrangements could be made for 'focusing' studies (projects, dissertations, internships, study service, problem-based curricula, undergraduate research opportunities, etc.) to give insight into the concerns of professions, could a case be made for alternative arrangements of initial and continuing education ? For example, would a 2 plus 2 pattern of studies be suitable for some professions?

2.8 What differences would be made to curricula and teaching methods in initial education for the professions if continuing education, systematically undertaken and equitably financed over an individual's lifetime, were to be assumed?

3. How may the mechanisms of accreditation and validation of education for the professions be based on appropriate evaluation of learning, and how may assessment measure legitimate professional competencies?

3.1 How may prior (experiential) learning be assessed for entry to professions at various possible levels of the educational process (cf Evans, 1981, 1983)?

3.2 Is there any evidence that the influence of professional bodies discourages innovation and initiative in education for the professions?

3.3 Do allegiances to professional associations or groupings impede or facilitate innovation and collaboration in industry, education, public services, or other spheres of life and work?

3.4 Do accreditation and validation procedures genuinely reflect what professionals actually do? (Or do they, for example, place excessive emphasis on memorization of facts?)

3.5 Once qualifying associations (Millerson 1964) have been empowered to grant licences to practise, are they adequately responsive to changing circumstances (public expectations, advances in theory, exigencies of practice)? If not, what can and should be done? Should there, for example, be state-funded 'performance standards review organizations'? (cf Burrage, p.33 above). Is there a case for, eg, a 'Privy Council Inspectorate' to ensure principles of good practice in professions and to prevent ossification?

3.6 Is formal professional status necessary or desirable in some occupations which may seek it and, indeed, for some which already have it? (cf Moore, p.74 above)?

3.7 What are the best ways of maintaining both high standards and flexibility in professional accreditation procedures? Could, for example, more use be made of external moderation of syllabuses (through the presence of representatives of professional bodies on examining boards) rather than promotion of uniformity through the publication of model syllabuses (cf Harrison, p.154 above)?

4. What are the most appropriate arrangements for continuing education for the professions, and how may these be suitably integrated with initial education?

4.1 Is there a case for re-licensing in any profession? If so, how should this be done?

4.2 Should more professions follow the accountants, surveyors, planners and others in requiring regular professional updating? If so, how should the updating be arranged and by whom? Who should pay? Does, for example, the Manpower Services Commission have a (funding, facilitating) role to play?

4.3 If re-licensing is neither desirable nor (politically) possible, how may professionals best be motivated to undertake continuing education (cf Innes-Williams, p.205 above)?

4.4 Is there a case for the creation of 'Deans of Professional Studies' to ensure continuity and integration between initial and continuing education? (Do, for example, the existing Regional Postgraduate Medical Deans offer a possible model to other professions (cf Innes-Williams, p.202 above)?)

4.5 If a distinction can be made (cf Sparkes, p.212-3 above) between awareness, updating, upgrading, and practitioners' courses in education for the professions, what are the best methods for achieving the objects of each? What arrangements, for example, can specific professions contemplate for optimizing the use of the Open University, the Open Tech, universities, polytechnics, professional associations, etc.?

4.6 Can continuing education be effectively combined with other professional purposes — for example, a regular audit of the achievements of an organization (cf Innes-Williams, p.204 above), or career development or corporate strategy (cf Higgins, p.218 above)?

4.7 What arrangements can be made to permit and encourage career-change, re-training, and 'credit-transfer' (of professional and/or academic recognition) from one profession to another, or from one level of practice in an occupation to another (ie technician to engineer)?

4.8 Who should be responsible for 'inter-professional training' — to help professions to understand and work with each other, or to stimulate growth in new areas such as information technology?

4.9 How may employers of professionals best influence the form and content of continuing education courses to ensure that courses are available to meet changing demands?

4.10 What release policies should employers operate to permit and encourage professional updating? Is any legislation by government required in this area?

5. Is there a case for the creation of a 'staff college' for professional educators for the professions based, for example, on departments of higher education in universities?

5.1 How can course design in education for the professions be improved?

5.2 Where might 'architects' of professional education come from (cf Warren-Piper, p.240 above)? In view of the (perhaps excessive?) distribution of rewards in favour of research (or practice) rather than in favour of course design in institutions of higher education, is there now a case for the creation of more 'professors of professional education' – (professors of engineering education, medical education, social work education, etc.) – possibly on short-term contracts (cf Goodlad, p.15 above)?

5.3 How should the performance of any such appointees be judged if publications come to have less salience? Peer-review by panels representing both other (research-oriented) academics and practitioners? Low drop-out or failure rates from courses they might design? High ratings from students and/or employers of graduates?

6. Why do occupations wish to become professions?

6.1 If the motivation of practitioners is idealistic (concerned with offering service rather than with securing personal status, power, wealth, etc.) when and where can (or should) the moral basis of this idealism be examined and/or nourished? In what contexts could, for example, the underlying emphasis of this chapter (the concern expressed in question 2 for facilitation rather than control) be subjected to sustained criticism?

7. Is the direct intervention of Government in quality-control in the professions (or occupations aspiring to professional status) politically acceptable ? (cf the recent interventions of the Secretary of State for Education in the field of teacher-training.) If not, how should quality (of service to the public) be secured?

8. How can professions avoid ossification? How, for example, can the range of their interests be continuously reviewed and refreshed – extending, perhaps, to political action in favour of people not well provided for by existing social arrangements?

Concluding Remarks

Professions are influential vehicles not only for the dissemination of technical information, but also for the expression of fundamental social values and interests. As Terry Johnson has shown (Chapter 2 above), they often act as the medium for collective political will (shaping it as well as transmitting it). In a very real sense, professions are the guardians of public values. If they are perceived to be exercising this responsibility in a partisan fashion, the question embodied in the title of this book will become the central one, namely: *Quis custodiet ipsos custodes?* (Who is to guard the guards themselves?) In a liberal democracy, self-control (together with a plurality of points of initiative and centres of responsibility) is to be preferred to central or bureaucratic control. It is for this reason that systematic attention to political, economic, and social questions must be at the heart of education for the professions − not as indoctrination, but rather as moral debate.

Appendices

Appendix A

The Authors

Mr.IAN BRUCE, who is Director of the Barnett Consulting Group, was an overseas General Manager with Shell International before joining the London Business School at which he was Director of External Affairs until his retirement in 1983.

Dr.JOHN BURGOYNE is Research Director in the Centre for the Study of Management Learning at the University of Lancaster which is concerned with furthering the understanding and practice of education, training, and development of those involved in management processes in all kinds of organization. His many publications include *Developing Resourceful Managers* (1973) (with J.F. Morris); *Management Development : Context and Strategies* (1978) (with R.Stuart), and *A Manager's Guide to Self-Development* (1978)(with M.J.Pedler and T.H.Boydell).

Dr.MICHAEL BURRAGE currently lectures at the London School of Economics and the Institute of United States Studies. He was educated at the London School of Economics, and was ACLS Research Fellow at Harvard, 1968-1970. His main research interest is the comparative analysis of professional and industrial organizations; his articles on these topics have appeared in *Administrative Science Quarterly, American Sociological Review, Daedalus,* etc.

Dr.JOHN P.CHONG is a 1978 medical graduate of McMaster University. He is currently Assistant Professor in the Department of Clinical Epidemiology and Biostatistics and the Occupational Health Programme at the Faculty of Health Sciences, McMaster University, Canada. His current interests include the development of innovative learning materials in medical education, the prevention of occupational and environmental diseases, and the evaluation of health care services.

Dr.DONALD CLARKE is Director of the British Life Assurance Trust Centre for Health and Medical Education. He has qualifications in economics, education, and psychology, has twenty-five years of teaching experience in schools, teacher training institutions, universities, and adult education, and is author of more than fifty papers. He holds fellowships of the Royal Society of Medicine and the Royal Society of Health.

Sir JOHN ELLIS, who is retired, was Dean of the London Hospital Medical College, 1967-1981. He was founder-secretary of the Association for the Study of Medical Education, 1956-1971, and editor of the *British Journal of Medical Education*, 1966-1975. He was a member of the WHO Expert Advisory Panel on Health Manpower, 1963-1982; member of the UGC Medical Sub-Committee 1959-1969; and member of the Royal Commission on Medical Education, 1965-1968. He is author of numerous publications on medical education.

Sir MONTY FINNISTON, who is chairman of a number of companies, was Chairman of the Committee of Inquiry into the Engineering Profession. He is a Fellow of the Royal Society, of the Royal Society of Edinburgh, of the Royal Society of Arts, and of the Fellowship of Engineering, and he holds honorary doctorates from many universities. He is active in many spheres of public life including being Chairman of the Council of the Policy Studies Institute, Chancellor of the University of Stirling, and pro-Chancellor of the University of Surrey.

Mr.BARRY FIRTH, who is Senior Assistant Secretary (Qualifications) and London Officer for the Institution of Chemical Engineers UK, has worked in academic administration at the University of Liverpool, the Australian National University, and the University of Papua New Guinea, and as Registrar of the Libyan Higher Institute of Mechanical and Electrical Engineering. He organized the International Conference on Higher Education in Developing Countries, Malta 1979, and was Secretary to the EFCE International Symposium on Chemical Engineering Education, London 1981.

NANCY FOY is a management consultant specializing in Management Development. She was FME Research Fellow at the Oxford Centre for Management Studies, 1977-80, and a manager in STC Ltd. 1980-82. She is author of many papers and books including *The Yin and Yang of Organizations* (1980), *The Sun Never Sets on IBM* (1975), *Presidential Leadership and University Change* (1974) (with Warren Bennis), and *Management Education : Current Action and Future Needs* (1979).

Dr.OLIVER FULTON, who is Lecturer in the Institute for Post-Compulsory Education at Lancaster University, holds degrees from Oxford and the University of California. His major research interests at present are in comparative and policy aspects of access to higher education, and in higher education policy more generally. His publications include *Access to Higher Education* (1981), which he edited as convenor of the SRHE Leverhulme seminar on Demand and Access.

Dr.SINCLAIR GOODLAD, who is Senior Lecturer in the Presentation of Technical Information at the Imperial College of Science and Technology, University of London, studied at Cambridge and the London School of Economics, has taught at Delhi University and at MIT, and was founder-secretary of the Higher Education Foundation. His publications on higher education include *Conflict and Consensus in Higher Education* (1976) and *Learning by Teaching* (1979). He edited and contributed to *Education and Social Action* (1974), *Project Methods in Higher Education* (1975), *Study Service* (1982), and *Economies of Scale in Higher Education* (1983).

Mr.ANTHONY HAMBLIN, who is Lecturer and Placements Officer in the School of Management, University of Bath, studied at Oxford and at the London School of Economics. From 1959-1963 he worked with Keith Thurley at LSE, investigating the role of industrial supervisors. He is author of *Evaluation and Control of Training* (1974).

Professor CHARLES HANDY is Visiting Professor at the London Business School, a writer, and consultant to a wide variety of organizations in business, government, and the voluntary sector. He studied at Oxford and at MIT and held industrial posts in Shell International and Anglo-American Corporation before starting and directing the Sloan Programme at the London Business School. In 1977 he was appointed Warden of St.George's House, Windsor. He is author of *Understanding Organizations* (1976), *Gods of Management* (1979), *Taking Stock* (1983) and forthcoming books on The Future of Work and Understanding Schools.

Dr.LEE HARRISBERGER, who is Professor and Head of Mechanical Engineering at the University of Alabama, studied at the University of Oklahoma, the University of Colorado, and Purdue University. He has served as Dean of the College of Science and Engineering at the University of Texas, as Andrew Mellon Visiting Professor of Engineering at the Cooper Union, and as President of the American Society for Engineering Education. He is founder-director of the Mechanical Engineering Design Clinic, and is author of two textbooks and numerous publications on engineering design and instructional innovations.

Mr.ROGER HARRISON, who is Senior Lecturer in the Institute of Educational Technology in the Open University, was previously Senior Lecturer in Physics at Newcastle Polytechnic and contributed to the

Nuffield School Physics Project. He has written papers on applications of Educational Technology in the Open University as well as a number of course units. He wrote the chapter on Students and Validation in *Practice and Perspective in Validation* (ed.Church)(1983).

Professor CHRISTOPHER HIGGINS, who is Director of the Management Centre and Professor of Management Sciences, University of Bradford, was formerly Director of Economic Planning and Research, IPC Newspapers Ltd. His previous appointments include English Electric Company, Metra Consulting Group, and the Department of the Chief Scientist (RAF) Ministry of Defence. He is author of books and papers on operational research, corporate planning, management information systems, and management education. He is a member of the Final Selection Board of the Civil Service Commission and of the Business and Management Studies Sub-Committee of the University Grants Committee. He was founder-chairman of the Social Science Research Council's Accountancy Steering Committee and of the Committee on Operational Analysis of the Defence Scientific Advisory Council.

Dr.CYRIL HOULE, who is Senior Programme Consultant at the W.K. Kellogg Foundation, Michigan, retired in 1978 from the University of Chicago where he was a professor and administrator for forty years. He is a member of the National Academy of Education and has been awarded honorary doctorates by six universities. He is author of numerous papers and of *Continuing Education in the Professions* (1980) and *Patterns of Learning* (1984).

Dr.DAVID INNES-WILLIAMS, who is Director of the British Postgraduate Medical Federation, has held specialist posts in Urology and was Dean of the Institute of Urology, 1972-1978. He is a member of the General Medical Council, Chairman of the Imperial Cancer Research Fund, and Vice-President of the Royal College of Surgeons of England. He is holder of numerous awards and honorary posts, and has been author and/or editor of many books and papers including *Paediatric Urology* (1968 and 1982), *Operative Surgery* (1975), *Scientific Foundations of Urology* (joint editor)(1976 and 1982), and *Surgical Paediatric Urology* (joint editor)(1978).

Mr.TERRY JOHNSON, who is Senior Lecturer and Head of the Department of Sociology at the University of Leicester, spent some years as a journalist on the *Chicago Tribune* before reading Sociology at the University of Leicester. He has been Assistant Lecturer in Sociology at the University of Ghana, and Senior Research Fellow at the Institute of

Commonwealth Studies, University of London. His publications include *Professions and Power* (1972), *Community in the Making* (1973), and *The Structure of Social Theory* (forthcoming 1984).

NORMA McGAVERN joined the MIT Undergraduate Research Opportunities Programme staff in 1976 and became Associate Director in 1979. A graduate of St.Lawrence University and Boston University, she taught history and social studies in the Lexington, Massachusetts, public schools. Before going to MIT she also served as assistant to the president of Data Terminal Systems, Inc., and as a member of the staff of the Governor of Massachusetts.

Professor MARGARET MACVICAR, who was founder and is Director of the MIT Undergraduate Research Opportunities Programme, is Cecil and Ida Green Professor of Education at the Massachusetts Institute of Technology where she combines an active technical career in physics, metallurgy, and materials science with her educational interests. She has served as a Trustee of the Carnegie Foundation for the Advancement of Teaching and as a member of the visiting committee to the General Motors Institute. She has held the Chancellor's Distinguished Professorship at the Universty of California at Berkeley and won the Sizer prize for the most significant contribution to undergraduate education at MIT. Simultaneously with her MIT academic appointment, she has recently been appointed Vice-President of the Carnegie Institution of Washington.

Professor PETER MOORE, who is Principal elect and Professor of Statistics and Operational Research at the London Business School, is a member of the Prime Minister's Review Body on the Remuneration of Doctors and Dentists, and of the University Grants Committee (of which he is a former Vice-Chairman), and was a consultant to the Wilson Committee on Financial Institutions. He has been Assistant to the Economic Advisor to the National Coal Board; Senior Statistician and Head of Statistical and Mathematical Services of the Reed Paper Group; Visiting Professor in Operational Research at the Virginia Polytechnic Institute; and a Director of Shell UK Ltd. He has been Chairman of the Conference of University Management Schools and Chairman of the International Teachers Programme (for developing management teachers). He is author of numerous books and papers including *Basic Operational Research* (1968), *Risk in Business Decision* (1972), *The Anatomy of Decisions* (1976) (with H.Thomas) and *Reason by Numbers* (1980).

Mr.RICHARD MORRIS, who is Chairman of Brown and Root (UK) Ltd., is Industrial Adviser to the Barclays Bank Group and Pro-

Chancellor of Loughborough University and is Visiting Professor of Chemical Engineering at the University of Strathclyde. He has been President of the Institution of Chemical Engineers and Honorary Secretary of the Fellowship of Engineering. In 1980 he was Chairman of the National Conference on the Education and Training of Engineers.

Dr.VICTOR NEUFELD, who is Professor of Medicine and Clinical Epidemiology and Biostatistics at the Faculty of Health Sciences, McMaster University, Canada, studied at the University of Saskatchewan, the London School of Tropical Medicine, and Michigan State University (where he studied educational psychology). His interests include new methods of medical education and the assessment of clinical competence. He is the principal editor of *Clinical Competence : A Measurement Perspective*.

Professor COLIN ROBERTS, who is Professor of Biomedical Engineering at the King's College School of Medicine and Dentistry, London University, was formerly a research engineer with Associated Electrical Industries. A past-President of the Biological Engineering Society, he is at present the Chairman of the International Clinical Engineering Board. He is the author of a book on Blood Flow Measurement and of many scientific publications in the field of biomedical engineering. He is deputy editor and editor designate of *Medical and Biological Engineering and Computing*, the official·journal of the International Federation for Medical and Biological Engineering.

Professor PHILIP SEAGER, who is Professor of Psychiatry at the University of Sheffield, is Sub-Dean of the Royal College of Psychiatrists and Secretary of its Education Committee. He was a member of the General Nursing Council for England and Wales and of the Joint Board of Clinical Nursing Studies. His interests include neuro-physiological studies, suicide and attempted suicide, and medical and nursing education.

Dr.ROBERT SMITH, who has been Director of Kingston Polytechnic since 1982, was previously Professor of Physical Electronics and Dean of Engineering at Southampton University. He was Chairman of the Engineering Professors' Conference 1980-1982. He is a member of the Design Council and of the joint SERC/SSRC Committee.

Professor JOHN SPARKES, who is Professor of Electronics Design and Communications, was until recently Dean of the Faculty of Technology at the Open University, and is a member of the Engineering Professors Conference. He was Head of the Physics Section at British Telecommunications Research; Senior Lecturer in Electrical Engineering at Imperial College; and Reader in Electronics at the University of Essex. His many publications include *Junction Transistors* (1966) and *Transistor Switching and Sequential Circuits* (1969). At the Open University he has participated in the preparation of many distance-teaching courses using a variety of media; recently this has included courses for the professional updating of engineers.

Professor HENRY WALTON, who is Professor of Psychiatry at the University of Edinburgh and Director of the University Department of Psychiatry, is President of the World Federation for Medical Education and President of the Association for Medical Education in Europe. He is the Editor of *Medical Education*, was a founder member and past-Chairman of the Society for Research into Higher Education, and is a past-Chairman of the Association for the Study of Medical Education. He has been Chairman of the Joint Committee on Higher Psychiatric Training, and Chairman of the Association of University Teachers of Psychiatry. He is author of books on alcoholism and group psychotherapy, and has published extensively on personality disorder, alcoholism, eating disorders, psychotherapy, and higher education. He was also a consultant to the World Health Organization, on the Task Force preparing for the World Assembly's Technical Discussion in May 1984, on the theme of mobilizing universities for health care.

Mr.DAVID WARREN-PIPER is Head of the Centre for Staff Development in Higher Education at the Institute of Education of the University of London. (The Centre was previously the University Teaching Methods Unit, which he joined in 1971.) He has written, contributed to, or edited a number of books on higher education. His professional training was in occupational psychology; he has worked in an educational research unit, a university department of management, an art college, and an architectural school, and has undertaken a range of industrial consultancies on management training. He was Chairman of the Society for Research into Higher Education, 1982-83.

Appendix B

SRHE 1984 Conference Committee

Sir Hermann Bondi (Chairman) Natural Environment Research Council

Dr.John Calvert (Organizer) Department of Management Studies, Loughborough University of Technology

Mr.R.A.Barnett Council for National Academic Awards

Dr.D.W.Clarke BLAT Centre for Health and Medical Education

Dr.Sinclair Goodlad (Editor of Proceedings) Department of Humanities, Imperial College, London University

Mr.David Jaques Hatfield Polytechnic

Dr.Nick Rushby Computer Centre, Imperial College, London University

Dr.David Billing Polytechnic of Central London

Dr.Graham Stodd West Sussex Institute of Higher Education

SRHE Administration

Mr.Rowland Eustace SRHE Administrator

Mrs.Sally Kington SRHE Publications Officer

References

Abraham Lincoln School of Medicine (1973) *Curriculum Objectives* Abraham Lincoln School of Medicine, University of Illinois College of Medicine. London: British Medical Association Publishing Department

Ackerknecht,E.H. (1967) *Medicine at the Paris Hospital 1794-1848* Baltimore: Johns Hopkins

Ahlstrom,G. (1982) *Engineers and Industrial Growth: Higher Technical Education and the Engineering Profession During the Nineteenth and Early Twentieth Centuries. France, Germany, Sweden, and England* London: Croom Helm

AMA Source Document (1975) *Malpractice in Focus* Chicago: American Medical Associaton

APAP (Association of Physician Assistant Programs) (1980) *Selected Annotated Bibliography of the Physician Assistant Profession* Arlington: APAP

Areskog,N.H.(Ed.) (1977) *The Introduction of New Subjects in the Curriculum: A Case Study, Medical Engineering* Report of a Conference in Linkoping, Sweden, 1975. Dundee: Association for Medical Education in Europe

Artz,F. (1966) *The Development of Technical Education in France 1500-1850* Cambridge: MIT Press

Association for Medical Education in Europe (1968) *Survey of Medical Students in 1966* Summary Report. Appendix 19 of the Report of the Royal Commission on Medical Education Cmnd.3569. London: HMSO

Association for Medical Education in Europe (1982) Editorial *Medical Education* 16(1)1-2

Association for Medical Education in Europe (1975) *The Objectives of Undergraduate Medical Education* Report of a Workshop, Edinburgh 1974

Association of Medical Deans in Europe (1980) Editorial *Medical Education* 14(2) 95-96

Association of Teachers of Management (1983) *The Future of Management Education and Development: A Discussion Paper* London: Association of Teachers of Management

Ball,R.J. (1983) The business school perspective (Stockton Lecture) *London Business School Journal* 8(1)

Bannerman,R.H., Burton,J. and Wen-Chieh,C. (1983) *Traditional Medicine and Health Care Coverage* Geneva: World Health Organization

Barber,B. (1963) Some problems in the sociology of the professions *Daedalus* Fall,669-688

Barker,W.H.(Ed.) (1983) *Teaching Preventive Medicine in Primary Care* New York: Springer Publishing Co.

Barondess,J.A. (1983) The doctor, the patient and the system: reflections on education for clinical careers *Perspectives in Biological Medicine* 26,261-273

Barrington-Kaye,B.L. (1960) *The Development of the Architectural Profession in Britain* London

Barrows,H.S. and Mitchell,D.L.M. (1975) An innovative course in undergraduate neuroscience experiment in problem based learning with 'Problem Boxes' *British Journal of Medical Education* 9(4)223-230

Barrows,H.S., Norman,G.R., Neufeld,V.R. and Feightner,J.W. (1982) The clinical reasoning of randomly selected physicians in general medicine practice *Clinical and Investigative Medicine* 5(1) 49-55

Barrows,H.S., and Tamblyn,R.M. (1980) *Problem-based Learning: An Approach to Medical Education* New York: Springer Publishing Co.

Becker,H. (1962) The nature of the profession. In Henry,N.B.(Ed.) *Education for the Professions* Chicago: University of Chicago Press, pp.27-46

Becker,H.S., Geer,B., Hughes,E.C. and Strauss,A.L. (1961) *Boys in White. Student Culture in Medical School* New Brunswick,NJ: Transaction Books

Berlanstein,L.R. (1975) *The Barristers of Toulouse in the Eighteenth Century,1740-1793* Baltimore: Johns Hopkins

Biological Engineering Society (1981) *Education, Training and Careers in Biomedical Engineering in the 1980s* London: Biological Engineering Society

Black,J. (1971) *Radical Lawyers: Their Role in the Movement and in the Courts* New York: Avon

Blackburn,R.T. and Fox,T.G. (1976) The socialization of a medical faculty *Journal of Medical Education* 51,806

Blauch,L.E. (1955) *Education for the Professions* Washington, DC: US Department of Health Education and Welfare

Bledstein,B.J. (1976) *The Culture of Professionalism. The Middle Class and the Development of Higher Education in America* New York: W.W.Norton & Co.Inc.

Bligh,D.(Ed.) (1982) *Professionalism and Flexibility in Learning* Guildford: Society for Research into Higher Education

Bloom,S.W. (1958) Some implications of studies in the professionalization of the physician. In Jaco,E.G.(Ed.) *Patients, Physicians and Illness* New York: The Free Press of Glencoe

Boaz,M.(Ed.) (1981) *Issues in Higher Education and the Professions in the 1980s* Littleton, Colorado: Libraries Unlimited,Inc.

Boot,R.L. and Boxer,P.J. (1980) Reflective Learning. In Beck,J and Cox,C.(Eds) *Advances in Management Education* Chichester: Wiley, pp.231-252

Boot,R.L. and Reynolds,M. (Eds) (1983)*Learning and Experience in Formal Education* Manchester: Manchester University Monographs

Boyatzis,R.E. (1982) *The Competent Manager: a model for effective performance* New York: Wiley

Bridgstock,M. (1976) Professions and social background: the work organization of general practitioners *The Sociological Review* 24(2) 309-329

British Association (1977) *Education, Engineers, and Manufacturing Industry* Birmingham, University of Aston: British Association for the Advancement of Science

Bucher,R. and Strauss,A. (1961) Professions in process *American Journal of Sociology* 66 (Jan) 325-334

Burgoyne,J.G. (1977) *SSRC Area Review: general courses* Lancaster: CSML University of Lancaster

Burgoyne,J.G. (1982) Integration. In Cooper,C.(Ed.) *Developing Managers for the 1980s* London: Macmillan

Burgoyne,J.G. and Cooper,C.L. (1976) A classified bibliography of some research on teaching methods in management education and some inferences about the state of the art *International Management Review* 16(4)95-102

Bussard,E. (1982) *Professional Competence Development: The Cooper Union Experience* New York:Educational Facilities Laboratories, Academy for Educational Development

Campbell,J.P., Dunnette,M.D., Lawler,E.E. and Weick,K.E. (1970) *Managerial Behaviour, Performance and Effectiveness* New York: McGraw-Hill

Cannell,R.L. (1982) *The Updating of Professional Engineers* Loughborough: Centre for Extension Studies, Loughborough University of Technology

Caplow,T. and McGee,R.J. (1958) *The Academic Market-Place* New York: Basic Books

Carr-Saunders,A.M. and Wilson,P.A. (1933) *The Professions* (New edition 1964) London: Frank Cass

Cartwright,A. (1964) *Human Relations and Hospital Care* London: Routledge and Kegan Paul

Cartwright,L.K. (1972) Personality differences in male and female medical students *Psychiatry in Medicine* 3,213-218

Chaigneau,V.L. (1945) *Histoire de l'Organisation Professionelle en France. La Loi du 4 Octobre 1941* Paris: Plon

Chickering,A.(Ed.) (1981) *The Modern American College* San Francisco: Jossey-Bass

Christensen,C.R. (1981) *Teaching by the Case Method* Boston: Division of Research, Harvard Business School

Chroust,A.H. (1965) *The Rise of the Legal Profession in America. Vol.2. The Revolution and Postrevolutionary Era* Norman: University of Oklahoma

Church,C.H.(Ed.) (1983) *Practice and Perspective in Validation* Guildford: Society for Research into Higher Education

Cogan,M.L. (1953) Towards a definition of profession *Harvard Educational Review* 23 (Winter 1953) 33-50

Cogan,M.L. (1955) The problems of defining a profession *The Annals of the American Academy of Political and Social Science* 297 (January)

Collins,R. (1979) *The Credential Society* New York and London: Academic Press

Committee for Engineering in Polytechnics (1982) *Policy Statement*

Cook,T.G.(Ed.) (1973) *Education and the Professions* London: Methuen

Conley Hill,C. (1979) *Problem-solving: Learning and Teaching. An Annotated Bibliography* London: Francis Pinter (Publishers) Ltd.

Crequer,N. (1982) From the outside looking in *Times Higher Education Supplement* 5 November

Crotty,P.T. (1974) Continuing education and the experienced manager *California Management Review* 17 (1) 108-123

Dainton Report (1968) *Enquiry into the Flow of Candidates in Science and Technology into Higher Education* Council for Scientific Policy, Department of Education and Science.Cmnd.3541. London: HMSO

Dardier,E. (1973) Mohawk College physiotherapy program *Physiotherapy Canada* 25(4) 237-239

Dixon,N. (1976) *On the Psychology of Military Incompetence* London: Jonathan Cape

Donnan,S.P.B. (1976) British medical students in 1975 *Medical Education* 10,341-347

Dore,R. (1976) *The Diploma Disease, Education, Qualifications, and Development* London: George Allen & Unwin

Douarche,A. (1905) *Les Tribunaux Civils de Paris pendant la Revolution 1791-1800* Paris: Maison Quantin

Duman,D. (1983) *The English and Colonial Bars in the Nineteenth Century* London: Croom Helm

Elliott,P. (1972) *The Sociology of the Professions* London: Macmillan

Elstein,A.S., Shulmann,L.S. and Sprafka,S.A. (1978) *Medical Problem-Solving: An Analysis of Clinical Reasoning* Cambridge, Mass: Harvard University Press

Elton,L.R.B., Boud,D.J. and Nutall,J. (1973) Teach yourself paradigm: the Keller Plan *Chemistry in Britain* 9(4)

Engel,C.E. and Clarke,R.M. (1979) Medical education with a difference *Programmed Learning and Educational Technology* 16,70-87

Engel,G.V. and Hall,R.H. (1973) The growing industrialization of the professions. In Freidson,E.(Ed.) *The Professions and their Prospects* Beverley Hills and London: Sage

Engineering Professors Conference (1982) *Engineering Professors Conference 1982: Proceedings*

Entwistle,N.J. and Wilson,J.D. (1977) *Degrees of Excellence: The Academic Achievement Games* London: Hodder and Stoughton

Etzioni,A. (Ed) (1969) *The Semi-Professions and their Organization* New York: Free Press

Evans,J.R. (1970) Organizational patterns for new responsibilities *Journal of Medical Education* 45, 989-999

Evans,N. (1981) *The Knowledge Revolution: Making the Link Between Learning and Work* London: Grant McIntyre

Evans,N. (1983) *Curriculum Opportunity. A map of experiential learning in entry requirements to higher and further education award bearing courses* A Project Report. London: Further Education Unit, Department of Education and Science

Fabb,W.E. and Marshall,J.R. (1982) *The Assessment of Clinical Competence in General Family Practice* Lancaster: MTP Press Ltd.

Farrant,J. (1981) Trends in admission. In Fulton,O. (Ed.) *Access to Higher Education* Guildford: Society for Research into Higher Education

Feinstein,A.R. (1970) What kind of basic science for clinical medicine? *New England Journal of Medicine* 283,847-852

Ferrier,B.M. *et al* (1978) Selection of medical students at McMaster University *Journal of the Royal College of Physicians London* 12

Finniston,M. (1980) *Engineering Our Future* Report of the Committee of Inquiry into the Engineering Profession. Cmnd.7794 London: HMSO

Fisher,L.A. (1971) On the value of professional discourtesy. In Gilbert, J.A.L. (Ed.) *Evaluation in Medical Education* Edmonton Bulletin: Commercial Printers

Fleming,P.R., Sanderson,P.H., Stokes,J.F. and Walton,H.J. (1976) *Examinations in Medicine* Edinburgh: Churchill Livingston

Flexner,A. (1925) *Medical Education* London: MacMillan

Florman,S.C. (1968) *The Existential Pleasures of Engineering* New York: St.Martens

Foucault,M. (1973) *The Birth of the Clinic* London: Tavistock

Foy,Nancy (1978) *The Missing Links: The Future of British Management Education* Oxford: Oxford Centre for Management Studies

Fraenkel,G.J. (1978) McMaster revisited *British Medical Journal* 2,1072-1076

Fredericks,M. and Mundy,P. (1976) *The Making of a Physician* Chicago: Loyola University Press

Freidson,E.(Ed.)(1973) *The Professions and their Prospects* Beverly Hills and London: Sage

Freidson,E. (1975) *The Profession of Medicine* New York: Dodd, Mead & Co.

Fulop,T. (1979) *Continuing Education of Health Personnel and its Evaluation* Copenhagen: WHO Regional Office for Europe

Fulton,O. (1981) Principles and policies. In Fulton,O.(Ed.) *Access to Higher Education* Guildford: Society for Research into Higher Education

Funkenstein,D.H. (1978) *Medical Students,Medical Schools and Society During Five Eras* Cambridge,Mass.: Ballinger Publishing Company

Gelfand,T. (1974) From Guild to profession: The surgeons of France in the eighteenth century *Texas Reports on Biology and Medicine* 32,121-132

General Guide (1983) MD Program, Faculty of Health Sciences, McMaster University

General Medical Council (1977) *Basic Medical Education in the British Isles* (2 vols.)London: Nuffield Provincial Hospitals Trust

Gerson,A. (1982) Attorneys spend $6.5 million for TV ads *National Law Journal* 26 April,2

Goode,W.J. (1960) Encroachment, charlatanism, and the emerging professions: psychology, sociology, and medicine *American Sociological Review* 25(6 Dec) 902-914

Goode,W.J. (1975) Community within a community: the professions *American Sociological Review* 22, 194-200

Goodlad,S. (1973) *Science for Non-Scientists. An examination of objectives and constraints in the presentation of science to non-specialists* Oxford: Oxford University Press

Goodlad,S.(Ed.)(1974) *Education and Social Action* London: George Allen & Unwin

Goodlad,S. (1976) *Conflict and Consensus in Higher Eduction* London: Hodder & Stoughton Educational

Goodlad,S. (1977) *Socio-Technical Projects in Engineering Education* University of Stirling: General Education in Engineering (GEE) Project

Goodlad,S. (1979) *Learning by Teaching. An introduction to tutoring* London: Community Service Volunteers.

Goodlad,S.(Ed.)(1982a) *Study Service: an examination of community service as a method of study in higher education* Windsor: NFER-Nelson

Goodlad,S. (1982b) Communicating technical information *Physics Bulletin* 33,238-239

Goodlad,S., Bennett,C., Gladstone,M. and Stafford,B. (1983) The use of video for training engineers in the presentation of technical information *Journal of Educational Television* 9(2)103-115

Goodman,P.S., Pennings,J.M. and Associates (1977) *New Perspectives on Organizational Effectiveness* San Francisco: Jossey-Bass Inc.

Gould,J.(Ed.) (1968) *The Teaching of the Social Sciences in Higher Technical Education: an international survey* Paris: UNESCO

Granick,D. (1972) *Managerial Comparisons of Four Developed Countries: France, Britain, the United States and Russia* Cambridge: MIT

Grant,G. and Associates (1979) *On Competence* San Francisco: Jossey-Bass Inc.

Graves,D.(Ed.) (1983) *The Hidden Curriculum in Business Studies* Proceedings of a conference on Values in Business Education. London: Higher Education Foundation with the Council for National Academic Awards

Grayson,L.(Ed.) (1977) *The Design of Engineering Curricula* Paris: UNESCO

Greenwood,E. (1957) Attributes of a profession *Social Work* 2(3) 44-55

Grogan,W.R. (1978) Problems and opportunities in performance-based engineering education *Proceedings Eighth Annual Frontiers in Education Conference* American Society for Engineering Education

Guttsman,W.L. (1963) *The British Political Elite* London: MacGibbon and Kee

Gyarmati,G. (1975) Ideologies, roles, and aspirations, the doctrine of the profession: Basis of a power structure *International Social Science Journal* 27(4)629-654

Halmos,P. (1970) *The Personal Service Society* New York: Schocken Books

Halsey,A.H., and Trow,M.(1970) *The British Academics* London: Faber

Ham,T.H. (1976) *The Student as Colleague: Medical Education Experience at Case Western Reserve* (2 vols.) Ann Arbor, Michigan: University Microfilms International

Hamblin,A.C. (1974) *Evaluation and Control of Training* London: McGraw-Hill

Hamilton,D. *et al* (1977) *Beyond the Numbers Game* London: Collier Macmillan

Handy,C.B. (1976) *Understanding Organizations* Harmondsworth: Penguin

Harden,R.M. (1979) How to assess students: an overview *Medical Teacher* 1(2) 65-70

Hardy,K.R. (1974) Social origins of American scientists and scholars *Science* 185(4150) 497-506

Harrisberger,L. and Associates (1976) *Experiential Learning in Engineering Education* American Society for Engineering Education

Harrisberger,L. (1977) Creating a professional competency BS curriculum in engineering *Proceedings 1977 Frontiers in Education Conference* American Society for Engineering Education

Harrisberger,L. (1979) Developing the compleat engineer *Proceedings 1979 Frontiers in Education Conference* American Society for Engineering Education

Harrisberger,L. (1979a) A survival course in mechanical engineering *Proceedings 1979 ASEE Southeastern Section Conference* American Society for Engineering Education

Harrisberger,L. (1981) Learning outcomes in engineering *New Directions for Experiential Learning* 12, 51-60

Harrisberger,L. (1983) Hey, engineers are people, too! (The software of project engineering) *Proceedings 1983 Conference ASEE Southeastern Section* American Society for Engineering Education

Haug,M.R. (1973) Deprofessionalization: an alternate hypothesis for the future *Sociological Review Monograph* 20 (Dec) 195-211

Haug,M.R. (1975) The deprofessionalization of everyone? *Sociological Focus* 8 (3 Aug) 197-213

Haug,M.R., and Sussman,M.B. (1973) Professionalization and unionism: a jurisdictional dispute? In Freidson,E.(Ed.) *The Professions and their Prospects* Beverly Hills and London: Sage

Helfer,R.E. (1970) An objective comparison of pediatric interviewing skills of freshman and senior medical students *Pediatrics* 45, 623-627

Higgins,J.C. (1967) *The Contribution of the College of Technology to Management Training with particular reference to Management Science* Operational Research Society Annual Conference, University of Exeter

Hilgard,E.R., Irvine,R.P. and Whipple,J.E. (1953) Rote memorization, understanding, and transfer: an extension of Katona's card trick experiments *Journal of Experimental Psychology* 46 (4) 288-292

Houle,C. (1980) *Continuing Learning in the Professions* San Francisco: Jossey-Bass Inc.

Hubbard,J.P. (1978) *Measuring Medical Education: The Tests and Experience of the National Board of Medical Examiners* (2nd edition) Philadelphia: Lea and Febiger

Huczynski,A. (1983a) Grasping a grand mixture of methods *Times Higher Education Supplement* 25 March

Huczynski,A. (1983b) *Encyclopaedia of Management Development Methods* Aldershot: Gower Publishing Company

Hughes,E.C. (1958) *Men and Their Work* New York: Free Press

Hughes,E.C. (1963) Professions *Daedalus* Fall, 655-669

Illich,I. (1976a) *Medical Nemesis* London: Calder and Boyars

Illich,I. (1976b) *Deschooling Society* Harmondsworth: Penguin

Illich,I. (1977) *Disabling Professions* London: Marion Boyars

Indian Council of Social Science Research (1975) *Social Sciences in Professional Education* Proceedings of the Conference on the Role of Social Science in Professional Education, Delhi,1974. Delhi: Indian Council of Social Science Research

Institute of Directors (1961) *Who's On The Board* London: Institute of Directors, Medical Unit Survey

Institute of Directors (1973) *The Director* March

Institute of Employment Research (1983) *Review of the Economy and Employment 1983* University of Warwick: Institute of Employment Research

Institute of Manpower Studies (1979) *Determinants of Doctors' Career Decisions* Report by the Institute of Manpower Studies to the Department of Health and Social Security

Institution of Chemical Engineering (1983) *A Scheme for Degree Courses in Chemical Engineering*

Jackson,J.A.(Ed.) (1970) *Professions and Professionalization* Cambridge: Cambridge University Press

Jarvis,P. (1983) *Professional Education* London: Croom Helm

Jason,H. and Westberg,J. (1982) *Teachers and Teaching in US Medical Schools* Norwalk,Conn.: Appleton-Century-Crofts

Johnson,T.J. (1972) *Professions and Power* London: Macmillan

Johnson,T.J. (1982) The state and the professions: peculiarities of the British. In Giddens,A. and McKenszie,G.(Eds) *Social Class and the Division of Labour* Cambridge: Cambridge University Press

Johnson,T.J. and Caygill,M. (1972) *The Royal Institute of British Architects and the Commonwealth Profession* London: Institute of Commonwealth Studies. Working Paper 5

Johnson,M.L. (1971) Non-academic factors in medical school selection *British Journal of Medical Education* 5(4) 264-268

Johnstone,Q. and Hopson,D. (1967) *Lawyers and their Work: an analysis of the legal profession in the United States and England* Indianapolis: Bobbs-Merrill

Jones,F.E. (1976) Social origins of four professions: a comparative study *International Journal of Comparative Sociology* 17(3-4) 143-163

Karatzas,N. and Walton,H.J.(Eds) (1980) Medical education and health care. Proceedings of the Conference of the Association for Medical Education in Europe at Athens, 1979. *Medical Education* 14(5) Supplement

Katona,C. (1940) *Organizing and Memorizing* New York: Columbia University Press

Kaufman,A. *et al* (1982) Undergraduate medical education for primary care: a case study in New Mexico *Southern Medical Journal* 75 (9) 1110-1117

Kehl,C. (1956) L'histoire de la profession d'avocat *Annales Juridiques, Politiques, Economiques et Sociales No 3* Alger: Librairie Ferraris

Keller,F.S. (1968) Goodbye teacher... *Journal of Applied Behaviour Analysis* 1 (Spring), 78-89

Kelsall,R.K. (1954) Self-recruitment in four professions. In Glass, D.V.(Ed.) *Social Mobility in Britain* London: Routledge and Kegan Paul

Kelsall,R.K. *et al* (1972) *The Sociology of an Elite* London: Methuen

Kennedy,I. (1981) *The Unmasking of Medicine* London: Allen and Unwin

Knowles,M. (1975) *Self-Directed Learning: A Guide for Learners and Teachers* New York: Association Press

Knowles,M. (1978) *The Adult Learner: A Neglected Species* (2nd edition) Houston: Gulf Publishing Co.

Koch,L. and French,J. (1948) Overcoming resistance to change *Human Relations* 1,512-532

Kolb,D. (1976) *The Learning Style Inventory: Technical Manual* Boston: McBer

Kolb,D. (1981) Learning styles and disciplinary differences. In Chickering,A.(Ed) *The Modern American College* San Francisco: Jossey-Bass Inc.

Kolb,D.A. Rubin,I.M. and McIntyre,J.M. (1979) *Organizational Psychology: an experiential approach* (3rd edition) Englewood Cliffs,NJ: Prentice-Hall

Korn Ferry International (1983) *Boards of Directors Study 1983* London: Korn Ferry International

Labour Force Survey (1981) *Labour Force Survey 1981* London: Office of Population Census and Surveys

Land, Edwin H. (1957) *Generation of Greatness: The Idea of a University in an Age of Science* Ninth Annual Arthur Dehon Little Memorial Lecture

Larkin,G. (1983) *Occupational Monopoly and Modern Medicine* London: Tavistock

Larson,M.S. (1977) *The Rise of Professionalism* Berkeley: University of California Press

Last,J.M., and Stanley,G.R. (1968) Career preference of young British doctors *British Journal of Medical Education* 2 (2) 137-155

Layton,E.T. (1971) *The Revolt of the Engineers: Social Responsibility and the American Engineering Profession* Cleveland: Case Western Reserve University Press

LeBreton,P.P. *et al* (Eds) (1979) *The Evaluation of Continuing Education for Professionals. A Systems View*

Leeder,S.R. *et al* Assessment: help or hurdle? *Programmed Learning and Educational Technology* 16(4) 308-315

Lees,D.S. (1966) *The Economic Consequences of the Professions* London: Institute of Economic Affairs

Le Mee,J., Stecher,M and Shannon,T. (1977) Liberal professional education: a proposal for the holistic approach to the engineering curriculum *Proceedings 1977 Frontiers in Education Conference* American Society for Engineering Education

Leonard,J (1977) *La Via Quotidienne du Medicin de Province Au XIXeme Siecle* Paris: Hachette

Leverhulme Report (1983) *Excellence in Diversity. Towards a New Strategy for Higher Education* Guildford: Society for Research into Higher Education

Lewis,R. and Maude,A. (1953) *Professional People in England* Cambridge, Mass: Harvard University Press

Ley,P. (1977) Psychological studies of doctor-patient communication. In Rachman,S.(Ed.) *Contributions to Medical Psychology* Oxford: Pergamon

Ley,P. (1982) Satisfaction, compliance and communication *British Journal of Clinical Psychology* 21,241-254

Loveluck,C. (1975) The construction, operation, and evaluation of management games. In Taylor,B. and Lippitt,G.L. (Eds) *Management Development and Training Handbook* London: McGraw-Hill

Lupton,T. (1982) *Management Development in Western Europe* Paper read at the East/West Meeting on Recent Trends in Management Education, Helsinki

McCaulley,M.H. and Associates (1982) ASEE-MBTI engineering school consortium: year two report *Proceedings 1982 ASEE Annual Conference, June 1982* American Society for Engineering Education

McCaulley,M.H. and Associates (1983) Applications of psychological type in engineering education *Engineering Education* Feb,394-400

McDaniel,W.B. (1958) A brief sketch of the rise of American medical societies. In Marti-Ibanex, Felix(Ed.) *History of American Medicine* New York: M.D. Publications

McDermott,W (1978) Medicine: the public good and one's own *Perspect. Biol.Med.* 21,167

McKean,D.D. (1963) *The Integrated Bar* Boston: Houghton Mifflin

McKeown,T. (1961) Limitations of medical care attributable to medical education *Lancet* ii,1-4

McKeown,T. (1979) *The Role of Medicine: Dream, Mirage, or Nemesis?* London: Nuffield Provincial Hospitals Trust

McMaster University (See General Guide)

Maddison,D. (1980) A medical school for the future: the Newcastle experiment *World Health Forum* 1 (1,2) 133-138

Maddison,D.C. (1978) What's wrong with medical education? *Medical Education* 12, 97-102

Mantech (no date) *Personalysis* Mantech Technologies, 1200 South Post Oak, Suite 34, Houston, Texas 77056

Mangham,I.L. (1978) *Interactions and Interventions in Organizations* London: Wiley

Marshall,T.H. (1939) The recent history of professionalism in relation to social structure and social policy *Canadian Journal of Economics and Political Science* 5 (August) 325-340

Marshall,T.H. (1963) *Sociology at the Crossroads* London: Heinemann

Marton,F. and Saljo,R. (1976) On qualitative differences in learning 1 and 2 *British Journal of Educational Psychology* 46, 4-11 and 115-172

Mawardi,B. (1979) *Physicians and their Careers* Ann Arbor, Mich: University Microfilms International

Mayhew,L.B. (1971) *Changing Practices in Education for the Professions* Atlanta, Georgia: Southern Regional Education Board

Mayhew,L.B. and Ford,P.J. (1974) *Reform in Graduate and Professional Education* San Francisco: Jossey-Bass

Medawar,P. (1975) Scientific method in science and medicine *Perspect. Biol.Med.* 18,345-352

Melone,A.P. (1979) *Lawyers, Public Policy and Interest Group Politics* Washington: University Press of America

Merton,R.K., Reader,G.G. and Kendall,P.L. (1957) *The Student-Physician: Introductory Studies in the Sociology of Medical Education* Cambridge, Mass: Harvard University Press

Metz,J.M.C., Moll,J and Walton,H.J. (1981) *Examinations in Medical Education: A Necessary Evil?* Utrecht: Wetenschappelijke uitgeverij Bunge. Proceedings of the 1980 Conference of the Association for Medical Education in Europe at Nijmegen, The Netherlands

Miller,G.E. (1962) An inquiry into medical teaching *Journal of Medical Education* 37(3) 185-191

Miller,G.E. (1978) The contribution of research in the learning process *Medical Education* 12(5) 28

Miller,G.E. (1980) *Educating Medical Teachers* Cambridge, Mass: Harvard University Press

Millerson,G. (1964) *The Qualifying Associations: A Study in Professionalization* London: Routledge and Kegan Paul

Mills,C.Wright (1956) *White Collar* New York: Oxford University Press

Mintzberg,H. (1979) *The Stucturing of Organizations* Englewood Cliffs, NJ: Prentice-Hall

Mintzberg,H. (1980) *Managerial Effectiveness* New York: McGraw-Hill

Monopolies Commission (1970) *Professional Services* (2 Parts) Cmnd.4462-3. London: HMSO

Morris,J.F. (1972) *Notes on Joint Development Activities* Lecture to ATM Annual Conference

Morris,J.F. (1980) Joint development activities: from practice to theory. In Beck,J. and Cox, C. (Eds) *Advances in Management Education* London: Wiley

Morrissey,E. and Gillespie,D.F. (1975) Technology and the conflict of professionals in bureaucratic organizations *The Sociological Quarterly* 16(3) 319-332

Moore,W.E. (1970) *The Professions: Roles and Rules* New York: Russell Sage Foundation

Mustard,J.F., Neufeld,V.R., Walsh,W.I. and Cochran,J.(Eds) (1982) *New Trends in Health Sciences, Education and Services: The McMaster Experience* New York: Praeger Publishers

National Academy of Engineering (1980) *Issues in Engineering Education. A Framework for Analysis* Washington,DC: National Academy of Engineering

National Opinion Polls (NOP) (1978) *National Opinion Polls Omnibus Survey* Policy Studies Institute. May 1978

Neame,R.L.B. (1981) How to construct a problem-based course *Medical Teachers* 3(3) 94-99

Nelson,B.H.(Ed.) (1962) *Education for the Professions* Chicago: University of Chicago Press

Neufeld,V.R. and Barrows,H.S. (1974) McMaster philosophy: an approach to medical education *Journal of Medical Education* 49(11) 1040-1050

Neufeld,V.R. *et al* (1978) What are the new schools doing about curriculum evaluation *Annual Conference of Research in Medical Education* 17, 449-459

Neufeld,V.R., Norman,G.R., Feightner,J.W. and Barrows,H.S. (1981) Clinical problem-solving by medical students: a cross-sectional and longitudinal analysis *Medical Education* 15,315-322

Newble,D.I. (1979) *Evaluation of Clinical Competence* Adelaide, Australia: Advisory Centre for University Education, University of Adelaide

Nilson,L.B. (1979) An application of the occupational 'uncertainty principle' to the professions *Social Problems* 26 (5 June) 570-581

Noack,H. (Ed.) (1976) *Medical Education and Primary Health Care* Proceedings of the Conference of the Association for Medical Education in Europe in Berne in 1976. London: Croom Helm

Norwood,W.F. (1944) *Medical Education in the United States* Philadelphia: University of Pennsylvania Press

O'Connor,J.G. and Meadows, A. (1976) Specialization and professionalization in British geology *Social Studies of Science* 6 (1 Feb) 77-89

Ohio State University College of Medicine (1976) *Individualizing the Study of Medicine* New York: Westinghouse Learning Corporation

Oppenheimer,M. (1973) The proletarianization of the professional *Sociological Review Monograph* 20 (Dec) 213-227

Paillie,W. and Brain,E. (1978) 'Modules' in morphology for self study: a system for learning in an under-graduate medical programme *Journal of Medical Education*

Painvin,C. *et al* (1979) The 'Triple Jump' exercise — a structured measure of problem-solving and self-directed learning *Proceedings of the Annual Conference on Medical Education* 18,73-77

Parsons,T. (1968) The professions. In *The International Encyclopaedia of the Social Sciences* New York: Macmillan

Pask,G. (1976) Styles and strategies of learning *British Journal of Educational Psychology* 46, 128-148

Payson,H.E and Barchas,J.D. (1965) A time study of medical teaching rounds *New England Journal of Medicine* 273, 1468-1471

Perry,W. (1970) *Forms of Intellectual and Ethical Development in the College Years: A Scheme* New York: Holt, Rinehart and Winston

Perry,W. (1981) Cognitive and ethical growth; the making of meaning. In Chickering,A.W.(Ed.) *The Modern American College* San Francisco: Jossey-Bass

Personnel Training Bulletin (1983) *Personnel Training Bulletin* Didasko, Warboys, Huntingdon

Peterson,O.L., Andrews,L.P., Spain,R.S. and Greenberg,B.G. (1956) An analytic study of North Carolina general practice *Journal of Medical Education* 31(12) Part 1

Pocock Committee Report (1977) *Educational and Training Needs of European Managers* European Foundation for Management Development

Powles,J. (1971) On the limitations of modern medicine *Science, Medicine, and Man* 1, 1-30

Pritchard,W.H. (1982) Instructional compiling in 2001: A scenario *Phi Delta Kappa* January, 322-325

Rayack,E. (1967) *Professional Power and American Medicine: The Economics of the American Medical Association* Cleveland: World Publishing

Reader,W.J. (1966) *Professional Men: The Rise of the Professional Classes in Nineteenth-Century England* London: Weidenfeld and Nicolson

Reason,P. and Rowan, J. (1981) *Human Inquiry: A sourcebook of New Paradigm Research* London: Wiley

Reddin,W.J. (1970) *Managerial Effectiveness* New York: McGraw-Hill

Reed,A.Z. (1921) *Training for the Public Profession of the Law* Carnegie Foundation for the Advancement of Teaching Bulletin No.15, New York.

Relman,A.S. (1980) Here come the women *New England Journal of Medicine* 302, 1252-1253

Revans,R.W. (1982) *The Origins and Growth of Action Learning* Bromley: Chatwell-Bratt

Riesman,D. (1961) *The Lonely Crowd* New Haven: Yale University Press

Rippey,R. (1981) *The Evaluation of Teaching in Medical Schools* New York: Springer Publishing Company

Rippey,R.M., Thal,S. and Bongard,S.J. (1981) A study of the University of Connecticut's criteria for admission to medical school *Medical Education* 298-305

Robbins Committee (1963) *Higher Education* Committee on Higher Education, Ministry of Education. Cmnd.2154. London: HMSO

Roberts,V.C., Aubry-Frize,M. Irnich,W., Katona,Z. and Oberg,P.A. (1982) International registration of clinical engineers *Medical Progress Through Technology* 9, 171-175

Rogers,C. (1969) *Freedom to Learn* Columbus, Ohio: Merrill

Rogers,D.E. (1980) On preparing academic health centers for the very different 1980s *Journal of Medical Education* 55,1-12

Roizen,J. and Jepson,M. (1983) *Expectations of Higher Education: An Employers' Perspective* London: Brunel University, Department of Education and Science

Rotem,A., Craig,P., Cox,K. and Garrick,C. (1979) *In Search of Criteria for the Assessment of Medical Education in Australia* Kensington, NSW, Australia: Centre for Medical Education, Research and Development, University of New South Wales

Rothstein,W.G. (1972) *American Physicians in the Nineteenth Century: from Sects to Science* Baltimore: Johns Hopkins

Rowbottom,R. and Billis,D. (1977) The stratification of work and organizational design *Human Relations* 30 (1) 53-76

Royal Commission on the National Health Service (1979) *Report of the Royal Commission on the National Health Service* Cmnd.7615. London: HMSO

Royal Commission on Medical Education (See Todd)

Rueschemeyer,D. (1978) The legal profession in comparative perspective. In Johnson,H.M.(Ed.) *Social System and Legal Process* San Francisco: Jossey-Bass.97-127

Sayles,L.R. (1979) *Leadership: what effective managers really do...and how they do it* New York: McGraw-Hill

Schein,E.H. (1972) *Professional Education: Some New Directions* Carnegie Commission on Higher Education. New York and London: McGraw-Hill

Schmidt,W.H.O. (1965) Processes of learning in relation to different kinds of material to be learnt. In Reid,J.V.O. and Wilmot,A.J. (Eds) *Medical Education in South Africa* Pietermaritzburg: Natal University Press, 228-232

Schwartz,H (1981) The AMA isn't what it used to be *Wall Street Journal* March 12-26

Seebohm Report (1968) *Report of the Committee on Local Authority and Allied Personal Social Services* Cmnd.3703. London: HMSO

Servan-Schreiber,J.J. (1967) *The American Challenge* London: Dutton

Sherlock.B.J. and Morris,R.T. (1967) The evolution of the professional: a paradigm *Social Inquiry* 37 (Winter) 27-46

Simpson,M.A. (1976) Medical student evaluation in the absence of examinations *Medical Education* 10 (1) 22-26

Snyder,B.R. (1971) *The Hidden Curriculum* New York: Knopf

Society for Research into Higher Education (1983) *Excellence in Diversity, Towards a New Strategy for Higher Education* (Leverhulme Report) Guildford: Society for Research into Higher Education

Stacey,N. (1954) *English Accountancy 1800-1954* London: Gee and Co.

Stevens,R. (1970) Two Cheers for 1870: The American Law School. In Fleming,D. and Bailyn,B.(Eds) *Perspectives in American History Vol.5. Law in American History* Cambridge, Mass: Harvard University Press, pp.405-548

Stevens,R. (1971) *American Medicine and the Public Interest* New Haven: Yale University Press

Stretton,T.B., Hall,R and Owen,S.G. (1967) Programmed instruction in medical education — comparison of teaching machine and programmed textbook *British Journal of Medical Education* 1,165-168

Strom,G., and Walton,H.J.(Eds) (1978) Innovations in medical education. Proceedings of the Conference of the Association for Medical Education in Europe at Uppsala, 1976 *Medical Education* 12(5) Supplement

Stuart,R. and Burgoyne,J. (1977) The learning goals and outcomes of management development programmes *Personnel Review* 6(1) 5-16

Svensson,L. (1977) On qualitative differences in learning: III Study skills and learning *British Journal of Educational Psychology* 47, 233-243

Swann Committee (1968) *The Flow into Employment of Scientists, Engineers and Technologists* Committee on Manpower Resources for Science and Technology, Department of Education and Science. Report of the working group on manpower for scientific growth. Cmnd.3760. London: HMSO

Tierney,K. (1979) *Darrow: A Biography* New York: Crowell

Todd, Lord (Chairman) (1968) *Royal Commission on Medical Education 1965-1968* Cmnd.3569. London: HMSO

Trouillat,R. (1979) *Les Conseils Juridiques* Paris: Presses Universitaires de France

Turner,R.H. (1960) Sponsored and contest mobility and the school system *American Sociological Review* 25(6) 855-867

Turner,J.D. and Rushton,J.(Eds) (1976) *Education for the Professions* Manchester: Manchester University Press

United States of America Department of Education (1983) *A Nation at Risk: The Imperative for Educational Reform* Washington: National Commission on Excellence in Education. US Government Printing Office

University Central Council on Admissions (1981) *Statistical Supplement to the Nineteenth Report, 1980-81* Cheltenham, Glos.

Veall,D. (1970) *The Popular Movement for Law Reform 1640 − 1660* Oxford: Oxford University Press

Vess,D.M. (1975) *Medical Revolution in France 1789-1796* Gainesville: Florida State University

Volmer,H.M. and Mills,D.L. (1966) *Professionalization* Englewood Cliffs, NJ: Prentice-Hall

Vu,Nu Viet (1980) Describing, teaching and predicting medical problem-solving: a review *Evaluation and the Health Professions* 3(4) 435-459

Wall,C., Cameron,C.H. and Ashworth Underwood,E. (1963) *A History of the Worshipful Society of Apothecaries of London. Vol.1.1617-1815* London: Oxford University Press

Walton,H.J. (1968) Sex differences in ability and outlook of senior medical students *British Journal of Medical Education* 2, 156-162

Walton,H.J. (1969) An experimental study of different methods for teaching medical students *Proceedings of the Royal Society of Medicine* 61,109-112

Walton,H.J. (1980) Introducing a new curriculum in an established medical school. In Katz,F.M. and Fulop,T.(Eds) *Personnel for Health Care: Case Studies of Educational Programmes* 2, 131-142. Geneva: World Health Organization

Walton,H.J. (1983) The place of primary health care in medical education in the United Kingdom: a survey *Medical Education* 17,141-147

Warren-Piper,D.(Ed.) (1981) *Is Higher Education Fair?* Papers presented to the 17th Annual Conference of the Society for Research into Higher Education. Guildford: Society for Research into Higher Education

Ways,P.O., (1973) Focal problem-teaching in medical education *Journal of Medical Education* 48,565-570

Weick,K.E. (1977) Re-punctuating the problem. In Goodman,P.S., Pennings,J.M. and Associates (1977) *New Perspectives on Organizational Effectiveness* San Francisco: Jossey-Bass Inc.

Weigel,C.J. (1974) Medical malpractice in America's middle years *Texas Reports on Biology and Medicine* 32(1) 191-205

Wiener,M. (1981) *English Culture and the Decline of the Industrial Spirit 1850-1980* Cambridge: Cambridge University Press

Wilding,P. (1982) *Professional Power and Social Welfare* London: Routledge and Kegan Paul

Wilensky,H.L. (1964) The professionalization of everyone? *American Journal of Sociology* 70, 137-158

Williams,G. (1980) *Western Reserve's Experiment in Medical Education and its Outcome* Oxford: Oxford University Press

Williamson,P. (1981) *Early Careers of 1970 Graduates* London: Unit for Manpower Studies, Department of Employment

Williamson.W. (1981) Class bias. In Warren-Piper,D.(Ed.) *Is Higher Education Fair?* Guildford: Society for Research into Higher Education.

Woodward,C.A. and Ferrier,B.M. (1982) Perspectives of graduates two and five years after graduation from a three-year medical school *Journal of Medical Education* 57, 294-302

Woodward,C.A. and McAuley,R.D. (1981) Performance of McMaster medical student graduates during the first post-graduate year *Final Report, Ontario Ministry of Health* Grant DM 370

Woodworth,J.R. (1973) Some influences on the reform of schools of law and medicine 1890 to 1930 *Sociological Quarterly* 14, 495-516

World Health Organization (1979) *Continuing Education of Health Personnel and its Evaluation* Copenhagen Regional Office for Europe, World Health Organization

World Health Organization (1980) *The Assessment of Competence of Students in the Health Field* Copenhagen Regional Office for Europe: World Health Organization

Wright,P. and Treacher,A. (Eds) (1982) *The Problem of Medical Knowledge: Examining the Social Construction of Medicine* Edinburgh: Edinburgh University Press

Yorkshire and Humberside Regional Management Centre (1981) *Management Development Needs in Yorkshire and Humberside* Summary Report

Zeldin,T. (1973) *France 1848-1945. Vol.1. Ambition, Love and Politics* London: Oxford University Press